C. B. MACPHERSON AND
OF LIBERAL DEMOCRACY

FOR BRON

C. B. MACPHERSON AND THE PROBLEM OF LIBERAL DEMOCRACY

JULES TOWNSHEND

EDINBURGH UNIVERSITY PRESS

© Jules Townshend, 2000

Edinburgh University Press Ltd
22 George Square, Edinburgh

Typeset in Goudy Old Style
by Bibliocraft Ltd, Dundee, and
printed and bound in Great Britain by
MPG Books, Bodmin

A CIP Record for this book is available from the British Library

ISBN 1 85331 213 4 (paperback)

The right of Jules Townshend
to be identified as the author of this work
has been asserted in accordance with
the Copyright, Designs and Patents Act 1988

CONTENTS

PREFACE

C. B. Macpherson liked to talk about academia as an 'industry'. I am painfully aware that this book about him may be just another contribution to the academic 'heritage industry'. No doubt he would have given a wry smile at the thought that he was continuing to keep scholars gainfully employed. Yet the ultimate purpose of this work is to show that he remains a relevant thinker. The triumphalism surrounding the the victory of Western liberal democratic capitalism over its Communist adversary has begun to subside. The same old uncertainties, as well as new ones, about the viability of Western political and economic institutions have begun to assert themselves. These institutions seem unable to deal with a large number of deep-seated problems. They include enormous disparities of wealth within and between nations, the prospect of global economic meltdown, the threat of trade wars, the seemingly unstoppable ecological degradation of our planet along with uncontrollable profit-driven technological innovation, de-industrialisation in the Western heartlands and the growth of labour forces 'surplus to requirements', the rise of all-powerful transnational corporations and omnipotent global financial markets, and the failure of Western instititutions to take firm root in the former Communist countries. These problems and their consequences we bequeath to unborn generations.

These problems call starkly into question the legitimacy of the prevailing ideology of liberal democracy, which specifies a particular relation between democracy and capitalism. Generically, democracy means rule by the people; capitalism demands the sovereignty of profit. Liberal democratic ideology says that both these imperatives can be reconciled through the welfare state and the state regulation and protection of the private activities of capital, enabling a mutually beneficial compromise between capitalism and the will of the people. The global problems referred to above raise the issue of whether capitalism and liberal democracy will continue to tango, and if so whether it will be a pretty sight.

For Macpherson the diagnosis of and remedy for this potentially unhappy relation was material and moral, and ultimately what he termed 'ontological': material, because political institutions (liberal democracy) and their overall imperatives were shaped by how we produce and reproduce our means of existence (private property, capitalism); moral, because individuals and societies can make choices about how they can lead the good life; and 'ontological', because such choices are based on the image of ourselves, of our 'human nature'. His argument and insight sharply contrast with Fukuyama's bored and anomic 'last man'. If we continue to see ourselves as 'infinite' consumers and appropriators – in short, as 'possessive individualists' – if we continue to embrace an ideology functional to the capitalist market, the problems already alluded to would persist or intensify. Instead, human freedom and the abundant material resources we already have ought to be used to achieve human ends through the exercise of our human powers. All this was predicated upon the assumption of a common humanity. In the modern world a material and moral equilibrium could only be sustained by a fundamental recasting of the relationship between democracy and property: the only chance that a common humanity could have to control its destiny was through the common control of its productive assets. Only then would we have a democracy worthy of the name. This simple, if potentially disturbing, message seemed to get lost in the plethora of criticism that greeted his work.

Macpherson raised fundamental questions not merely about the practical shortcomings of the institutions of liberal democratic capitalism and its justificatory ideology; he was also concerned with the purpose of academic inquiry, with the relation between value and factual postulates, and with the feasibility and desirability of a unified field of political and economic study. This book focuses on the diverse objections levelled against Macpherson to demonstrate that in many respects they were not as decisive as his critics hoped. Indeed, I intend to demonstrate that tables can be turned, that a Macphersonian critique of current intellectual trends is apposite, that Macpherson is our contemporary. I am fully aware that my venture involves taking on much of the heavy artillery of modern political philosophy. But it is inspired by the belief that Macpherson was saying something politically important about political philosophy and its role in the promotion of human flourishing, that political philosophy is too important to be left to the political philosophers.

The aim, then, is to contribute to the consolidation of Macpherson's reputation as a major twentieth-century political theorist through a critical defence of his work. My hope is to show that a map of modern political theory which does not include Macpherson is not worth looking at. There are some signs that hostility to his work has begun to abate. Nevertheless, his ideas still suffer from unwarranted neglect within the contemporary academic world. Where one would expect to see a discussion of his work in commentaries on liberal and democratic theory, or on the history of political thought, especially on Hobbes and Locke, his name is often absent. And strangely, when Fukuyama's *The End of History and the Last Man* was published in 1992 no one bothered to note that Macpherson's little *Life and Times of Liberal Democracy* (1977) was the perfect and effortless antidote. My argument will be that this neglect should not be attributed to any notion that his critics had successfully undermined his project. And equally, if this neglect is because he is regarded as old-fashioned, as a wilted flower from the optimistic 1960s, this too is an underestimation of his value as a political thinker. Now that we live in a global, capitalist world his work is of even greater relevance.

This book can also be read in another way. It demonstrates that academic discussion in the human sciences is not always about the disinterested search for clarification or truth. This is especially so when confronted with a project such as Macpherson's, which was an overt political intervention. Equally, the book can be read as a chronicle of the changes in academic fashion that occurred in the postwar Anglophone world, as many a young academic cut their teeth on the 'Macpherson thesis'. In a sense the controversy he created is itself a commentary upon the history of postwar Anglophone political philosophy. There is also a slightly less respectable motive for writing a defence of Macpherson. A reputable academic in the 1970s spoke of Macpherson's 'vulgar appeal'. I must confess to my continuing lapse of taste, and hope that after reading this volume my indulgence will be treated with greater sympathy.

As for the book's scope, it does not cover all the criticisms of Macpherson's work, such as his account of the Levellers, Harrington, Hume and Burke, or his first book, *Democracy in Alberta*. The reason for these omissions is that I have attempted to examine criticisms of the core parts of his project.

The manuscript has been improved by many people, who have either read various chapters and have commented incisively on them, or who have helped me clarify, change or confirm my ideas on Macpherson. They include Ed Andrew, Alan Apperley, Gary Browning, Frank Cunningham, Alistair Edwards, Joe Femia, Tim Kenyon, Alkis Kontos, Peter Lamb, Dave McNally, David Morrice, Leo Panitch, Raia Prokhovnik, Dave Shugarman, Hillel Steiner, Reg Whitaker and Larry Wilde. They are of course not responsible for the book's remaining shortcomings.

Further, thanks to Colin Mooers for his hospitality in Toronto, as well as his continuing friendship and intellectual stimulation. I want in addition to acknowledge the continuing support of the the Department of Politics and Philosophy at Manchester Metropolitan University, which has unfailingly helped me in my academic endeavours over the years. Also thanks to Anne

Davies for unearthing the wealth of critical literature on Macpherson. Last but not least special thanks to Bron Williams for having to share me with an incorporeal 'Brough'.

LIST OF ABBREVIATIONS

DP   J. Tully, *A Discourse on Property: John Locke and His Adversaries* (Cambridge: Cambridge University Press, 1980).

DT   C. B. Macpherson, *Democratic Theory: Essays in Retrieval* (Oxford: Oxford University Press, 1973).

HSS   E. Laclau and C. Mouffe, *Hegemony and Socialist Strategy: Towards a Radical Democratic Politics* (London: Verso, 1985).

LTLD   C. B. Macpherson, *Life and Times of Liberal Democracy* (Oxford: Oxford University Press, 1977).

PI   C. B. Macperhson, *The Political Theory of Possesive Individualism* (Oxford: Oxford University Press, 1962).

PTJL   J. Dunn, *The Political Theory of John Locke* (Cambridge: Cambridge University Press, 1969).

RFEJ   C. B Macpherson, *The Rise and Fall of Economic Justice* (Oxford: Oxford University Press, 1984).

RWD   C. B. Macpherson, *The Real World of Democracy* (Oxford: Oxford University Press, 1965).

TJ   J. Rawls, *A Theory of Justice* (Cambridge, MA: Harvard University Press, 1971).

CHAPTER 1

LIFE AND PROJECT

'Possessive individualism' was Crawford Brough Macpherson's theoretical signature. It stood at the centre of his lifelong preoccupation with the relationship between property and democracy. Yet 'possessive individualism' was also shorthand for a multifaceted project, taking him into a terrain that cut across many of today's academic disciplines within the human sciences. Macpherson has been described as a 'hedgehog', who has one big idea, in contrast to a 'fox', who has various small insights. He accepted this description with good humour. Compared with many contemporary academics, who are often fully paid up members of the hedgehog tendency, Macpherson was a rather large hedgehog. Political philosophy, the history of political thought, political science and last but by no means least economics all came within his intellectual sweep. He was no academic under-labourer, working within and contributing to an increasing academic division of labour. For him big questions mattered, in particular: what kind of principles, consistent with human flourishing, should inform our political and economic institutions? This led him to focus on the relation between democracy and capitalist property. The exploration of this multifaceted relationship, which required an interdisciplinary approach, commanded his exceptionally powerful analytic and creative gifts. And for him ideas mattered. As a child of the ancient Greek thinkers, especially Aristotle, and of the Enlightenment, he firmly believed in the reasoning capacity of human beings to solve problems with which they were confronted. If Macpherson's ultimate purpose can be summarily described, it was to puncture ideas that falsely defined and analysed these problems – for they legitimated practices that caused human oppression and exploitation. Simultaneously, he reaffirmed humanity's potential to create a world of individual and collective human flourishing.

His holistic vantage point meant that he had a healthy disregard for ideological and disciplinary labels. Whether in the realms of politics or academia these labels stultified the emancipatory spirit through the establishing of artificial barriers, either producing intolerance or only a partial view of reality. Politically, liberalism was too good to be left to liberals, and Marxism was too good to be left to Marxists. Academically, intellectual history was too good to be left the intellectual historians, political science to the political scientists, political philosophy to the political philosophers and economics to the economists. Beyond all this, the function of ideas was to improve upon human practice, which disregarded these enervating political and academic distinctions.

Not surprisingly his holistic approach to the study of human beings and their institutions came to look increasingly both transgressive and old-fashioned in the postwar era. The world polarised into liberal and Marxist camps as a result of the Cold War, which had its effect on academic discourse. Simultaneously, and to some extent relatedly, the academy became increasingly fragmented, especially in the human sciences. The rise of positivism, or 'behaviouralism' as it was called, split scientific concerns from normative ones.[1] And by the early 'fifties even philosophy had succumbed to positivism and the view that values were arbitrary and could not be justified in factual terms, by reference for example to human nature. The 'death' of political philosophy, as 'first order' theorising was announced. Divisions within the human sciences that were noticeable in the prewar era became more pronounced, with economics, politics, philosophy and history becoming increasingly separated. A holistic view of the human sciences, such as Macpherson's, could be viewed as a quaint relic from a bygone era. Although Macpherson attempted to put such a perspective into practice in *Democracy in Alberta* (1953),[2] he moved into the international limelight with the publication of *The Political Theory of Possessive Individualism* (hereafter *PI*) in 1962.[3] Anglophone academics quickly realised that they were dealing with a thinker of exceptional talent who combined a sharp critical intelligence with a historical sensibility. He also expressed himself in a direct manner in lucid and elegant prose. Fellow academics praised him for all this. And perhaps they could even have accepted his explicit political commitments, which seemed incompatible with the disinterested pursuit of truth, if they had been of a conservative or unequivocally liberal sort, of an Oakshottian or Popperian kind. What they found hard to license was his exposure of liberal democracy's darker side – its 'possessive individualism' – and his argument that it was built on unstable, capitalist foundations. Although they were tempted to write him off as a Marxist,[4] they realised that something more than the *ad hominem* was required, not merely because of his acuity. He spoke the liberal language, albeit with a heavy Marxist inflection, and took liberalism seriously enough to embrace some of its core values and he built his argument on a close textual reading, particularly of Hobbes and Locke.

If *PI* announced to the world a new major intellectual talent, his *Democratic Theory: Essays in Retrieval* (hereafter *DT*), published in 1973, consolidated his reputation as a careful, analytical thinker with a strong egalitarian message.[5] This book, along with *Life and Times of Liberal Democracy* (hereafter *LTLD*)[6] (1977), dealt with themes already enunciated in the lectures, *The Real World of Democracy* (hereafter *RWD*), publicly broadcast in 1965.[7] *DT* looked closely at questions of democratic theory and property, and subjected leading liberal theorists – Rawls, Berlin and Milton Friedman – to trenchant critique. *LTLD* examined different models of liberal democracy. Macpherson also felt obliged to make a rare excursion into utopian theorising on his own behalf, in offering his own (sketchy) model of participatory democracy. His last book, *The Rise and Fall of Economic Justice* (hereafter *RFEJ*) (1984),[8] did not add much to his previous work, although it contained a number of oblique replies to some of his critics, displayed a number of subtle changes of position and also showed that he was keeping abreast with certain aspects of modern scholarship.

Initially, only liberals criticised him. However, the student revolt in the 1960s produced scholars with firm anti-liberal, Marxist commitments, who attacked him for not being sufficiently Marxist and disliked his liberal attachments. And as academic fashions and concerns changed, his reputation was such that scholars often felt the need to define their own perspectives against what he said. Thus he became the target of criticism from communitarians, 'deliberative' democrats, 'radical' democrats, feminists and ecologists. As we shall see he responded in a true Millian vein to many, but not all, his critics, however minor within the academic firmament. Sadly, the liberals he criticised did not subscribe to this Millian ethos and did not reply to his arguments.

— MACPHERSON'S LIFE AND TIMES —

Macpherson was born in Toronto in November 1911, and died there in July 1987 of emphysema. He was born into a comfortable middle-class family. Both his parents were teachers. He was educated at the University of Toronto Schools. His undergraduate studies (1929–32) were primarily in political economy, although he had won a couple of scholarships in the Classics. He then took a Masters at the London School of Economics under Harold Laski (1932–5) and returned to Canada to become a lecturer, mainly in the history of ideas, in the Department of Political Economy at the University of Toronto. He had a good working relationship with Harold Innis, the head of department for many years, who maintained a 'political economy' approach, despite the growing fragmentation of interests within the department into economics and political science. Macpherson taught for a year at the University of New

Brunswick (1942–3), where he met his future wife Kathleen Margaret Walker ('Kay'), who was a physiotherapist and later to become an important figure in the Canadian peace and women's movements. The next year he worked for the Canadian Wartime Information Board in Ottawa, afterwards returning to the University of Toronto. There he remained for the rest of his academic career, apart from a couple of sabbaticals in England (Oxford, 1952–3 – becoming a good friend of the historian Christopher Hill – and Cambridge, 1967–8) and short visits to universities in Israel (1972), Australia (1973), Holland (1975) and the United States (1979).

His book, *The Political Theory of Possessive Individualism*, was the making of his international reputation. It received enormous critical acclaim in the Anglophone world and was soon translated into many languages. Subsequently came various honours, such as the Fellow of the Royal Historical Society (1973) and Order of Canada (1976). In 1965 he gave the Massey Lectures for the Canadian Broadcasting Company, lectures later published as *The Real World of Democracy*. However, he did not follow an exclusive path of lonely scholarship. He undertook a great deal of professional activity, serving on the Executive of the International Political Science Association (1950–8), as President of the Canadian Political Science Association (1963–4), as well as vice-chairman and chairman of the Conference for Study of Political Thought (1972–8) and President of the Canadian Association of University Teachers. Added to all this, he was a member of various university committees at the University of Toronto in the 1960s and 1970s, the most important of which dealt with university reform in 1967. This committee, known as the 'Macpherson Committee', recommended a less elitist form of undergraduate instruction and more student participation in university governance.

Although he left most political activity to his wife, Kay, he did not leave it all to her. He campaigned within the university against the Vietnam War (1966–8), was a founder of the Committee of Socialist Studies in 1967, and took an active part in supporting the Marxist political philosopher Istvan Meszaros, who was having difficulties with the Canadian immigration authorities in 1973. He also wrote letters to the press on such matters as student finance, Canadian neutrality and nuclear disarmament, and was a Director of the Canadian CND (1963–4). We have already noted that he played the role of a public intellectual in his Massey Lecture broadcasts in 1965. Earlier, when the Cold War was intense in January 1949, he defended the Soviet Union in a broadcast debate. He was, though, never a member of the Canadian Communist Party.[9]

His most significant contribution to Canadian political life as an activist was in 1946, surrounding the so-called 'Gouzenko Affair', which became an important catalyst for the Cold War. A military intelligence officer, Igor

Gouzenko, had defected from the Soviet embassy, accusing various Canadians of spying for the Soviet Union. Thirteen people were interrogated without civil rights. Macpherson was a key figure in establishing an Emergency Civil Liberties Association, which organised a none too popular campaign against the Canadian government. Apparently, there were pressures to have Macpherson sacked which his head of department, Harold Innis, successfully resisted.

What of Macpherson's character? Although a rigorous and tough-minded scholar with exceptional reasoning powers he had little of the arrogance that can accompany these qualities, even when he became famous. He seemed to conduct himself as though he had taken Mill's *On Liberty* to heart. Nothing less than the passionate but disinterested pursuit of truth would do. And truth would make the world a better place. He believed that human beings ultimately wanted to know the truth, and this could only be achieved through reasoned debate. His letters demonstrate an unfailing courtesy even to those with whom he strongly disagreed, or who strongly disagreed with him. Although he had strong convictions, he was also a bridge-builder, and could work with fellow academics such as Leo Strauss whose overall views could be sharply at odds with his own, as well as being very much the peacemaker within his own family. Yet ultimately truth mattered more than personal relationships or the hurt feelings of those he criticised. So, for example, Isaiah Berlin wrote to him in 1971 paying him huge compliments.

> You do not need my praise: all the same I am not going to deny myself the pleasure ... of saying that you are one of the very few rational and lucid, and altogether admirable writers on topics, and in a field where mush, gush, frightful fumisme prevail, and that when the future generation sort things out the difference between your kind of writing and the hideous inflated prose of the Germans and their followers will be duly noted ... There now, I could go on, but I had better not.[10]

These blandishments did not prevent Macpherson from delivering one of the sharpest critiques of Berlin's celebrated thesis on 'negative' and 'positive' liberty, two years later in *DT* ('Berlin's Division of Liberty'). He was not only one of Mill's rational debaters from *On Liberty*, he was also as equally committed to the book's other key value: human toleration. His historical approach and his re-working of the concept of democracy were intended to promote a toleration of difference, most vividly seen in his *RWD*. Macpherson urged his Western audience to respect different political and economic institutions of the Second and Third Worlds because their object was human flourishing.

What is also apparent from some of his writings is a strong, if quiet, sense of humour, a little on the (self-)deflating, caustic side. Thus, he could joke about his obsession with possessive individualism in the preface to his last book, *RFEJ*. He could refer to academic work as akin to 'industry' as in a review article 'Progress in the Locke Industry', or as in his attack on Linguistic analysis in political philosophy. We must not, he urged, accept such Analysis at its own evaluation. This would condemn us to a 'treadmill that may give us continuous and agreeable employment, but will not add much to our knowledge of the wheel. It is more likely to induce a myopia that is satisfied with its close scrutiny of the treads.'[11] Nevertheless, as William Leiss has rightly emphasised in his intellectual biography of Macpherson, he undertook his scholarly vocation with extreme seriousness, arising out of deep moral and political commitment.[12]

– *Early influences* –

What and who were Macpherson's formative influences? The mature Macpherson could rightly claim that he was no one's disciple – indeed, he probably would not be worth studying if he was. And 'possessive individualism' was a unique, composite concept, an amalgam of Hobbes, Locke and Marx. Yet circumstances, events and individuals helped define the shape of Macpherson's intellectual trajectory. From all accounts he seems to have been endowed with a strong sense of social justice and social responsibility. This has to be seen against the backdrop of mass unemployment and the rise of Fascism in the capitalist world of the 1930s, which he saw at first hand during his sojourn in England between 1932 and 1935, pushing him in a leftward direction.

As for individual influences, while an undergraduate Otto B. van der Sprenkel made the greatest impact on him. A refugee from Europe, he taught political theory for two years at the University of Toronto, and Macpherson took his courses in both years. He wrote to Otto's wife after his death in 1978, that 'whatever success I have as a political theorist owes its start to the enthusiasm with which he then infected me ... he made [political theory] come alive with an intellectual acumen and an immediacy, to a degree unequalled in all my subsequent experience.'[13]

Van der Sprenkel had been a student and disciple of Harold Laski. And on the strength of this and reading some of Laski's works Macpherson decided to study under him at the LSE. He then came under Laski's influence. Later, in a letter to van der Sprenkel, he stated that he was 'under Laski's spell back in the 1930s and 1940s'.[14] His stay in London proved pivotal to his intellectual development. While he had a strong independence of mind, there is little doubt that the broad parameters of his thought were shaped by his experience at the LSE, where he came into contact not only with Laski, but R. H. Tawney and Morris Ginsburg, and was introduced to the British left-of-centre ethos.

The importance of this period between 1932 and 1935 for Macpherson's intellectual evolution can be guaged in a number of ways. There is first his stance as to what it meant to be a scholar. With Laski, Tawney and many other progressive intellectuals to be a good scholar and simultaneously be politically committed was unproblematic. Indeed, the whole *purpose* of scholarship was not to pursue knowledge for its own sake, but to make the world a better place, and political allegiances did not have to cloud scholarly analysis and judgement. This was a point that Macpherson came to insist upon, and referred to Adam Smith, Burke and Marx as 'solid thinkers' who were also pamphleteers.[15] Furthermore, one could be a serious scholar and a public intellectual. And here Laski was an obvious role model, as a founder of the National Council for Civil Liberties and of the Socialist League in 1932, member of the Labour Party National Executive Committee from 1937 and eventually becoming chairman of the Labour Party in 1945, active in the Workers' Education Association and speaker at countless trade union meetings.[16]

The possibility of combining scholarship with protagonism was perhaps facilitated by the view that the scholar was a free thinker, who defied simplistic political doctrines and formulas. In other words, a broad humanist commitment did not entail unquestioned allegiance to any particular 'ism'. This is why Macpherson's thought resists easy labelling, except in a general kind of way. This is also why he had no compunction in attempting to reconcile the two warring siblings of the Enlightenment: liberalism and socialism. In the intellectual climate experienced by Macpherson great thinkers of the past were neither swallowed whole or spat out. Rather, they were discriminatingly ingested. They were an intellectual resource, a raw material, whose values and substantive and methodological insights could be utilised in order to promote human progress. This could be seen particularly in the works of Tawney and Laski, and in one of their precursors, J. A. Hobson. They had all been nurtured on a strong ethical liberalism inspired by J. S. Mill, T. H. Green, Ruskin and others, and yet they were not afraid of, nor hostile to, Marx, and could distinguish between Bolshevism and what Marx wrote and intended.[17] While thinkers such as Hobson and Tawney were indebted to Marx's insights into capitalism, and derived their ethical frameworks from either Christianity (in Tawney's case) or from Ruskin (in Hobson's case), Laski from the 1930s onwards saw in Marx a humanism. Thus, Laski, although firmly committed to what he deemed to be liberal values, had no problem in writing a lengthy and complimentary introduction to the *Communist Manifesto* in 1948. Not surprisingly, therefore, Macpherson, in replying to one of his earliest critics, could assert that one could borrow the 'analytical insights of Marx the scholar and the ethical insights of Marx the humanist' without being driven by a 'Marxist apostolic fervour'.[18] From the start Macpherson did not feel a compulsion to make Marx the touchstone of his political creed and felt at home with a synthetic approach to political values and analysis, which combined historical materialism, especially Marx's famous 'Preface' to a

Contribution to the Critique of Political Economy, with a Mill-inspired ideal of individual self-development.

Arguably, Macpherson's social, historical and ideological analysis was framed by this 'Preface': the historical primacy of the development of human productive forces, the stress on the relation between the economic structure and the political, legal and ideological superstructure, and between 'social being' and 'consciousness' (albeit non-deterministic), which meant that whether certain ideas were taken up on a mass scale depended on material conditions. 'Mankind always sets itself only such tasks as it can solve; since ... it will always be found that the task itself arises only when the material conditions for its solution already exist or are at least in the process of formation.'[19] All this presupposed a teleological reading of history, in which the 'real' and the 'good' would coalesce. The 'good', however, for Macpherson had much of the Mill about it, and unlike orthodox Marxists he did not display an unquestioning confidence in the working class in achieving it. We can also see in the 'Preface' a 'realist' treatment of political thought that Macpherson adopted. 'Just as our opinion of an individual is not based on what he thinks of himself, so can we not judge of such a period of transformation by its own consciousness ...'[20] Thus, contra to the so-called British, 'Cambridge School', Macpherson's approach to the history of political thought was not based upon authorial intention, but on a presumption that a full account of the motive forces impelling the writer to write in a certain way may well be obscure to the writer. Moreover, they may be unaware of the social significance of their thought in propagating an (unintentional) world-view that serves to legitimate various political, social and economic processes.[21]

Just as important, Macpherson's conceptual coordinates became firmly set in this period: property and democracy and their interrelation. Laski by the time Macpherson came into close contact with him had firmly moved into the (undogmatic) Marxist camp, which entailed a distancing from, but not an abandonment of, his former pluralism.[22] By the late 1920s he had conceded the Marxist (and Aristotelian) argument that 'political power is the handmaid of economic power' and that 'a mere ballot-box democracy is, as a consequence, utterly unreal in the presence of large inequalities of property'.[23] The relationship between private property and democracy was relatively unproblematic during capitalism's expansionary phase, when the demands for social reforms by the newly enfranchised masses could be met. But he stated in *Democracy in Crisis* (1933) that capitalist decline meant that this was no longer so hence the 'crisis', and that he feared that Fascism could result, with the 'men in possession of actual sovereignty' choosing 'to fight rather than to abdicate'.[24] Thus private property and democracy became juxtaposed. In his preface to the third edition of the *Grammar of Politics* (1925), published in

1934, he acknowledged 'the antithesis between individual property rights and the fulfilment of the democratic idea'. He then stated that 'Fascism in its various national forms, is simply the expedient adopted by capitalism in distress to defeat the democratic political foundation with which it could be successfully linked in its period of creative expansion.'[25] As a consequence of this he saw liberalism in crisis owing to its ultimate attachment to private property. This crisis was the product of the intense conflict between the forces and relations of production.[26] Nevertheless, in his pamphlet, *The Decline of Liberalism*, published in 1940, he argued that liberalism could survive through a 'reinvigoration of [its] doctrinal content' based upon a 'new conception of property in which social ownership and control replace individual ownership and control.'[27]

Ultimately, stability could only be restored if the state's legitimacy was based on a democracy grounded in turn upon legitimate property relations, that is, a state whose function was *not* to protect the interests of a wealthy minority. Private ownership ultimately meant, especially through inheritance, that it had no moral basis. It broke the link between reward and effort, and therefore undermined the correlation between reward and social function.[28] Similarly, the rise of finance capital, more interested in profit than production, meant that 'functionless property is the controlling factor in industrial production'.[29] What was needed was a system of property that satisfied an individual's basic material needs for the 'realisation of personality',[30] as well as the 'needs of citizenship'.[31]

Tawney's treatment of the property question may have had an even greater impact on the young Macpherson. He later stated that his concept of 'possessive individualism' arose from the desire to make Tawney's notion of acquisitiveness, as expounded in *The Acquisitive Society* (1921), more precise.[32] Like Laski, his ethical position on work and property was founded on a functional perspective, especially their contribution to a general social purpose (although he never specified precisely how it was constituted – Tawney was more interested in the *idea* of social purpose[33]). In a crucial passage, he argued that the doctrine of an 'acquisitive society' implies that the

> foundation of society is found not in functions, but in rights; that rights are not deductible from the discharge of functions, so that the acquisition of wealth and the enjoyment of property are contingent upon the performance of services, but that the individual enters the world equipped with rights to the disposal of his property and the pursuit of his economic self-interest, and that these rights are anterior to, and independent of, any service which he may render.[34]

The individual became the 'centre of his own universe' and moral principles were dissolved into a 'choice of expediences'.[35] Rewards became divorced from services, and economic activity became an end in itself, rather than a means to an end. Rather than abolishing private property, he argued, following J. A. Hobson, a distinction had to be made between property and 'improperty'.[36] Entitlements were due only if the work performed fulfilled a social purpose, declaring agricultural rent, windfall profits, monopoly profits, urban ground rents and property in mineral royalties as 'improperty'.

The political conclusions from this Laski–Tawney discussion on property were not lost on Macpherson. They were not calling upon the abolition of private property consequential upon a successful class struggle by the proletariat. Rather, following the tradition established by New Liberals such as L. T. Hobhouse and J. A. Hobson, they wanted a progressive middle-class/working-class alliance, based upon a platform that combined liberal and socialist principles.[37] These principles meant that the individual contributed to a society whose ultimate end was the promotion of individual flourishing. To keep both the middle classes and the working class on board – this union of workers by hand and by brain – meant proposing a property system that gave both what they wanted. Although Laski and Tawney did much educational work with trade unions, they also devoted much of their time to impressing their ideas on the middle-class elite – their students. Getting the intellectual elite on board – or as Gramsci would say, 'organic intellectuals' – was vital if a 'revolution by consent' was to be achieved. This class alliance strategy from the mid-1930s onwards was reinforced by the Popular Front campaign, initiated by the Third International against Fascism. Laski, although critical of Communist Parties because of their opposition to liberal values and commitment to violent revolution, nevertheless participated.[38] Macpherson after his return to Canada contributed book reviews to the Popular Front journal *New Frontier*.

A final, if more speculative, consideration about Macpherson's intellectual development is that Laski and Tawney may have either wittingly or unwittingly helped generate or reinforce an Aristotelian approach to the study of politics. As already indicated Macpherson had won a couple of Classics scholarships, and E. J. Urwick, originally from the LSE, who taught him political economy was initially a Classics scholar. Laski was a student of the great Classics scholar Ernest Barker at Oxford. Laski strongly urged his own students to read Aristotle, for he thought that 'Aristotle made the greatest showing mind has been capable of.'[39] Laski also wrote to a friend Justice Holmes in 1918, outlining his planning for his *Grammar of Politics*, although he did not stick to it.

It will begin by a discussion of the bearing of philosophy on politics and discuss the idealistic canon of T. H. Green and Bosanquet. Then it will go on to discuss the purpose of the state (a) historically, (b) in theory, and show that (b) must, in Aristotelian fashion, be derived from (a).[40]

We have also already noted how both Laski and Tawney saw the state, labour and property in terms of its proper functioning, its telos. What we see in Macpherson's writings is the same insistence upon function (or the Greek *ergon*), along with concepts such as essence and potentiality. And like Aristotle he held, implicitly at least, a concept of virtue, which meant that what potentials were realised in human beings could be discovered through reason and experience. And possibly at the root of his willingness to combine liberalism and Marxism was the Aristotelian notion of virtue as a mean between extremes, involving judgement and choice. This exercise of the peculiarly human faculty of practical reason, for Aristotle, best occurred in a political community concerned to promote this flourishing, which minimally required material goods and physical energy, and consisted in the pleasures gained from the free, purposive exercise of these faculties for their own sake, often done in conjunction with others. Thus, the good life had to consist of autonomous choices rather than being subject to external forces.[41] Equally significant, Aristotle was one of the earliest critics of a developed market economy, condemning the accumulation of money for its own sake, rather than as a means to an end, that is as a medium of exchange for use.[42] By the same token property should not be accumulated but seen as a means to the end of the good life of the citizen. Such a perspective was directly at odds with the utilitarian tradition from Locke to Bentham, which Macpherson strongly criticised.[43] The Aristotelian dimension to Macpherson's thought could easily have been reinforced by Marx's own affinity to this thinker.[44]

The importance of function and purpose may also have affected his attitude towards what it meant to be a scholar. Scholarship had a role in society, because ideas influenced it. Thus scholarship was an activity that had to be undertaken with the utmost seriousness. And in the field of the human sciences scholars had a choice whether consciously or unconsciously to support existing power relationships that buttressed exploitation and oppression or subvert them. The method of subversion was partly through 'immanent critique', derived from Socrates, and was in effect democratic. It involved demonstrating how holding a certain set of ideas was self-contradictory, especially as between means and ends, rather than criticising the ends themselves. As we shall see Macpherson argued that one cannot be a committed Millian liberal and be at the same time committed to the capitalist market. In so far as the Millian conception of individual human flourishing was the goal of Western liberal democracy, it could not be achieved by capitalist means. Although he often used this form of argument he was also prepared to specify what constituted good and bad forms of human flourishing. In so far as Macpherson can be described as a liberal, he was a liberal with 'attitude', of a pre-Rawlsian kind. He was prepared to cut the knot between liberalism and capitalism. There could be no neutrality over competing conceptions of the good, when the capitalist dispensation could not confer upon its citizens the dignity of exerters, developers and enjoyers of their human powers, but only their freedom as consumers. And in so far as he was a Marxist, he was a Marxist by stealth. His understanding of society and history was based upon a Marxist concepts in which production relations, productive forces and exploitation were dominant. Yet, as we shall see, Macpherson's own distinctive vocabulary used to describe them – 'possessive market society', 'transfer of powers', 'extractive powers' and so on – could in part be construed as an attempt to get his ideas taken seriously by a liberal audience in the Cold War period.

– Before possessive individualism –

Macpherson took time to develop his own unique voice summed up in the phrase 'possessive individualism', which first appeared in his article, 'The Deceptive Task of Political Theory' in 1954.[45] Yet his concerns were visible in this period of gestation. In a substantive sense, they were announced in his Masters dissertation written under Laski's supervision. They were property and democracy. His dissertation, which he submitted in April 1935, had the ungainly title of 'Voluntary Associations within the state, 1900–1934, with special reference to the place of Trade Unions in relation to the state in Great Britain'. His thesis sought to make a simple point: within a 'capitalist democracy' variations in the regulation of voluntary associations were explicable in terms of their real or potential impact on private property. He then contrasted the state regulation of trade unions with the British Medical Association.[46] He concluded that:

> In no case does [the state] recognise [the trade unions'] claim to have a freer and larger place in society in virtue of the fact that they are voluntary associations which have arisen spontaneously to give expression to certain needs of individuals, needs which the state itself as a universal and compulsory association, cannot express.[47]

In other words, democratic voluntary associations, if they happened to be trade unions, were legally regulated by the capitalist state to ensure that they did not threaten the institution of private property. That the property/democracy relation would became his central concern was articulated in a review of Michael Oakshott's Social and Political Doctrines of Contemporary Europe.[48] Macpherson noted that there was

> no analysis of the implications of the property structure for democracy, or of the place of the concept of property in democratic theory ... not only the genesis of democracy but also its present and future are bound up with the problem of property relations. An examination of the presuppositions of democratic theory with regard to property is therefore of major importance.[49]

He was working out his own perspective on the property/democracy relation, a vision destined to become a permanent feature of his thought. He viewed democracy not merely as a means, as a set of institutions, but as a 'set of purposes or ends to which these institutions are but means'.[50] For him 'economic democracy' was essential in promoting ends which democratic theorists and movements have 'always sought'. This normative goal consisted of

> an equal humanity of every individual, the belief that each human being has a right to live as much as any other human being, and therefore that each has a right to live as fully as his capacities allow, always of course, so far as is consistent with others having the same rights.

Democracy meant, in other words, 'equal access to the means of self-development'.[51] This democratic end could not coexist with the institution of private property. Although formal democratic rights (means) existed, the 'modern concentration of wealth and economic power' distorted the democratic process. 'Political power still tends to follow property, in spite of the completely democratic franchise.'[52] This occurred through the control of the press and the ability to finance political parties and pressure groups. Thus these concentrations of wealth were able to prevent 'equality of opportunity and equality of consideration within the economic sphere of individuals.'[53] This means/end definition of democracy he saw as contained in the political theory of the United Farmers of Alberta (UFA), which governed Alberta from 1921 until 1935.[54]

A crucial consequence of his insistence on seeing democracy as an end became apparent by the late 1940s. He referred to the 'democratic revolutions' of Cromwell, Robespierre and Lenin on the grounds that they promoted the 'moral, intellectual, and active worth of all individuals', because they released 'the productive forces of society from previous obstacles' and developed 'wide participation in administration'.[55] This view enabled him publicly to defend the Soviet Union in a broadcast for the Canadian Broadcasting Company of the same year, claiming that the original aim of the Russian Revolution was the promotion of 'positive' liberty, and that dictatorship would disappear once the Soviet Union became a classless society.[56] Later in RWD he again argued that democracy and dictatorship were not necessarily antithetical on the grounds that Second and Third World regimes were promoting the democratic end of individual self-development. Not only was he insistent upon the notion that democracy could take different forms, he argued that the 'alternate-party' liberal democratic system was a 'special case of democracy'. It fulfilled needs specific to 'class-divided societies': the moderation of the 'conflict of class interests'.[57] It provided 'if not the satisfaction for one class, at least continual hope of further satisfaction for both.'[58]

Further, it continually provides a 'potential alternative government' and is therefore a 'constant check on any government's abusing its power', especially in the interests of a specific class.[59] In a classless society, such a system would be unnecessary because a 'general will' could sustain democracy. He saw this idea embodied in UFA's concept of democracy.[60] He extended this analysis of the 'alternate-party' system in his 'protective' and 'equilibrium' models of democracy, which appeared in his later work, especially *LTLD*.

If his substantive concerns with property and democracy were clearly Marxist-informed, like Laski,[61] his approach to the study of politics rejected any deterministic reading of historical materialism. 'It is time that the straw man of strict [Marxian] economic determinism was left alone.'[62] The scope for conscious human agency was central to Macpherson's project. The interaction of human beings and their circumstances in which ideas played a vital part should be the object of theoretical and empirical analysis. Thus, the modern state had to be understood as the

> product of the interaction of men's ideas and men's actions and the circumstances from which these have arisen and with which they have been confronted. This understanding must be sought in the study of the history of political ideas considered not as abstract philosophies but as, at each stage, both cause and effect of political, social and economic situations and activity.[63]

He wanted the 'study of the development in interaction of political ideas and concrete political facts' to be the 'new principle of unity' within political science. The study of political ideas ought, he urged, to be at the 'centre of the teaching of politics', enabling it to become a 'coherent intellectual discipline' as it ' aspired to be fifty years ago'.[64] He was dismayed by the detachment of economics, history and law from the study of politics at the University of Toronto. His demand, however, for a 'new principle of unity' was not merely for methodological reasons. As already suggested for Macpherson ideas, circumstances and institutions interacted with each other. And as he said a little later, a 'new period' had arisen, indicated by the 'emergence of the new practical problems'.[65] The 'decline of economic expansion' left 'less leeway for contending groups' and therefore a political philosophy of political pluralism. Changing 'economic realities' demanded a 'new social philosophy', which entailed a 'radical revision of the prevailing philosophy of liberalism'.[66] The Second World War and its aftermath would expose the contradiction contained within liberalism between 'free economic enterprise and other freedoms usually described as democratic.'[67] 'Class issues' were likely to become 'increasingly important in Canada'.[68] Following Marx's injunction in the famous eleventh of his *Theses on Feuerbach* about philosophers and the need to change the world, he argued that the political scientist could be 'at the same time a scholar and a protagonist of a political philosophy demanding change, and he will be a better scholar if he is a protagonist of, or feeling his way towards, a more adequate philosophy.'[69] His view of the study of politics was therefore premised upon a belief that he knew where the world was heading, that ideas could have a beneficial impact on a changing world and the prevailing liberal ideology was not up to the job and required revision since the value of all political ideas was 'relative to the needs of different periods'.[70] In such periods of transition, these ideas could only be properly evaluated if an 'inclusive historical method' were adopted.[71]

Various aspects of Macpherson's critique of orthodox political science can be noted in this period. First, he described its conservative, anti-Marxist orientation. The 'disturbing tendency' among political scientists was that they accepted ideological and national 'alignments as given' and assumed 'that the problem is to find a theoretical basis to shore up the defences of western society against the encroachments of philosophic materialism.'[72] As he was later to say, however, this was not because political scientists were necessarily fully aware of what they were doing. The observer in the social sciences

> is part of the total social situation, all or part of which he is observing. His whole attitude is shaped to some extent by the mental climate of his group and his period, and his own feelings and desires pull him this way and that within this general attitude.[73]

Political scientists were not completely sensitised to the fact that 'social and historical thought is to a peculiar degree formed by the very forces it seeks to interpret.'[74] And if they were not fully aware of the fact that they were part of this process, self-deception could arise, causing them unwittingly to become 'ideological' rather than scientific in outlook. Later in 'The Deceptive Task of Political Theory' he asserted 'solid political theorists in the liberal tradition have been compelled to deceive themselves'.[75] Although they had from J. S. Mill onwards seen beyond possessive individualism, they did not make their theorising consistent with this observation.

Secondly, linked to the fact that the political scientist was not above, but part of, society, he rejected the notion that political science could become value-free, modelled on the natural sciences. Not surprisingly, he had little time for the empiricist obsessions of American political science. In Aristotelian fashion he commented that it was

> so intent on empirical analysis that for the most part it eschews any inquiry into adequacy, since that would involve 'value judgement'. The prevailing view . . . is that it is necessary not only that political science should be done, but also that it should appear to be done, and here 'science' is predominantly taken to mean purely empirical investigation and generalization. [Thus, concern for techniques of power,

opinion formation, and so on had] turned attention away from the purposes of the political process, the needs of the ruled, and the potentialities for satisfying these needs. The prevailing focus of attention is the mechanics rather than the purposes or potentialities of the political process.[76]

The preoccupation with testing empirical hypotheses was, he argued, ultimately self-defeating, because only those hypotheses were chosen where uniformities could be identified, and research projects were considered valuable only if they employed empirical methods. Political science ought, however, to be evaluated in terms of whether it was pursuing 'with the requisite consciousness of the need to rethink a political philosophy adequate to the new moral problems posed by changes in society.'[77] The basic challenge was to keep a balance between systematic and particular inquiries on the one hand, and a 'political philosophy thought out in relation to a new set of social relations and problems', on the other.[78] Macpherson's only attempt to integrate rigorously the normative and empirical aspects of political science was in *Democracy in Alberta* (1953).

Macpherson a little later resisted the positivist move within political philosophy. He objected to the current fad of Linguistic Analysis that endeavoured to sort out linguistic muddles surrounding derivations of values from facts. Linguistic Analysts, such as T. D. Weldon, maintained that according to the rules of grammar there were only two types of meaningful statement: those that were factual, or those which were tautologous, modelled on mathematics. Macpherson argued that rules of grammar were themselves different in different societies, and the gap between the 'is' and the 'ought' did not arise in primitive societies. Rather, this gap suited class-divided societies, because otherwise obligations would follow from the facts of equal human 'wants' – physical, spiritual, emotional and aesthetic – and therefore prompt criticisms of existing class-based systems of rights. However, the problem with Linguistic Analysis, he maintained, was not that it was too empirical, but that it was not empirical enough: it did not fully recognise the social nature of language and logic.[79] For Macpherson the ought/is derivation was to play a significant part in his interpretation of Hobbes in *PI*, as a conceptual revolutionist.[80]

To sum up his main concerns before 'possessive individualism': his analysis of the relationship between property and democracy formed the focus of his work, in descriptive, explanatory and normative senses. These concerns had implications for what it meant to be a political scientist, especially given the relationship between thought and social, economic and political realities. The political scientist, whether he or she liked it or not, was part of the thought/reality 'loop', as cause and effect. And ultimately there could be no fact/value dichotomy, because the political scientist was too deeply implicated in the world. Not to recognise this amounted to self-deception, especially as thought could lag behind reality. Consequently, the political scientist had a choice as to how he or she might affect the world in which he or she lived. The relationship between the world and thought also had to be viewed historically, as both were subject to change. Understanding this relationship historically meant current political ideas could be more clearly evaluated, especially liberalism, to see which elements were 'living' and 'dead' when contrasted with contemporary reality and given the nature of human beings. Furthermore, the world had to be seen holistically, because it was a totality: different disciplines within the human sciences had to remain in contact with each other. By the 1960s and 1970s he bemoaned the fact that political science had become separated from economics: there was no longer a 'political economy', which was of course explicit in his property/democracy focus.[81]

— Possessive individualism and after —

His object was to formulate a post-capitalist revised liberal political philosophy through a deconstruction of the liberal democratic tradition, by showing how two contradictory ontologies beat in its breast. The purpose of his analysis of Hobbes and Locke in particular, examined in the next two chapters, was to expose the possessive individualist roots of modern liberalism, by revealing what can be called its 'negative' ontology. Hobbes and Locke between them had in effect fashioned an ideological mind-set that had been historically appropriate, at once realistic and ethically suited to a capitalist, market society. He sought to free liberalism from this possessive ontology, based upon private property, and run with Mill's 'positive' ontology of individual self-development, which required a new set of property relations along with a new concept of democracy.

Let us first look Macpherson's concept of 'possessive individualism' as outlined in *PI*. The concept had its first outing in 1954, but full elaboration had to wait until *PI* in 1962. The 'Deceptive Task of Political Theory' was very much a first approximation and was Marx–Locke inspired, whereas in *PI* Hobbes came fully into the frame.[82] For Macpherson 'possessive individualism' was *the* political philosophy of a capitalist society. And the concept consisted of an amalgam of Hobbes, Locke and Marx. He itemised the essential 'postulates' of a possessive market (capitalist) society as follows. First, there existed, unlike in 'customary or status' societies, no authoritative allocation of work and rewards for work; only contracts were authoritatively defined and enforced. Secondly, all individuals seek rationally to maximise their utilities, and some individuals want more utilities or powers than they have. Thirdly, each individual owns his capacity to labour which he can sell, that is alienate. Fourthly, land and other resources are owned by individuals, and are alienable. Fifthly, some individuals have more energy, skill or possessions than others.[83] All these postulates are required for a competitive market society consisting of commodity owners, whether of capital (land or other means of production) or labour.

However, Macpherson argued that the competitive exchanges that occur between the owners of capital and labour are intrinsically unfair, because the owners of labour cannot resort to independent production.

> They cannot demand in wages an amount equal to what would have been the product of their labour on land or capital of their own. Those who have the capital and the land can, therefore, by employing the labour of others, get a net transfer of the labour of others (or some of the product of those powers) to themselves.[84]

The wage-worker's powers (defined in Hobbes' terms as present means to obtain future apparent goods) are thereby reduced because access to the means of production, which enable 'him' to exercise his powers, is restricted. They are reduced 'by the price he has to pay for access, and that price measures the amount of his power that is transferred to another'.[85] This price of access then for Macpherson constitutes the 'net transfer of powers'. The job of the state, whether it pursues mercantilist or laissez-faire economic policies, was at the very least to administer a compulsory framework of law, which protects life and property and defines and enforces contracts.

Here we move into the realm of justification, of political philosophy. Macpherson summed up the 'assumptions' of possessive individualism in seven propositions:

> (i) What makes a man human is freedom from dependence on the wills of others. (ii) Freedom from dependence on others means freedom from any relations with others except those relations which the individual enters voluntarily with a view to his own interest. (iii) The individual is essentially the proprietor of his own person and capacities, for which he owes nothing to society. (iv) Although the individual cannot alienate the whole of his property in his own person, he may alienate his capacity to labour. (v) Human society consists of a series of market relations. (vi) Since freedom from the wills of others is what makes a man human, each individual's freedom can rightfully be limited only by such obligations and rules as are necessary to secure the same freedom for others. (vii) Political society is a human contrivance for the protection of the individual's property in his person and goods, and (therefore) for the maintenance of orderly relations of exchange between individuals regarded as proprietors of themselves.[86]

These assumptions were 'clearest and fullest in Hobbes'.[87] They were 'not unalloyed' in Locke, who did not 'entirely let go of traditional natural law.'[88]

Macpherson's theory of possessive individualism drew on Marx as well as Hobbes and Locke. The general methodological approach was clearly Marxist, the use of economic models, the economic base/political-legal superstructure relation, a concept of exploitation based on free exchange between proprietors, and the correlating of Hobbes' and Locke's thought with the rise of capitalism. Yet, there was more than this. In his first article on Hobbes, he detected in his thought manifestations of Marx's concept of 'commodity fetishism'.[89] Social interdependence, through capitalist exchange relations, appears as an impersonal relation between commodities, that is between things. Hobbes saw individuals as free of all relations of personal mutual dependence and 'so constituted that they are not fit for society, but only for the competitive struggle for existence, unless there is an artificially constructed power sufficient to overawe them all.'[90] At the heart of possessive individualism is a society of atomised, free and equal individuals – self-proprietors – whose obligations are based upon rational self-interest. Relations of domination, subordination and exploitation are rendered, at least at the formal level, invisible. Hobbes' contribution to the theory was in a sense to reflect the emergence of a possessive individualist society, not only the idea of it consisting of free and equal competitive individuals, but also at the ontological level. These individuals were utility maximisers ('infinite consumers' he was later to say), and given limitless appetites, had to be power maximisers. Although Macpherson downplayed Locke's contribution to the theory in PI, it can nevertheless be seen in his emphasis of individuals as self-proprietors, and the function of the state to protect 'property' in the broad sense of the term to include 'lives, liberties and estates'. Here again freedom is conceived in the 'negative' sense of being free from the will of others. Just as significant was Locke's contribution to legitimising the idea of 'infinite appropriation': the never-ending accumulation of wealth was morally permissible.

This possessive individualist ontology was, Macpherson argued, at the root of the twentieth-century liberal difficulty in offering a coherent theory of obligation. Broadly speaking, it was viable while the working class were not granted the franchise: cohesion could be maintained provided only the possessing classes had a political voice, for they were the beneficiaries of the property-protecting state, of a capitalist market society. But once the working class was brought within the pale of the constitution in Britain from the mid-nineteenth century onwards, not all those with a political voice felt equally content with being equally subject to the market. There was in other words a developing mismatch between political equality and the formal economic equality of self-proprietorship. For the working class, why support a state whose function was to facilitate a substantive inequality of outcome?[91] Macpherson stated that the dilemma for twentieth-century liberalism was either to reject possessive individualist assumptions, which is unrealistic because market relations are deeply embedded, or to retain them in which case 'we cannot get a valid theory of obligation'.[92] However, writing when nuclear war seemed a real possibility, especially under the shadow of the Cuban missile crisis, led to an abrupt change of direction at the end of *PI*. The threat of nuclear annihilation had created a new global equality of insecurity that required allegiance to a 'wider political authority'.[93]

In a number of ways *PI* did not give the full flavour of the Macpherson project indicative in his earlier work. The core thematic of property/democracy is more implicit than explicit. He focused primarily on applying the possessive individualist concept to Hobbes, Locke, Harrington and the Levellers. And his discussion of the contradictions of liberal democracy is only touched upon briefly when discussing the problem of obligation. After *PI*, along with criticisms of contemporary political science, we continue to get commentary on past and present thinkers as seen through the possessive individualist optic – Hume, Bentham, James and John Stuart Mill, T. H. Green, Chapman, Rawls, Freidman and Berlin. However, his attention is more obviously devoted to revising liberal democratic theory and practice by an examination of its contradictions arising from the problematic relation between property and democracy. These contradictions were manifest at a number of levels. The most basic was ontological. What becomes starkly posed in his post-*PI* works is the opposition between the Hobbesian and Lockean 'essence' of 'man' as 'infinite' consumer and appropriator, deriving from possessive individualist, utilitarian assumptions, and the Millian concept of man as purposive 'exerter' and 'developer' of human capacities, deriving ultimately from Aristotle. Although Mill could be criticised for not having abandoned capitalist market assumptions, he nevertheless articulated the 'central ethical principle of liberalism – the freedom of the individual to realize his or her human capacities.'[94] The capacities that Macpherson had in mind included those

> for rational understanding, for moral judgement and action, for aesthetic creation or contemplation, for the emotional activities of friendship and love, and sometimes religious experience . . . for transforming what is given by Nature . . . for wonder or curiosity . . . for laughter . . . for controlled physical/mental/aesthetic activity . . . .'[95]

Macpherson's argument was that liberal democracy claimed to maximise the powers necessary to satisfy both these images.[96] Yet, they were, he said, fundamentally contradictory, because the infinite consumer/appropriator image, built upon the assumption of infinite scarcity, justified a possessive individualist view of the world, and therefore in effect the net transfer of powers. This net transfer diminished people's developmental essences, in the sense that it reduced their ability and energy to engage in freely chosen activities. Macpherson contrasted what he deemed to be this 'ethical concept' of power, where no net transfer occurred because all had equal access to the means of production, with the prevailing liberal 'descriptive' concept based upon Hobbes. This consisted of the present means however acquired to obtain a future apparent, appetite-driven good.[97] The contradiction between these two images was in reality in the process of being overcome. World society was on the threshold of technologically-created abundance, rendering the image of 'man' as infinite consumer and appropriator redundant. The concomitant assumption of infinite scarcity, which served as an incentive to boost productivity, was about to be undermined.[98] With the prospect of abundance, 'the appetite for human freedom has outgrown its capitalist market envelope'.[99] A society free of 'compulsory labour' which provided 'a fully human life for all' was now a distinct possibility.[100]

These two competing ontologies, Macpherson held, were mirrored in liberal democratic theory. Macpherson argued that liberal democracy had two meanings: *either* procedural, as a system of *government*, which he termed 'protective democracy', a mechanism for protecting citizens and their possessions from the state and from each other, and suited to a market society, *or* substantive, which referred to a *society* of self-developers, which he termed 'developmental democracy'.[101] Under capitalism he saw both models as contradictory because universal suffrage had not produced equal participation in the political process, and was thus 'unable to promote that personal development and moral community, which was the main rationale offered for liberal democracy'.[102] The party system that arose after the granting of universal suffrage created political apathy. This was so for a number of reasons. First, Macpherson used his earlier critique of liberal democracy, already noted, to argue that the party system enabled the capitalist minority to maintain their power because it blunted class conflict.[103] Parties to get elected had to move to the middle ground, and appeal to notions of the 'common good' (especially economic growth) which transcended particular class interests. Although Macpherson did not spell out the significance of this, he seemed to have meant that with the attenuation of class issues came a lack of expectation by the majority, working class that voting would make a great deal of difference to the fundamental structure of society. Secondly, he maintained that the rise of the party machine had ensured that constituency rank and files have little say in the selection and conduct of MPs. A third cause of apathy was that party leaders needed room for manoeuvre to effect class compromises and therefore could not be directly accountable to the party rank and file.

Optimistically, Macpherson suggested that the developmental model was in the process of superseding the protective model, at least in the effectively Hegelian, dialectical sense of preservation and transcendence (or 'sublation'). The procedural liberal democratic model prevalent in the West was now challenged by the Second (socialist) and Third (populist) worlds, which were successfully establishing the developmental model:[104] by successfully exploiting modern technology and overcoming scarcity they were promoting egalitarian self-development. Once the Second and Third Worlds had caught up in individual civil and political rights, and given the nuclear stalemate, the Western regimes would only be able to compete 'morally' if they promoted developmental democracy.[105] Macpherson, in seeking to eradicate the global schism, believed that both (including the Third world) models issued from the same stable: liberalism. The goals of Western liberalism and Eastern socialism were identical: the fostering of individual self-development. In a historical sense, he argued, the East was nearer reaching this goal because through economic planning they would be more adept at utilising modern technology.

In hoping to facilitate this process of undermining the exclusively protective model of liberal democracy, he challenged the main justificatory theory of liberal democracy in political science, first formulated by Joseph Schumpeter in *Capitalism, Socialism and Democracy* (1942). Macpherson called it the 'equilibrium model'. Schumpeter held that the electoral system was analogous to the marketplace. Political parties (entrepreneurs) competed in the selling of their political goods to the electorate (consumers), who registered their preferences by voting. Elections, analogous to the price system, equilibrated supply and demand. The ultimate justification of this process is that it protected the people from tyranny through periodic elections.[106] The strength of this theory, Macpherson maintained, was its realism. As a description of how the party system operates this may be true, he argued. Yet this descriptive accuracy should not be confused with its immutability and its commendatory assumption of optimality and consumer sovereignty. The political ability of the average person was taken as a 'fixed datum' instead of dependent upon circumstances. Indeed, social inequality might account for voter apathy as well as the absence of real choice. The optimality claim also had to be rejected because the electoral system only equilibrated supply with the *effective* demand of those who financed the political parties and had the time and energy to play an active part in the political process.[107] And consumer sovereignty was hardly evident because the suppliers (parties) of political goods were few, and therefore did not have to respond to demand. The political initiative lay with such suppliers who in effect create their own demand, because they consisted of political elites who determined the political agenda.[108]

What was ultimately pivotal to a democratic *society* was the transformation of property relations, both in theory and practice. He boldly announced that 'all roads lead to property'.[109] Private property relations were obviously appropriate to a possessive market society, but some kind of socialised property relations would be required for a society of self-developers, where a net transfer of powers or 'extractive powers' was absent. In brief, his argument was that capitalist property relations, which developed from the seventeenth century onwards, were characterised by the individual or corporate right to exclude others from the use or benefit of a thing, and a right in or to a material thing, rather than as a right to a revenue. Private property also served as an incentive to work, as well as a means to exercise human capacities.[110] The kind of property relations entailed for a fully democratic society would require 'retrieving' the pre-capitalist concept of property as a right to a revenue, derived from labour or what he called 'common property'. The idea behind this was Aristotelian inspired, that property should not be an end in itself but a means to the exercise of one's human capacities. Thus, it had also to include the notion of not being excluded from the means of life and labour. Beyond this it meant the right to a 'fully human life', which entailed a right to share in the political power that controlled society's productive assets, and a right to participate in a 'satisfying set of social relations', beyond access to material things.[111] The transition to this type of property was now feasible because of the possibility of technologically-created abundance. Private property as an incentive to labour would not be redundant, as the need to labour would become less significant. Hence democratic control over productive assets would be necessary to ensure the equal right to self-development.

Macpherson argued that this shift in the theory and practice of property was actually in train. A 'quasi-market society' was already in existence, whereby income was not exclusively allocated by the market. Democratic pressure on modern states had led to an increase in welfare responsibilities, people expecting a right to a job[112] or a right to a revenue, a guaranteed income. And environmental pressures, such as demands for clean air and water, were also putting restrictions on private ownership.[113] Nevertheless, technological advance was still the key to broadening the concept of property.

Macpherson advocated an ideal democratic model consonant with this socialised notion of property and the Millian developmental ontology. He proposed a participatory system, with direct participation at the base, at the level of neighbourhood and workplace, constituting the ground for indirect, 'pyramidal' representation at higher levels. Within this framework parties would compete, although in the future they might be replaced by other representative groupings.[114]

He admitted that the developmental ontology that such a system would uphold entailed the 'staggering' assumption of social harmony, or non-contentiousness, such that no one prevented others from developing their essentially human capacities.[115] He admitted that this postulate of non-opposition might be 'too good to be true', but it was 'necessary to any fully democratic theory'.[116] And the truth of this proposition could be only proved or disproved 'by trial'.[117] Appeal to past or present empirical experience was not, he argued, decisive, because such human capacities were 'as yet nowhere realized'.[118]

His optimism was also manifest in that he did not see the problem as how such a society would be run so much as how to arrive: the journey rather than the destination was the problem.[119] Human beings would develop such capacities on the way. He did, however, mention two prerequisites for such a transition. One was an alteration of the image people had of themselves, from consumer to doer, which required a sense of community, because capacities were largely developed in conjunction with others. Such a sense of community was also necessary for participatory democracy.[120] The other prerequisite was a substantial reduction in social and economic inequality to reduce political apathy. He acknowledged that to establish these requisites involved him in a vicious circle, because only more democratic participation would in fact achieve this.[121] He rejected Marx's theory of transition because workers in the West were too affluent, and where they did exhibit class consciousness it was not in a revolutionary form.[122]

Nevertheless, he maintained there were at least three 'loopholes' in the vicious circle. First, people were beginning to recognise the costs of economic growth, of environmental degradation.[123] Second, neighbourhood and community movements were developing in cities in opposition to the 'urban commercial-political complex', as were movements for industrial democracy.[124] Thirdly, in a way that slightly contradicted his dismissal of a Marxist view of transition, he suggested that world capitalism was entering into deepening crises, which was leading to greater working-class trade union and political activity.[125] Thus, he contemplated the possibility of both a 'partial breakdown (national or international) of the political order of the market society' and a 'partial breakthrough of consciousness', leading to the 'cumulative realization of democracy'.[126] Yet he was not wholeheartedly optimistic about such an outcome. The chances were 50/50, owing to the power of the multinationals, state intelligence services such as the CIA, and popular support for a police state to combat political terrorism by left- or right-wing minorities. And finally an economic downturn might occur before popular pressures had managed to reduce economic inequalities.[127]

Before concluding this chapter we can take note of Macpherson's strategy of argument. First, there is an appeal to human nature – his essentialist, 'ontological' argument that conceives the proper function of human beings, *qua* humans, as 'doing' rather than 'getting'. Second, there is the immanent critique of 'adequacy', whether some desired (liberal) ends are consistent with the (capitalist) means. Third, there is the historical perspective, to 'de-reify' or demythologise pro-capitalist concepts. This involved showing how such concepts arose to serve the needs of a dominant class, and how their actual meaning should not assume lapidary status, and how past traditions of thought are still valuable to the emancipatory project. Fourth, 'new facts' arose which challenged accepted institutions and ideas, demanding new ways of thinking. Finally, this 'new' way of thinking was in part reflected in Macpherson's own terminology, 'possessive individualism', 'net transfer of powers', 'ethical powers', 'extractive power', 'protective democracy' and 'developmental democracy'. As well as providing fresh insight, by using these terms he hoped to move the reader onto more neutral territory, especially away from the emotive Marxist terms such as 'exploitation' or 'bourgeois democracy'.

We can now conclude by briefly summarising the conceptual structure of his thought with democracy and property its centre. The 'bad' couplet was capitalism/democracy. Here human beings were conceived as acquisitive, possessive, self-owning individualists, as 'infinite' consumers and appropriators. Such a conception derived from a capitalist system built upon exclusive, private property. Human powers were conceived in a descriptive, Hobbesian sense of present means to acquire future apparent goods, and as such licensed the 'net transfers of powers'. Democracy was essentially 'protective', defending individuals against each other and against the state, and the party system functioned to blur class division. Freedom meant being independent of the will of others. The 'good' couplet was common property/participatory democracy. Here, human beings were seen as exerters, enjoyers and developers of their own powers, individually and collectively. Powers were viewed 'ethically', as fufilling human potentials that were neither harmful to oneself or others, and required a system of common, inclusive property, to enable equal access to the means of life and labour. Freedom meant not merely being independent of the will of others, but also being able to freely exert, enjoy and develop one's human powers. While Macpherson was hesistant about what kind of agency could bring about the transition from the 'bad' to the 'good' couplet and the form it would take, he was certain about one thing. Technological development created the necessary preconditions.

NOTES

1. See D. M. Ricci, *The Tragedy of Political Science, Politics, Scholarship, and Democracy* (New Haven, CT: Yale University Press, 1984), ch. 5, *passim*.
2. C. B. Macpherson, *Democracy in Alberta* (Toronto: University of Toronto Press, 1953).
3. C. B. Macpherson, *The Political Theory of Possessive Individualism* (Oxford: Oxford University Press, 1962).

4. Jacob Viner wrote: 'If only [Macpherson] had not tightly integrated his scholarly endeavour with his apostolic mission I am sure that this book could have been a superlative manifestation of top-level intellectual history' ' "Possessive Individualism" as Original Sin', *Canadian Journal of Economic and Political Science*, 29, 1963, p. 559). Peter Laslett commented, Macpherson 'may best be described as a dogmatic, economic sociologist of a familiar, but refined, Marxian cast ...' ('Market Society and Political Theory', *Historical Journal*, 7/1, 1964, p. 154).

5. Oxford: Oxford University Press, 1973.

6. Oxford: Oxford University Press, 1977.

7. Oxford: Oxford University Press, 1965.

8. Oxford: Oxford University Press, 1984.

9. K. Macpherson, *When in Doubt Do Both: The Times of My Life* (Toronto: University of Toronto Press, 1994), p. 79.

10. Berlin to Macpherson, 25 June 1971, Macpherson papers, Robarts Library, University of Toronto.

11. 'The Treadmill', *The Canadian Forum*, January, 1958, p. 232.

12. *C. B. Macpherson: Dilemmas of Liberalism and Socialism* (New York: St. Martin's Press, 1988), ch. 1, *passim*.

13. Macpherson to Pamela van der Sprenkel, 28 August 1978, Macpherson papers. He may also have inspired in Macpherson a lifelong passion for the music of Bach.

14. 17 May 1976, Macpherson papers.

15. C. B. Macpherson, 'The Position of Political Science', *Culture*, 3, 1942, p. 458.

16. See also R. Miliband, 'Harold Laski: An Exemplary Public Intellectual', *New Left Review*, 200, 1993, pp. 179-80.

17. See 'Introduction' to *The Communist Manifesto* [1848] (London: Allen & Unwin, 1948), pp. 86-7, p. 94.

18. 'Scholars and Spectres: A Rejoinder to Viner', *Canadian Journal of Economics and Political Science*, 29, November 1963, p. 592.

19. K. Marx, 'Preface to *A Contribution to the Critique of Political Economy*', *Marx and Engels, Selected Works* (Moscow: Foreign Languages Publishing House, 1962), vol. 1, p. 363.

20. Ibid.

21. See I. Shapiro, 'Realism in the Study of the History of Ideas', *History of Political Thought*, 3/3, November 1982, pp. 535-78.

22. P. Lamb, 'Laski on Sovereignty: Removing the Mask from Class Dominance', *History of Political Thought*, 17/2, 1997, pp. 326-42.

23. Quoted Ibid., pp. 329-30.

24. Quoted Ibid., p. 337.

25. London: Allen & Unwin, 1934, p. i.

26. *The Rise of European Liberalism* (London: Allen & Unwin, [1936] 1962), pp. 168-71. Macpherson's general attitude towards liberalism may have been influenced by the fact that Laski delivered lectures which became *The Rise of European Liberalism* while he was at the LSE. I. Kramnick and B. Sherman, *Harold Laski: A Life on the Left* (London: Allen Lane/Penguin, 1993), p. 362.

27. Quoted in M. Freeden, *Liberalism Divided* (Oxford: Clarendon Press, 1986), p. 310.
28. *Grammar of Politics*, p. 188.
29. Ibid., p. 208.
30. Ibid., p. 184.
31. Ibid., p. 183.
32. Leiss, *C. B. Macpherson*, p. 28.
33. A. Wright, *R. H. Tawney* (Manchester: Manchester University Press, 1987), p. 60.
34. R. H. Tawney, *The Acquisitive Society* (London: Fontana, [1921] 1962), p. 25.
35. Ibid., p. 33.
36. Ibid., p. 58, and see Hobson's later *Property and Improperty* (London: Gollancz, 1937).
37. See J. Townshend, *J. A. Hobson* (Manchester: Manchester University Press, 1990), chs 4 and 6, *passim*.
38. M. Newman, *Harold Laski* (London: Macmillan, 1993), p. 178.
39. M. De Wolfe-Howe (ed.), *Holmes–Laski Letters, The Correspondence of Mr. Justice Holmes and Harold J. Laski, 1916–1935* (London: Oxford University Press), p. 68.
40. Ibid., p. 156.
41. See for a summary R. Miller, 'Marx and Aristotle. A Kind of Consequentialism', in G. E. McCarthy (ed.), *Marx and Aristotle*, (Savage, MD: Rowman & Littlefield, 1992), pp. 276-7.
42. See, for example, *RFEJ*, pp. 5-7.
43. Macpherson, 'Property as Means or End', in A. Parel and T. Flanagan (eds), *Theories of Property: Aristotle to the Present* (Waterloo, Ontario: Wilfred Laurier Press, 1979), pp. 3-4.
44. For example, McCarthy (ed.), *Marx and Aristotle*.
45. *Cambridge Journal*, 7, 1954, pp. 560-8, reprinted in *DT*, pp. 195-203.
46. For example, p. 282, p. 290, Macpherson papers.
47. Ibid., p. 316.
48. Toronto: Macmillan, 1939.
49. 'History of Political Ideas', *Canadian Journal of Economic and Political Science*, 7, 1941, pp. 576-7.
50. 'The Meaning of Economic Democracy', *University of Toronto Quarterly*, 11, 1942, p. 404.
51. Ibid., p. 404.
52. Ibid., p. 407.
53. Ibid., p. 406.
54. Macpherson, *Democracy in Alberta: Social Credit and the Party System* (original subtitle: *The Theory and Practice of a Quasi-party System*) (Toronto: University of Toronto Press, [1953] 1962), pp. 46-8.
55. 'The Political Theory of Social Credit', *Canadian Journal of Economics and Political Science*, 15, 1949, p. 390.
56. CBC archives, 26 January 1949.
57. 'The Political Theory of Social Credit', p. 390.

58. Ibid.
59. Ibid., p. 391.
60. *Democracy in Alberta*, pp. 46–50.
61. Lamb, 'Laski on Sovereignty', pp. 330–1.
62. 'History of Political Ideas', p. 574.
63. 'On the Study of Politics in Canada', in H. A. Innis (ed.), *Essays in Political Economy, in Honour of E. J. Urwick* (Toronto: University of Toronto Press, 1938), p. 164.
64. Ibid., p. 164.
65. 'The Position of Political Science', *Culture*, 3, 1942, p. 453.
66. Ibid., pp. 456–7.
67. Ibid., p. 457.
68. Ibid., p. 459.
69. Ibid., p. 458.
70. 'History of Political Ideas', p. 566.
71. Ibid., p. 577.
72. 'A Disturbing Tendency in Political Science', *Canadian Journal of Economic and Political Science*, 16, 1950, p. 98.
73. 'Pareto's "General Sociology": the Problem of Method in the Social Sciences', *Canadian Journal of Economics and Political Science*, 3, 1937, p. 470.
74. 'The Social Sciences', in J. Park (ed.), *The Culture of Contemporary Canada* (Ithaca, NY: Cornell University Press, 1957), p. 181.
75. *DT*, p. 203.
76. 'World Trends in Political Science Research', *American Political Science Review*, 47, 1954, p. 433.
77. Ibid., pp. 448–9.
78. Ibid., p. 449.
79. 'The Treadmill', *The Canadian Forum*, January 1958, pp. 230–2.
80. Yet, interpreting Hobbes as such should have led him to modify his suggestion that the separation of 'is' from 'ought' is a feature of all class societies.
81. For example, *DT*, p. 46, and 'After Strange Gods: Canadian Political Science 1973', in T. N. Guinsburg and G. L. Reuber (eds), *Perspectives on the Social Sciences in Canada* (Toronto: University of Toronto Press, 1974), pp. 63–7.
82. In the 'Deceptive Task ...' the theory contained three elements. First, the individual was seen as 'absolute natural proprietor of his own capacities, owing nothing to society for them. Man's essence is freedom to use his capacities in search of satisfactions' (*DT*, p. 199). Freedom was identified with domination over things, not over men, that is with possession. Freedom is universal because everyone at least owns their own capacities. Second, society consists of free property owners, who relate to each other through their possessions, as owners of capacities and what they have produced and accumulated through exercising these capacities. Market exchange is the fundamental social relation. Third, the state's function is to protect property, including capacities, and 'even life and liberty are considered as possessions, rather than as social rights with correlative

duties' (ibid.). At this stage, he saw Locke as properly the first possessive individualist thinker. He had just written two pieces on Locke ('Locke on Capitalist Appropriation', *Western Political Quarterly*, 4, 1951, pp. 550–66, and 'The Social Bearing of Locke's Political Theory', *Western Political Quarterly*, 7, 1954, pp. 1–22). Although Hobbes went further than Locke in seeing individuals as commodities with exchange values, he saw domination as being over men rather than things, 'which is perhaps why he is not to be counted entirely in the liberal tradition' (*DT*, p. 199). However, by the time he wrote *PI* he held that possessive market assumptions were 'clearest and fullest in Hobbes' (*PI*, p. 264).

83. *PI*, p. 54.
84. Ibid., p. 56.
85. Ibid.
86. Ibid., pp. 263–4.
87. Ibid., p. 264.
88. Ibid., p. 269.
89. *DT*, p. 248.
90. *PI*, pp. 248–9.
91. Ibid., pp. 272–5.
92. Ibid., p. 275.
93. Ibid., p. 276.
94. *LTLD*, p. 2.
95. *DT*, pp. 53–4, also ibid., p. 4.
96. Ibid., ch. 1, *passim.*
97. Ibid., p. 9.
98. Ibid., p. 31.
99. *LTLD*, p. 2.
100. *DT*, p. 22.
101. Ibid., p. 51.
102. *LTLD*, p. 64.
103. *DT*, p. 191; *LTLD*, pp. 66–9.
104. *DT*, pp. 34–5.
105. *RWD*, pp. 65–7.
106. *LTLD*, p. 78.
107. Ibid., p. 87.
108. Ibid., pp. 90–1.
109. *DT*, p. 121.
110. Ibid., p. 122.
111. Ibid., p. 139.
112. Ibid., p. 134.
113. Ibid., p. 135.
114. *LTLD*, ch. 5, *passim.*
115. *DT*, p. 54. See also *Democracy in Alberta*, pp. 46–8.
116. Ibid., p. 55.

117. Ibid.
118. Ibid.
119. Ibid., p. 74; *LTLD*, p. 98.
120. Ibid., p. 99.
121. Ibid., p. 100.
122. Ibid., p. 101, footnote.
123. Ibid., p. 102; *DT*, p. 76.
124. *LTLD*, p. 103.
125. Ibid., p. 106.
126. *DT*, p. 76.
127. *LTLD*, p. 107

CHAPTER 2

HOBBES AS POSSESSIVE INDIVIDUALIST

Before looking at Macpherson's treatment of Hobbes and Locke and the critical response in this and the next chapter, a number of general considerations ought to be borne in mind. The first is that, like the format of nearly all his works, *PI* consisted of a collection of essays, written over a ten-year period. Not surprisingly, lines of questioning and levels of assertion undergo subtle changes in different chapters, although the possessive individualism motif pulls them together. The second consideration is that while possessive individualism constitutes the main theme, Macpherson uses it to establish a number of disparate claims, which could create certain tensions, especially in his treatment of Locke. As we shall see, his critics often dealt with one or two of these claims, implying that if these could be rejected, then all could be rejected, for few were prepared to say where they agreed with him. Macpherson used the possessive individualist optic to substantiate the following propositions:

1. To demonstrate the significance of Hobbes and Locke – as possessive individualists – for the later nineteenth- and twentieth-century liberal tradition, which created problems for its theory and practice.
2. To assess the theoretical strengths and weaknesses of Hobbes and Locke in terms of whether they provided a satisfactory ideology for a possessive market society, both as it was emerging and as it would be constituted in a mature form. Thus, Macpherson was not only necessarily asking a directly historical question as to whether their ideas were immediately appropriate, but also whether or not they corresponded to a more pure, abstract model of a possessive market society, as Britain and other countries were later to become.
3. To identify the role of unwitting possessive individualist assumptions, which (a) helped solve the problems arising from the diverse interpretations of their thought, and (b) explained their ambiguities and tensions.

4. To offer a historical explanation of their thinking in terms of their response, albeit it at a semi-conscious level, to the problems posed by an emerging possessive market society. This tended to involve a mixture of causal propositions, moving along a determination/correlation/contingency spectrum.

These two chapters seek to do a number of things: first, to establish what Macpherson's interpretation of Hobbes and Locke actually was given his critics' propensity for distortion; secondly, to show how Macpherson responded to his critics; thirdly, to assess the extent to which critics were correct, and see where his thesis has to be modified to meet these criticisms. What will become apparent is that how well Macpherson performed depended on the kind of question he was asking and claim he was making. Finally, at the end of these two chapters there will be a brief discussion of the possessive individualist approach to the history of political thought in general. Hopefully, both these chapters will have implicitly shown that it is a defensible methodology, if handled with care. The result of this discussion will be that, although Macpherson was a little overambitious in his employment of the possessive individualist postulate, it remains a plausible interpretation of a significant facet of the liberal tradition as a whole. It also contains valuable insights into Hobbes and Locke as well as into the nature of their contribution to this tradition. And beyond this Macpherson affirms the importance of a so-called 'realist' perspective on the history of political thought, which does not take authorial intention as the key item of a history of political thought research agenda.

– HOBBES: FIRST APPROXIMATION –

We can note that Macpherson's first attempt to correlate in some way Hobbes' thought with the rise of capitalism appeared in 1945. It laid the basis for his later interpretation of Hobbes in *PI*.[1] In this article he built on Leo Strauss' characterisation of Hobbes' political philosophy as essentially 'bourgeois'.[2] According to Strauss, whatever Hobbes' own aristocratic values and preferences may have been, he was writing for a bourgeois society. And if he was anti-bourgeois, it was only in the sense that he opposed its policies of unbridled self-aggrandisement, which were against its long-term interests. Hobbes' state, Strauss argued, was not just about individual physical protection. It had to enable citizens to go about unhindered in their 'Trades and Callings', as Hobbes called them. In other words the state should promote 'freedom for individual enrichment'.[3] It was also to encourage private thrift through taxation on consumption rather than income and, in keeping with the Protestant ethic, to force the able-bodied to work. Strauss further noted

SHIP TO:

ess

ERVICES

K14 4YN, U.K.
) 465555

I. Code No. 20 65 18
ount No. 2366053

(009)

ADRIAN BUDD
SOUTH BANK UNIVERSITY
103 BOROUGH ROAD
LONDON
SE1 0AA

ype	Account No.	Date/Tax Point	Payment Terms	Document No.	Page
voice	10045000	18-APR-00	Terms: 0 Days	I58359591	1

Customer Reference	QTY	Retail Price	Net *	Discount	Value	VAT	VAT Amount
ments of The Publisher							
UD/LON	1	16.95	*				
UD/LON	1	14.95	*				

Total Quantity	2

VAT Codes	

SUB TOTAL	
CARRIAGE	
TOTAL VAT	
TOTAL TO PAY	

1. DEFINITIONS

1.1 'Buyer' means the person, firm or company whose name appears on the invoice or credit note.

1.2 'Conditions' means the terms and conditions of the sales of Publications set out below.

1.3 'Document' means the invoice or credit note on the reverse of which the Conditions are printed.

1.4 'Marston' means Marston Book Services Limited.

1.5 'the Publishers' means those publishers for whom Marston is the agent in the sales of Publications.

1.6 'Publications' means the articles which the Buyer agrees to buy from Marston the quantity and description which is set out on the invoice.

2. CONDITIONS APPLICABLE

2.1 These Conditions shall apply to all contracts for the sale of Publications to the exclusion of all other conditions including any conditions which the Buyer may purport to apply under any purchase order or confirmation of order or similar document.

2.2 Any variation to these Conditions (including any special terms and conditions agreed between the parties) shall be inapplicable unless agreed in writing by Marston or the Publisher.

2.3 All orders of Publications shall be deemed to be an offer by the Buyer to purchase the Publications pursuant to these Conditions.

2.4 Acceptance of delivery for the Publications shall be deemed as conclusive evidence of the Buyer's acceptance of these Conditions.

2.5 The Buyer agrees and accepts that Marston is the agent of the Publishers in relation to all aspects of the sale of the Publications.

3. PRICE AND PAYMENT

3.1 The price for the Publications is set out on the document overleaf and in the Publisher's catalogue and unless indicated otherwise is exclusive of VAT.

3.2 The Buyer shall pay for the Publications within the number of days stipulated on the Document, such number of days to be calculated from the end of the month in which the Document is dated.

3.3 Interest on overdue invoices shall accrue from the date when payment becomes due, from day to day until the date of payment at a rate of 2% above Barclays Bank Plc's base rate from time to time in force and shall accrue at such a rate after as before any judgement.

3.4 Any discounts to the price of the Publications are to be agreed with the Publishers.

3.5 All unavailable titles are re
cancelled on the invoice.

3.6 The Buyer may instruct M
instruction will be implemente
instruction for any particular o

3.7 Marston may at their discre
unavailable titles will be noted

3.8 The Buyer may only return
done in accordance with the re
prior authorisation has been gi

4. THE PUBLICATIONS

4.1 The quantity and descriptio
out on the invoice overleaf (su
shortages).

5. WARRANTIES

5.1 All terms, conditions and w
expressively) whether by Mars
or in relation to the quality and
Publications or any of the Publ

6. DELIVERY

6.1 Time for delivery of any Pu
for delivery is not of essence in

6.2 Marston shall not be liable
unavailable items.

6.3 Marston shall arrange for th
Buyer's delivery address. The
to take delivery of the Publicati
delivery.

7. ACCEPTANCE

7.1 The Buyer shall be deemed
hours after delivery to the Buye

7.2 Where the Buyer accepts or
any publications Marston shall
Buyer in respect of the Publicat
publications).

7.3 Any claim for damaged Pub
Publications must be notified in
days of receipt of the Publicatio
considered.

7.4 Where dues are recorded, as
deemed to be accepted by the B
cancel them within 72 hours of

not to record dues. This
ss the Buyer countermands the

lect not to record dues. All
ncelled on the invoice.

cations for credit when this is
Publishers returns policy and

he Publications shall be as set
o any temporary stock

ies (whether implied or made
its servants or agents otherwise
ness for the purpose of the
ns are excluded.

ions is not guaranteed and time
order.

buyer for late delivery or

lication to be delivered to the
shall make all the arrangements
whenever they are tended for

ve accepted the Publications 72

been deemed to have accepted
no liability whatever to the
except for any defective

ons or for shortage of
ng to Marston within seven
therwise no claim will be

vn on the invoice, they will be
unless Marston is requested to
ot of the invoice.

8. TITLE AND RISK

8.1 The Publications shall be at the Buyer's risk as from delivery to the Buyer's premises or to the Buyer's appointed shippers, whichever occurs first.

8.2 In spite of delivery having been made, the property in any of the Publication supplied by Marston shall not pass from the Publisher to the Buyer until:

8.2.1 The Buyer shall have paid the sum invoiced by Marston in respect of the relevant order for that publication in full; and

8.2.2 No other sums whatever shall be overdue in the Buyer's accounts with Marston in respect of Publications supplied by Marston on behalf of any of the Publishers.

8.3 The Buyer shall not pledge or in anyway charge, borrow or offer any security for any indebtedness any of the Publications which are the property of the Publishers. Without Prejudice to the other rights of Marston or the Publishers, if the Buyer does so, then all sums whatever owing by the Buyer to Marston shall immediately become due and payable.

9. INSURANCE

9.1 The Buyer shall insure and keep the Publications insured to their full price against "all risks" to the reasonable satisfaction of Marston until the date when the property in the Publications passes to the Buyer.

9.2 If the Buyer fails to insure or keep insured the Publications under this clause, then all sums owing to Marston shall be immediately payable.

10. REMEDIES OF THE BUYER

10.1 Where the Buyer rejects any Publications the Buyer shall have no further rights whatever in respect of supply to the Buyer of such Publications or the failure by Marston to supply any other Publications which conform to the details set out on the invoice.

11. LIMITATION OF LIABILITY

11.1 In the event of any breach of the Conditions by Marston, the remedies of the Buyer shall be limited to damages. Marston shall be under no liability whatever to the Buyer for any indirect loss and or expense (including the loss of profit) suffered by the Buyer arising out of a breach by Marston of this contract.

11.2 Under no circumstances shall Marstons liability to the Buyer exceed the net price of the Publications set out on the invoice overleaf.

12. PROPER LAW

12.1 The Conditions are subject to the law of England and Wales

SOLD TO:

ADRIAN BUDD
SOUTH BANK UNIVERSITY
103 BOROUGH ROAD
LONDON
SE1   0AA

Original
Quality is our bu

INVESTOR IN PEOPLE

MARSTON BOO
Marston Book Services Ltd.
PO Box 269, Abingdon, Ox
Tel: (01235) 465500 Fax: (

VAT No. GB 532 5222 78

Bank Accounts: Barclays,
Account No. 00636835 Gi

10045000   10045000   AA;203358 I58359591 OGI

Pick Batch				Batch/Doc.	Trans
GN1 60776	BUD/LON		ORP 0002	69215/019	Gratis

Pub. Code	Edition Binding	Standard Book No.	Author/Title
			GRATIS INVOICE
			These title(s) are being sent with the com
			ENC 69215/19
EU	1P	1 85331 213 4	TOWNSHEND\C B MACPHERSON
EU	1P	0 7486 1268 8	HARVEY\SPACES OF HOPE

E & OE

TOTAL
DUES

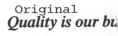

58359591

1.0

5835

that in Hobbes there were no real goods outside sensual goods and the means to acquire them.[4] In this article, Macpherson used many of Strauss' quotations from Hobbes, as well as adding to Strauss' perspective. Macpherson was keen to underline just how 'bourgeois' Hobbes' 'man' was. Hobbes' emphasis on individual 'vainglory', although an 'old trait', had become generalised throughout society once capitalism became dominant, dissolving old feudal hierarchies.[5] Similarly, although the search for gain was not new, because 'scarcity had always existed', by the seventeenth century men were so conscious of it and were ' so determined to avoid it ... that their actions are dominated by this consciousness. This is the mark of a bourgeois society, in contrast to pre-capitalist societies.'[6] Furthermore, he embraced the bourgeois view that human appetites were limitless, and that no moral restraint could be put on them (although this is not to discount prudential reasons for doing so). In addition, human relations had become reduced to market relations. For Hobbes, the value of an individual was his 'price'.[7] A strong state now became an imperative as these emergent capitalist relations were rapidly breaking down the old feudal social ties. Macpherson also argued that Hobbes' materialism and mathematics were the product of a developing bourgeois society, for both were congruous with the reduction of men to the equality of the market.[8] Finally, Hobbes' thought reflected the growth of the market, because it was unconsciously influenced by commodity fetishism. This ideological phenomenon in effect rendered invisible social relationships of mutual personal dependence by viewing society as consisting of free and equal, asocial commodity owners, as a relationship between things.

The difference between this article and his later interpretation in *PI* was that in the latter work he wanted to apply his concept of possessive individualism, highlighting its market motif, which he had first articulated in 1954,[9] relating it to the liberal tradition in general and to Hobbes, Locke and others in particular. Various elements did, however, drop out of his later interpretation of Hobbes at the formal level, namely the concept of commodity fetishism and the significance attached to the role of scarcity in generating human conflict. Nevertheless, as suggested in the previous chapter, commodity fetishism was woven into his possessive individualism thesis, and scarcity became a vital consideration in his later work.

– HOBBES IN *POSSESSIVE INDIVIDUALISM* –

To understand fully Macpherson's interpretation of Hobbes as a possessive individualist in *PI* means we have to remember that he had set himself a number of tasks. At one level this consisted of exposing the seventeenth-century roots of the problem of legitimacy for twentieth-century liberal democracy, by showing how possessive individualism was built into its foundations. On this score Hobbes' significance was as an obvious forerunner of the Utilitarian philosophy of Bentham and his followers, the liberal philosophy *par excellence* for a market society. According to Macpherson, 'Bentham built on Hobbes'.[10] Hobbes' view of human nature and of the functions of the state provided some of the crucial intellectual foundations and justifications of the liberal capitalist state. A second task was to demonstrate the problem-solving capacity of his possessive individualist hypothesis through an analysis of Hobbes. He sought to show how it provided the conceptual masterkey in unlocking the unresolved problems in interpreting Hobbes, namely the tension between his materialism and his deontology, and his supposed logical error in deriving political and moral obligation from factual premises.

A third consideration was explanatory, aiming to indicate how Hobbes' thought was shaped by the socio-economic context of early British capitalism. For Macpherson this did not entail economic reductionism. He stated that in stressing the possessive individualist roots of modern liberal theory, the concepts of freedom, rights, obligation, justice and so on were not reducible to the 'concept of possession', although they were 'powerfully shaped by it'.[11] Equally significant, he was not concerned with Hobbes' 'motives', but with the 'social content of some of his assumptions', or more specifically with 'historically the probable content of unstated or unclear assumptions that are contained or necessarily implied in [Hobbes'] theory'. Macpherson stated that he was undertaking a 'logical and historical' inquiry.[12] Thus and this will be a important point in later discussion – Hobbes' ideas were not viewed as simple epiphenomena of emerging capitalist production relations, *either* in the sense that he actually advocated them, *or* that he was fully aware of them. Macpherson was merely concerned to detail how possessive individualist assumptions worked in Hobbes' political philosophy, and assess their historical significance both for Hobbes' own society and for future generations. Macpherson argued that Hobbes' possessive individualism was revealed most clearly in two areas: first, in his account of the state of nature, which imported assumptions derived from contemporary society; secondly, in the way in which he folded social postulates into his justification of the state after starting from explicitly physiological and psychological premises.

In his interpretation of Hobbes' state of nature, Macpherson in effect exposed the superficiality of Hobbes' abstract individualist assumptions, and showed that they could only have been derived from his observations of human behaviour in modern society. Hobbes treated the state of nature as a 'logical' and not a 'historical' hypothesis.[13] He used it to demonstrate how contemporary 'civilized' men would behave in the absence of law and its enforcement, while not jettisoning the 'socially acquired behaviour and desires of men'.[14] Macpherson argued that intuitively Hobbes could not have deduced the state of nature from psychological or physiological postulates alone, because he had to persuade contemporary men of the need for an all-powerful sovereign, and therefore appealed to their own experience of their own society.[15] In the famous chapter 13 of the *Leviathan*, Hobbes when employing examples of the 'natural tendency' of men to destroy and invade one another – his inferences 'made from the passions' – used evidence from contemporary society:

> Let him therefore consider with himselfe, when taking a journey, he armes himselfe, and seeks to go well accompanied; when going to sleep, he locks his dores; when even in his house he locks his chests; and this when he knowes there bee Lawes and publike Officers, to revenge all injuries shall bee done him; what opinion has of his fellow subjects, when he rides armed; of his fellow Citizens, when he locks his dores; and of his children, and servants, when he locks his chests.[16]

Further, that Hobbes had contemporary society in mind was evidenced by the 'full state of nature' being reached by 'successive degrees of abstraction from civilized society'.[17] For its complete negation occurred when there was 'no industry, no culture of the earth, no navigation, no commodius building, no arts, no letters, no society'.[18] This outcome arises from passions that have been fostered by civilisation. The three causes of contention derived from living in a civilised society. Men do not merely want to live, but live 'commodiously', which causes competition and diffidence. Competition is about the 'invasion' of men who 'plant, sow, build or possesse a convenient Seat'.[19] Naturally, this gave rise to diffidence. And the third cause of conflict, namely 'glory', was a socially acquired characteristic, stemming from people being undervalued in contemporary society.[20] Finally, Hobbes suggested that men in the state of nature would 'lack' all the means to a 'commodious living' – such things as property, industry and commerce – hardly the desires of primitive men.[21]

The second element in Hobbes' political philosophy which embodied unarticulated social assumptions was in his discussion of power. Hobbes in the *Leviathan* and elsewhere assumed that when he was discussing 'natural' man as self-moving, self-directing appetitive machines he was applying physiological and psychological analysis. Yet by the time he described man in the state of nature, he had unwittingly introduced social assumptions that postulated universal competition, and therefore the need for an all-powerful state. Macpherson undertook a highly detailed analysis of chapters 10 and 11 of the *Leviathan* to make his point. The penetration of unwitting social assumptions was manifested by the shifting definition of power that occurred in these two chapters. Chapter 10 starts with a neutral, 'absolute' definition of power as a 'present means to obtain some future apparent good'. However, in chapter 11 power becomes comparative by implication when Hobbes describes power as power over other men, as in 'I put for a generall inclination of all mankind, a perpetuall and restlesse desire of Power after power, that ceaseth onely in Death'.[22] After his neutral and absolute definition of power in chapter 10, Hobbes immediately proceeded to endow it with a comparative property by introducing the term 'eminence' of natural ability, such as 'Strength, Forme, Prudence, Arts, Eloquence, Liberality, Nobility'. It was the 'eminence' of ability over that of others that enabled a man to acquire 'instrumental' powers, such as 'Riches, Reputation and Friends'.[23] Thus, power was no longer neutral in terms of a person's capacities plus control over things acquired by these capacities, but relative. It was, as he stated in the *Elements of Law*, an 'excess' of personal capacities and what could be obtained as a result of this 'excess'. This 'excess' presumed an opposition of powers, because if there was no opposition, then an excess would not be needed. This postulated opposition of powers was also confirmed by Hobbes' perception of the significance of wealth and reputation, which gave the individual an offensive or defensive strength against other individuals.[24] And this strength consisted in the ability to command some of the powers of other individuals, and this in turn implied the possibility of a transfer of the power of some individuals to others. Macpherson quoted Hobbes on the valuing and honouring of an individual's power to demonstrate that he must have assumed that these transfers of power must have been so usual that there must have been a market in power:

> The *Value*, or WORTH of man, is as of all other things, his Price; that is to say, so much as would be given for the use of his Power: and therefore is not absolute; but a thing dependant on the need and judgement of another ... And as in other things, so in men, not the seller, but the buyer determines the Price.[25]

As for honouring and dishonouring, this was dependent on the valuation by others of a person's power, which consisted primarily in the ability to command the services of others: '*Honourable* is whatsoever possession, action, or quality, is an argument and signe of Power. [So] Dominion, and Victory is Honourable; because acquired by Power ... Riches, are honourable; for they are power ...'.[26] Macpherson deduced that all men make estimates, that is valuations, of other men's powers and the converse. Out of these independent value judgements an 'objective value' of a person's power was established, and this presumed that every man's power was regarded as a commodity, offered in competitive exchange.[27] The same idea, Macpherson maintained, was repeated by Hobbes in the *Elements of Law*.

In positing the notion of a universal opposition of powers, however, Macpherson was not interpreting Hobbes as consistently implying that all men innately sought an excess of power over others, merely that some men may do so. This meant that the rest, to maintain their existing power and derivative level of satisfactions, have to defend themselves against such people. The concept of possessive individualism now entered the discussion because Macpherson argued that if society is to exist, given this universal opposition of powers and the simultaneous need for men's natural powers to be invaded, there must be a mechanism to ensure that this 'invasion' or transfer occurs peacefully. A possessive market society, where a market mechanism presupposes a universal competition of powers and their peaceful transfer, is the only type of society that could meet these requirements. Market relations either permeated or shaped all social relations, because not only were the products of labour commodities, so was labour itself. In 'status' or 'customary' societies competition and the forcible invasion of powers occurred at the top of society, since below this level the allocation of power and goods occurred in a customary fashion. Hence there was no universal competition for power between all members of society. Only in capitalist market societies are all individuals engaged in a 'continual competitive relationship'.[28]

Seventeenth-century England 'approximated closely to a possessive market society' with nearly half the adult male population as wage earners, increasing to two-thirds if cottagers were counted as part-time wage earners. Moreover, land was increasingly exploited as capital, and state regulations were introduced to offset some of the socially deleterious effects of the market. Yet, there remains the question of the extent to which Hobbes was aware of this emerging market society. Macpherson argued that he seemed to have discerned a number of important features, whether or not he had a possessive market in mind.[29] First, labour was a 'commodity, exchangeable for benefit, as well as any other thing.'[30] Although Hobbes discussed this in relation to foreign trade, there was 'presumptive evidence that he was taking for granted the normality of the wage relationship.'[31]

Just as significantly, he rejected the medieval notions of commutative justice (exchange based upon equality of values) and distributive justice (equal rewards for equal merit) on the grounds that they did not accord with the new realities of the market: 'As if it were injustice to sell dearer than we buy; or to give more to a man than he merits.'[32] Finally, Hobbes in *Behemoth* described the civil war as the product of the propertied classes in the City of London and in other corporation towns seeking to create a constitution 'favourable to new market interests'.[33]

Macpherson conjectured that Hobbes might not have thought that his market assumptions were antithetical to those of the ancient Greeks and Romans, because competitive power struggles at the top of their societies 'approximated to market relations.'[34] Nevertheless, Macpherson was willing to concede that Hobbes may not have 'consciously' drawn his model of society from his 'appreciation of the market attributes of seventeenth century society', although 'his model approximates most nearly to the model of the possessive market society.'[35]

Macpherson aimed to demonstrate Hobbes' modernity in another way that amounted to a 'leap in political theory', a 'revolution in moral and political theory'.[36] Modern interpreters had problems with Hobbes' derivation of values from facts. Hobbes was the 'first to deduce rights from facts without putting something fanciful into the facts' such as God or Nature.[37] Thus, grand teleological assumptions were abandoned. His theory of obligation was grounded on the postulate of the equality of ability in men to kill each other, and an equal expectation in the satisfaction of their wants, and thus in a state of nature an equal fear for their continued motion. Therefore an equality of rights was necessary to ensure the maintainence of individual motions. These facts about human beings – equal physical vulnerability, equal expectation of want satisfaction and the desire for continued motion – could be utilised to formulate a philosophy of the state. Whether such a philosophy was prudential or moral, Macpherson equivocated, but he inferred that in the light of human experience of civil disorder it was 'as moral an obligation as could be found.'[38] It was the 'highest morality of which market men are capable.'[39]

He extended this argument, hoping to demonstrate the problem-solving potential of his possessive individualism thesis. He thought he could show that one of the traditional problems of interpretation that suggested a separation of Hobbes' scientific materialism from his political theory could be remedied. For Macpherson, Hobbes' materialism and political theory were intimately connected. Once human beings were conceived as self-moving mechanisms, with no other desire but to keep moving, then morality could be deduced from an equal desire for continued motion. A system of moral obligation was required to ensure the non-collision of motions. The market assumption now entered the argument, because only in a competitive market society was there a universal opposition of motions and equal insecurity.

Hobbes' derivation of obligation from fact was shaped by market assumptions in another sense: no measure of value external to the market system, such as contained in medieval notions of distributative and commutative justice, was required. 'A standard of value was provided by the facts of the market system.'[40] It could be taken as a standard of justice, since it met the requirements of any moral principle, namely that it transcended each man's subjective desires. The value of every individual was determined by the objective workings of the market.

Macpherson concluded therefore that Hobbes' theory of obligation was most appropriate to a market society, because everyone would see it as in their interest to submit to a political authority with sufficient power to enforce the rules of a competitive society. Not only did people recognise equal insecurity, they also acknowledged equal subordination to the market. Everyone was subject to the competitive market for powers, and accepted all values and entitlements established by the market mechanism.[41] Hence, a rational basis for obligation existed, because all were equally subject to the market, which meant that individuals could see themselves 'as equal in some respect more vital than all their inequalities'.[42] Such obligation was rational so long as possessive market relations prevailed and were thought to be inevitable.

Although Hobbes himself thought that he had based his theory on a generic human nature and would not have been satisfied with such a historicist interpretation, he 'opened a new way in political theory. And he penetrated closer to the nature of modern society than any of his contemporaries and many of his successors', because he dispensed with the teleologically inspired idea of an outside will or purpose.[43] Nothing was imported outside the observed facts: the growing equality before the law of the market which was replacing the old social hierarchy with its unequal rights for different ranks. Thus, Hobbes' deduction of obligation from fact was on the whole both logically and historically unobjectionable, except that his theory did not allow for a non-self-perpetuating sovereign. He failed to recognise the degree of class cohesiveness among the ruling class that would counteract the fissiparous tendencies of the market. Nevertheless, a centralised state was needed to cope with these effects, especially in the transition from a status to a market society, especially to protect the right of possession, thereby ensuring a peaceful invasion of individual powers through the exchange process. Macpherson concluded that Hobbes' political theory was definitely 'of and for a possessive market society'.[44]

— CRITICISM —

Diverse types of criticism were mounted against Macpherson's version of Hobbes. Most critics ignored Macpherson's claim that a possessive individualist reading of Hobbes would solve the problems of interpretation arising from various tensions in Hobbes' writings.[45] Rather they focused on Hobbes' supposed championing of bourgeois values, on whether his thought was shaped by emerging market relations, on whether England in the seventeenth century was significantly a possessive market society and on Macpherson's use of market models. Interestingly, a consensus soon emerged and became hardened into an orthodoxy, which suggested that Macpherson's thesis was irrevocably flawed.

− Hobbes as champion of the bourgeoisie −

This line of criticism, based on the question of Hobbes' intentions, appeared the easiest way to discredit Macpherson's analysis. Textual evidence merely had to be examined to discover whether Hobbes was variously a 'spokesman of the bourgeoisie',[46] 'spokesman for "bourgeois" values'[47] or 'an apologist for capitalism'.[48] If such intentions could not be clearly ascertained, then Hobbes' thought was 'unbourgeois'. The primary assumption, or implication, of these critics was that Macpherson was effectively a mechanical Marxist, who had not merely swallowed wholesale the crude base/superstructure model of social and ideational analysis, but who also had attributed to Hobbes the mantle of spokesman for a rising capitalist class. Further, they suggested that Macpherson had assumed that this class had a single, fixed and transparent interest and common agreement as to how it could be promoted.

Keith Thomas' article, 'The Social Origins of Hobbes's Political Thought', became the keystone of this kind of critical orthodoxy.[49] He offered a wealth of material to prove, contra Macpherson (and to a lesser extent Strauss), that Hobbes could not have championed capitalist interests. For Thomas the 'social affiliations of Hobbes' thought' were primarily aristocratic or feudal rather than bourgeois. Although there were bourgeois elements, his thought contained many pre-capitalist values. Hobbes' thought was complex and reflected the transitional nature of the English economy and society in the seventeenth century from feudalism to capitalism. So although he assumed in some ways a 'relatively advanced economy' in which labour was sold, the market stimulated manufacturing and 'all things obey money', there was no mention of the role of capital, and labour was viewed as the basic factor of production.[50] And in wanting to imitate the Dutch, who grew rich through trade rather than the exploitation of natural resources, Hobbes' thought was pre-industrial.

Thomas, however, focused mainly, but not exclusively, on Hobbes' non-capitalist values and perceptions. Not only did Hobbes espouse the virtues of the patriarchal family, resisting the idea that it should be put on an individualistic, contractual basis,[51] his values and perceptions were pre-eminently aristocratic. The mainspring of human motivation was not the pursuit of wealth and power stemming from acquisitiveness, but pride, associated with the aristocratic virtue of honour. He also favoured the aristocratic elements in the constitution, such as the judicial powers of the House of Lords; he applauded the aristocratic cult of reputation and a hierarchy built on honour and approved of individuals concerned with their posthumous reputation. In addition, the aristocratic virtue of courage was important for national defence. And aristocrats were good for governing, providing they were properly trained. Furthermore, if money-making and accumulation of property were his goal, why did he stipulate that the right of resistance against the sovereign be based on the violation of life rather than property? He opposed the acquisitiveness of the propertied classes generally and favoured sumptuary legislation. He also maintained that it was permissible for the starving to steal. Indeed, life could not be seen as a commodity because all members of society had the right to subsistence. What is more, his whole idea of covenanting, which in effect legitimated contracts made under duress, especially in the case of sovereignty by acquisition, patently displayed an 'unbourgeois' attitude towards contracts.[52] And conversely, contracts that led to one's self-destruction could also be broken.[53] In personal terms he was happy to fit into an aristocratic milieu, despite his relatively humble origins, and preferred the non-bourgeois activity of pursuing knowledge and a retired, rural life to money-making in an urban setting.

Nevertheless, Thomas did concede that 'in many respects his state can be regarded as a bulwark of property. The sovereign levies taxes so as to maintain private men in their callings and by upholding property rights against incursions of other subjects gives every citizen the security he requires.'[54] He also acknowledged that Hobbes expected internal laissez-faire to operate. Citizens were at liberty 'To buy, and sell, and otherwise contract with one another; to choose their own abode, their own diet, their own trade of life ...'[55] His attitude was that the 'commonwealth exists to provide a framework of security in which wealth may be pursued, but not to interfere with its distribution.'[56]

Yet, Thomas argued, for Hobbes the rich still had certain welfare obligations to the poor, and the right of subsistence could militate against unlimited accumulation. And although the state's function was to protect private property, his justification of it was not bourgeois: it prevented conflict, unlike communal property which could generate arguments. Equally significant, there were no individual property rights against the sovereign in Hobbes' state.[57] And he put 'power before plenty', or defence before opulence. Thus, there could be a limit to 'private acquisitive activity'.[58] And given the enormous authority invested in the state, theoretically the sovereign had the power to support either laissez-faire or state intervention. Thomas, however, admitted that Hobbes' 'economic position' constituted the 'most obviously *bourgeois* aspect of his thought'.[59] Finally, in his discussion of the value of a person being his price, Hobbes was not concerned with market relationships, but the 'nature of human reputation'.[60] This view echoed German medieval courtly literature, where men were judged by repute, not intrinsic value. Price meant *Pris*, which meant praise or fame. Furthermore, men could be valued in terms of dignity and worthiness, which were determined by the sovereign's will. For Hobbes the market did not reign supreme: all had to acknowledge each other's claims to life according to the laws of nature, and the state had to look after the poor and impotent. Nevertheless, Thomas conceded that Hobbes had rejected commutative and distributive standards of justice in favour of market criteria, and that he restricted the use of the word 'value' to when it was synonymous with price so as to 'inhibit judgement upon market transactions deriving from some external moral standard.'[61] And he concluded his article by recognising that the 'very economic trends which his political recommendations were perhaps best calculated to advance were precisely those with which he was personally most out of sympathy.'[62]

Macpherson's subsequent critics echoed Thomas' perspective concerning Hobbes' intentions, but did so in a far less nuanced manner to prove that Hobbes could not have been a bourgeois partisan. Thus, Hobbes' requirement that the state had ultimate control over private property was repeated on numerous occasions,[63] as was his espousal of aristocratic values of honour and reputation as opposed to what were effectively the bourgeois virtues of acquisitiveness and covetousness.[64] Indeed, Hobbes' political writings could be viewed as an attempt to regenerate a contentious aristocracy as a ruling class.[65] Critics held that market considerations were not uppermost in Hobbes' mind. In explaining human motivation, the incessant struggle for power could not be interpreted in terms of economic competition. Rather, wealth was an expression of competition for power, and the transfers of power were not the product of market competition between entrepreneurs, but of political competition to gain security.[66] Hobbes also upheld non-market values, such as the right of those in desperate need to steal from the rich.[67] The state moreover had a responsibility towards the sick and poor, even if this involved taking away some of the rich's property.[68] And in terms of economic policy, he was not an advocate of laissez-faire.[69] Indeed, he was not a keen advocate of merchants' interests.[70] Thus, Ryan has argued that Macpherson's argument was essentially 'circular': Hobbes lived in a market society; his thought must have reflected this; scrutiny of the text demonstrates that Hobbes was 'friendly to capitalism'.[71]

Other arguments were advanced to demonstrate that Hobbes was not a bourgeois apologist. For example, in his discussion of the value of a person as his price he was being 'deliberately satirical'.[72] And rather than speaking on behalf of the bourgeoisie, he thought he was speaking of human behaviour 'at most times and in most places'.[73] Further, his state of nature, rather than being an unconscious or conscious reflection of contemporary society, could just as easily be a real one.[74] And if he was defending a certain version of modernity, of 'industry, prosperity and science-propelled social advance', it was not a capitalist one.[75] Tuck went as far as to suggest that Hobbes' 'attitudes' could confirm a 'socialist' version of modernity.[76]

The upshot of this critical line of questioning over Hobbes' intentions was the suggestion that they were not economically driven. Rather, they were *political*. Tully proposed that 'What Macpherson saw as economic competition among self-interested consumers in Hobbes' state is now seen as competition for power to protect oneself in the English Civil War.'[77] Hobbes was concerned with the same problems as Grotius, namely how to build a strong state that subjects would obey in the face of a civil war caused by religious diversity. The job of the sovereign was to regulate trade and labour in order to preserve the population and strengthen the state in relation to other European states.

Macpherson's reply and commentary

In subsequent writings Macpherson denied that he had portrayed Hobbes as a capitalist apologist in two ways. First, he was unsure about whether Hobbes was 'aware' of the fact that he was analysing bourgeois man.[78] Hobbes' models of man and society were 'half consciously bourgeois models'.[79] Second, Macpherson argued that, although Hobbes took the capitalist model for granted, he 'disliked some aspects of it',[80] especially its bourgeois morality.[81] Further, he noted Hobbes' excoriation of merchant capitalists, and stated that he was not suggesting that 'Hobbes was consciously writing to support a capitalist takeover.'[82] Thus, he was not attributing capitalist partisanship to Hobbes.[83] He distanced himself from such a position on methodological grounds: 'The question of conscious intention to support a position as distinct from what one may, with historical hindsight, see as an objective support of that position, can rarely be conclusively answered.'[84]

On this issue critics got Macpherson simply wrong. As remarked at the beginning of the chapter, Macpherson stressed that he was not concerned with Hobbes' 'motives'. Rather, he explored Hobbes' unstated assumptions that unconsciously, or semi-consciously reflected the emergence of a possessive market society. And, logically it would have been odd for Macpherson to have interpreted Hobbes as a champion of the bourgeoisie given that he repeatedly noted that Hobbes was unaware of the existence of its cohesion as a class. Another logical point seems to have been overlooked by his critics: to interpret Hobbes' thought as a response to the emergence of a market society does not entail a corollary commitment of any form of class partisanship, bourgeois or otherwise. Further, Macpherson, like his earliest critic Thomas, was fully aware of the distinction between what may have been Hobbes' personal preferences and values on the one hand, and the actual human behaviour that he saw around him, and therefore the need to distance himself from the external, negative facticity of human existence. In *PI* as already noted, Macpherson observed Hobbes' antipathy towards the urban merchants as a result of their role in bringing about the Civil War. Hence, whether

Hobbes was opposed to covetousness, preferred a secluded rural existence, the aristocratic virtues of honour, worthiness and courage, supported patriarchy and sumptuary legislation and believed that the rich or that the state should be responsible for the welfare of the poor was beside the point. Thomas' interpretation could, indeed, partly be seen as confirming Macpherson's viewpoint in distinguishing between what Hobbes wanted and what he accepted. This also undermines Ryan's contention that Macpherson's argument was somehow 'circular' to the extent that this circularity is construed as entailing intentionality. Given Hobbes' proto-utilitarian account of human nature, his clear acknowledgement of the public/private distinction and conception of the state primarily as a ring-holder as far as economic activities were concerned, his ultimately non-judgemental attitude should be of no surprise. He was able to separate his own personal preferences from the desired structure of the state that would have to incorporate activities that he might find distasteful. Furthermore, there is no reason, in response to Ryan's argument, why Hobbes, à la Macpherson has to be saddled with an intentionally and specifically 'capitalist' version of 'modernity'. The *effect* of his intentions, whether he was fully conscious of it or not, through a broad acceptance of market valuations and a call on the state to defend private economic activities was to make a world safer for capitalism.

A less obvious point can be made on the question of Hobbes' modernity, which relates to Tuck's contention that his attitude can be taken as either capitalist or socialist. It concerns the relationship between capitalism and socialism. Socialists of a Marxist kind have viewed some of the ideas developing out of capitalism as historically progressive. Macpherson certainly acknowledged Hobbes' modernity in his positing of a post-feudal, non-teleological view of the world, in deriving his normative notion of the state from observable common human fears and satisfactions. Socialists were to build upon such an anthropocentric vision which, in recognising a fundamental factual equality between people, demanded equality of respect. Fundamental to Macpherson's thesis was the idea that the liberal, developmental equality of Mill, to be realised, required some kind of socialism.

More significantly, Hobbes' aristocratic preferences and concerns, contra Wood, can be integrated with his conscious or unconscious acknowledgement of a possessive market society. While he did not regard himself as a card carrying member of the bourgeoisie and wanted the aristocracy to reform itself – he viewed the *Leviathan* as a contribution to this process – the kind of state that he advocated was exceptionally well fitted for a possessive market society. The state, apart from protecting the lives of its members, secured the conditions for their private economic activities which involved the protection of private property, contracts and the rule of law. Interpreting Hobbes in this way can also account for the fact that he can be read in different ways: either aristocratic or bourgeois. Thus, he can uphold non-market values – honour, worthiness and so on – and he can see that those working for the state ought to fulfil the duties associated with their office in a way that transcends a simple contractual wage relationship.[85] Yet the kind of state that these aristocrats were meant to administer rested on the assumption that ordinary citizens need the security of their life and property in order to achieve a 'felicity' of a kind that Hobbes might not have approved.

Another difficulty, to use Marxist parlance, with the imputation of 'bourgeois' values, policies and interests to Hobbes is that the question of what actually constitutes them at any particular point in time, or whether there is common agreement about them within the 'bourgeoisie' itself, is not raised. Critics assume that because Hobbes did not advocate laissez-faire, he could not have been a 'bourgeois'.[86] This, however, is merely a matter of circumstance: different 'bourgeoisies' in different historical epochs have advocated different economic policies to promote capital accumulation, including mercantilism. This was something of which Macpherson was completely aware. Similarly, the 'bourgeisie' has had different attitudes towards thrift and consumption. Further, differences could arise within a 'bourgeoisie' over the prioritisation of its long- and short-term interests. To infer that Hobbes could not have been a partisan of the 'bourgeoisie' because he put state power before private accumulation, defence before opulence, is questionable since this is something that far-sighted members of the bourgeoisie might prefer to do. Additionally, historically 'bourgeois' states have always insisted that they control and regulate private property and taxation in the interests of internal and external order and economic expansion. Not too much should be made about the sanctity of private property from a bourgeois viewpoint. Even Locke gave the state ultimate power over private property through his doctrine of majority rule. Lastly, to assume that a 'bourgeoisie' would automatically oppose the idea of a welfare state is questionable: long-term political stability may be seen as preferable to short-term profit.

– Mirroring the market –

Critics went further than arguing that Hobbes' intention was not to promote capitalist market relations. They did not see that Hobbes' thought significantly reflected the emergence of such relations. Macpherson's interlocutors focused on Hobbes' theory of human nature and motivation to make their case. They also suggested that Hobbes' account of human nature was derived from non-market sources and that Hobbes assumed that he was establishing universal hypotheses about human behaviour. So many commentators maintained that for Hobbes the desire for self-preservation took precedence over the desire for 'commodious living'.[87] Equal physical vulnerability was the factor which prompted all reasonable 'men' to establish a contract, rather than market considerations.[88] Moreover, the psychological egoistic disposition to pursue power and honour was far more deeply rooted than the desire to satisfy material appetites.[89] Even if economic competition were eliminated, there would still be the desire for power and honour.[90] Critics held that for Hobbes the real question was how to curb pride rather than how to cope with the effects of market competition.[91]

They maintained that even when it came to looking at sources to confirm Hobbes' supposedly market-shaped views, Macpherson took evidence out of context. So in the passage relating to Hobbes' acknowledgement of the widespread existence of wage labour, he was only referring to the export industry,[92] and as for his recognition of market forms of justice, Hobbes was merely attacking its traditional notions.[93] The sources of Hobbes' thought were also probably non-market derived. His state of nature could just have easily been obtained from current observations of primitives[94] and many of his ideas and concerns could be seen in ancient Greek and Roman literature.[95]

Only one critic analysed the centrepiece of Macpherson's argument, based upon his examination of chapters 10 and 11 of the *Leviathan*, which attempted to demonstrate that Hobbes' theory of obligation only works with market assumptions. Carmichael,[96] expanding Goldsmith's criticisms,[97] suggested that Hobbes could not have even unconsciously utilised possessive market assumptions, which Macpherson had argued were necessary for Hobbes to postulate a universal opposition of powers in civil society. Nevertheless, Carmichael agreed that a universal opposition of powers could be hypothesised in the state of nature. He confined his remarks to Macpherson's interpretation in the *Leviathan*, and discounted evidence from other texts such as the *Elements of Law* on the grounds that they were earlier and less developed pieces. Carmichael argued that there was nothing in the *Leviathan* to show that Hobbes imputed a universal opposition in civil society – a limited opposition, yes, but not a universal opposition. He criticised Macpherson for proposing that Hobbes defined power in a double sense, as neutral, as a present means to attain some future apparent good, and in comparative, oppositional terms, which was possible once possessive market assumptions were introduced. First, when Hobbes discussed power in comparative terms, this referred to natural and not instrumental powers or power in general. 'Eminence', that is comparative power, referred to natural, not instrumental, power and referred to faculties of body and mind rather than the actual powers themselves. In any case, eminence had to become very pronounced to become an instrumental power. Further, although Macpherson assumed that for Hobbes instrumental power was acquired through natural power, it could also be acquired 'by fortune'. In addition, the notion of comparative powers was not essential to Hobbes' argument, because he posited a society in which there was only a limited opposition of powers. This could be viewed logically. One's power did not necessarily have to be opposed to others, although it *might* be. Hobbes also allowed for cooperation, or 'assistance'. And where comparisons of power occur, these arose from vanity rather than from calculations of potential enmity. Such use of comparisons were possible in any society. A limited opposition of powers existed in another sense: although acquired powers consisted in strength against others, this did not mean that every man's power was opposed to the power of every other man. Thus for Hobbes friendship, that is cooperation, constituted power. In all Hobbes' examples of power, limited, rather than universal, opposition was implied.

Carmichael also rejected the idea that in Hobbes there existed a market in powers. The valuing of another's power for Hobbes was merely the price that *would* be offered for their power, rather than an actual price, especially if the individual had an interest in cooperating. Moreover, this process of valuing was done on an individual, one-to-one basis, rather than in a collective, 'objective' manner. Just as significant, honouring did not refer in Hobbes to a price put on another's power, but on one's own power. And there was no reference in Hobbes to power holders actually selling their power.[98] Thus, Macpherson was reading into Hobbes market assumptions that were hypothetical and erroneous. Carmichael then questioned whether the notion of a universal opposition of powers required a possessive market society. If all men innately sought power, which needed regulating, this did not have to be explained solely by a possessive market model, because it was true for all societies. And even if a more limited explanation of power was adopted, that is a defensive strength by moderates against immoderates, again this was applicable to non-market societies.

Carmichael concluded by holding that the difference, for Hobbes, between limited and universal oppositions of power lay in the difference between civil society and the state of nature. Macpherson's crucial defect was that, in postulating of a universal opposition of powers in Hobbes, he obliterated the difference between these two situations.[99]

Macpherson's reply and commentary

Macpherson, in defending the idea that Hobbes' thought reflected an emerging capitalism, reiterated the textual evidence: Hobbes' assertion that the value of an individual was his price, his recognition that labour was a commodity and that market-determined values had superseded medieval notions of commutative justice and just price.[100] Equally important, Hobbes' views supported 'primary capital accumulation'.[101] This meant mercantilism rather than laissez-faire. In this period of English history mercantilism *was* capitalism.[102] Accordingly, he advocated state policies that would promote farming and fishing, encourage people to work through laws against idleness, and increase thrift through sumptuary laws. Nevertheless, the liberal elements of Hobbes' state policy were also evident in his favouring of competition as against monopolies and his assumption that the state would protect market freedoms. The state's primary economic aim was to increase the wealth of the nation through encouraging and facilitating private enrichment. So the individual could expect not merely the state's protection against foreign enemies, domestic peace and the enjoyment of 'a harmless liberty', but also to be 'enriched as much as may consist with public security'.[103] The state had to ensure not merely 'bare Preservation', but also 'all other Contentments of life, which every man by lawfull Industry, without danger, or hurt to the Commonwealth, shall acquire to himselfe.'[104] Not surprisingly that state's right to levy taxes lay in the need 'to defend private men in the exercise of severall Trades, and Callings',[105] which meant not merely physical safety, but the protection of private property and contract. The state, however, could intervene where the strength and wealth of the nation was undermined by such activities, which necessitated the possible regulation of monopolies, corporations and foreign trade. Macpherson, responding to one of his critics' arguments, acknowledged that Hobbes allowed the right of the state to interfere with individual property rights, but held that this was consistent with an era of primary capital accumulation. In the mid-seventeenth century the state, for Hobbes, had to have the right to establish the laws of property, contract and exchange favourable to a market system. For example, the state had to 'cut through all traditional restraints', namely feudal land rights of copyholders, cottagers and others, which had restricted the supply of marketable land. However, once primary capital accumulation was no longer the paramount problem in terms of economic development, as when Locke was writing forty years later, private property could be fully protected against the state. Yet, even for Locke, the state could encroach on private property, provided the sovereign was a non-self-perpetuating body of representatives from the property owning classes.[106]

His most specific and prolonged defence was against Carmichael.[107] He maintained that evidence from the *Elements* concerning the universal opposition of powers in society was admissible, because Hobbes himself saw this work as equally part of his doctrine along with the *Leviathan*, and this notion had been repeated in *De Cive* (1642), which was translated into English in 1651, the same time as the *Leviathan* was published. As for the *Leviathan* itself, a close textual reading of chapter 10 showed that Hobbes assumed that even in society there was a universal search for power. Instrumental powers such as riches, reputation and friends were comparative and oppositional, as were natural powers, and arose from the need for self-defence. Moreover, the significance of eminence in natural powers for Hobbes was that they were effective abilities or powers to obtain more protection or power against other men.

As for the question as to whether these powers were universally opposed, against Carmichael's argument favouring limited opposition, Macpherson held that Hobbes' argument supported the case for universal opposition. Diffidence arose because help from others could not be relied upon. Distrust was universal. And although men sought alliances, these could always fluctuate. Because of this there was no difference between the notion of a war of every man against every other man, and a confederacy of the weak against the strong. Thus, individuals always had to be on their guard. Cooperation was limited precisely because a universal opposition of powers existed.

Macpherson also defended the idea that there was a market in powers. Valuing was something which was generalised. Logically, the notion of a price was as a relation between *any* one person and another, rather than a limited relation between individuals, as was the notion of honouring, since both involved universal comparisons. Macpherson then denied that universal opposition of powers required market postulates extraneous to the text. Rather, he found it in Hobbes treatment of power.[108] The 'invasive' aspect of his definition got lost in the process of Hobbes employing the 'resolving' part of his resolutive/compositive method, but he clearly acknowledged that the society he was resolving was invasive. The object was to persuade men that they needed an all-powerful sovereign to ensure that these invasions, within a possessive market society, occurred peacefully. If he had aimed to prevent such invasions occurring at all, then he would have had to have changed the economic foundations of society as well.[109] In sum, Macpherson attempted to defend the link he had made between Hobbes' idea of universal opposition between individuals and the development of a possessive market society, which also postulated universal opposition.

Let us now assess the effectiveness of the criticisms and Macpherson's reply concerning the extent to which Hobbes' philosophy mirrored the market. A common method used to refute Macpherson on this matter was to pose issues in terms of juxtapositions, or through the introduction of certain distinctions to demonstrate that Hobbes' thought could not have been market oriented. Let us look at the discussion of human nature. Critics suggested that Hobbes could not have been a bourgeois because he valued self-preservation more than commodious living. Of course *anybody* would in a civil war situation, but Hobbes is not merely addressing what one might prefer in this situation, either life *or* commodious living. Logically, life has to come first in order to enjoy such living. In any case Hobbes' conception of human behaviour in terms of motion maximisation in intensity and duration involves both physical safety and appetite satisfaction. Or Hobbes supposedly explains the contract in terms of equal human vulnerability rather than the market.[110] While as we shall later argue, the market may not have been quite so pervasive in Hobbes' thought as Macpherson allows, it could still have an indirect effect in generating a feeling of equal vulnerability. Hobbes felt that material appetites in the face of relative scarcity created conflict and equal vulnerability. The effect of the market is to generate the zero-sum notions of possessive individualism and therefore equal vulnerability. Similarly critics prioritise the psychological over the material, with pride as the obvious candidate. Yet for Hobbes pride was significantly manifested through the acquisition of riches, including trade and land-ownership. This interrelation was expressed in another way: if pride could be curbed, either through self or state regulation, then material benefits would accrue to all who laboured and owned, who 'plant, sow, build or possesse a convenient seat'.[111]

Another false juxtaposition was to hold that Hobbes maintained that the search for power was more important than the satisfaction of material appetites.[112] Again for Hobbes these two facets were integrally related. His definition of power is an instrumental one: the present means to acquire a future apparent good. Such goods, while they may include some sense of psychological superiority over others – 'glory' –, quite evidently encompass the satisfaction of material appetites. Equally, the desire for power in a defensive/ offensive sense was generated by the existence of human appetites in the face of relative scarcity. There is also the larger question that even if Hobbes did in fact juxtapose the psychological and the material in his own mind, lending the former some universal significance, why cannot this be explained in material terms? The break-up of the feudal order, which had much to do with the rise of the market, created different kinds of ontologically individualistic perceptions of the world manifest in Hobbes' work, to the extent that the state could only appear as 'artificial'. Further, whatever perception Hobbes may have had about his own philosophy, that he was speaking to all men in all times, it is impossible to escape historical situatedness in which actors are acting in a kind of unselfconscious, unreflective way, and can have no knowledge about the later historical significance of their own thought. This was Macpherson's point: Hobbes' thought either unconsciously or half-consciously reflected the emergence of a market society.

One last example of questionable juxtaposition: Tully suggests that Hobbes, following a Grotian agenda, sharply separated the economic from the political. He wanted to build a strong state for self-preservation in the face of growing religious diversity. And like Grotius, Hobbes was part of the juridical tradition. Two questions can be posed: is Tully suggesting that the development of religious conflict had *nothing* to do with the emergence of a market society, notwithstanding the differences between Weberians and Marxists on this subject? And secondly, is he saying that the juridical tradition has *nothing* to do with economic activity? The institution of property is at once political *and* economic. A state (political) supported and organised legal framework defines individual and collective rights over objects, whether natural or human made (economic). Even Macpherson's fiercest critics were aware that for Hobbes a vital function of the state was the promotion of private economic activities through the protection of property.[113]

In response to Berlin's argument that Hobbes' thought was more influenced by the ancient Greeks than the market, if he was merely replicating ancient Greek thought, this would certainly undermine an absolute reductionist, 'market', methodology. Yet a more complex position can be advanced, which raises very general issues about how writers appropriate past thinkers. But first, an obvious point: Macpherson was attempting to explain an *aspect* of Hobbes' thought, its 'bourgeois' character manifested in, or coloured by, semi-conscious or unstated social assumptions rather than giving an account of all its features. Second, while writers may draw on different thinkers from the past, and they invariably do, there is the question of *why* they do so, that is in response to what circumstances. Current social practices may confirm the insights of past thinkers. And in response to societal changes, depending on value/cognitive preferences, different past writers may be invoked to confirm a radical or conservative perspective. In explaining 'influences' thought may be a mixture of both autonomy and social determination. Then there is the question of precisely *how* such thinkers are used, how they fit into a philosopher's overall theory, which may involve differences between them and the past thinker. For example, Marx is well known for his admiration of Aristotle. Yet at least we would have to say Marx combined Aristotle with other thinkers such as Hegel, Ricardo and Smith within his own unique overall system. So too for Hobbes. While, for example, Hobbes may have been influenced by Thucydides and the Sophists, he borrowed conceptions from more contemporary thinkers, such as materialism and a resolutive/compositive method from Galileo.[114] Furthermore, even if for the sake of argument Hobbes was writing in the tradition of the Sophists, this does not rule out the possibility of more contemporary determinations, which could generate his own unique slant on that tradition. This could easily be the result of the different socio-historical situation as well as the development of knowledge in comparison to the ancient Greeks. The precise way in which conflict is assumed to arise has to be acknowledged. For Hobbes it was in terms of mechanical materialism. Taking the case of Thucydides, while Hobbes' call for a strong state may have been echoing him, his specific form of argument, resting on materialism and a resolutive-compositive method, was different. Moreover, Hobbes' notion of the state as regulating the activities of private individuals within an autonomous civil society had little in common with Greek thought.

On the question of textual evidence, supposedly demonstrating that Hobbes' thought was influenced by market considerations, Macpherson was on both strong and weak ground depending on which quotation was in contention. His strongest position seems to relate to passages confirming Hobbes' dismissing of medieval notions of justice. Few critics have challenged Macpherson here. Although Letwin stated that Hobbes was merely attacking traditional notions of justice, Hobbes presumably thought that his readers would agree with him as a result of reflecting on the market nature of their society. Macpherson was on slightly weaker ground in discussing value as price in the sense that Hobbes may have derived this notion from medieval courtly literature, as Thomas suggested, and he may have been attempting to persuade contentious and egoistic aristocrats to take a more humble opinion of themselves. Yet, whatever his intentions, such a view could easily have been confirmed for him because of his awareness of existing in a market society. Again, the evidence to show that Hobbes had only a restricted awareness of the existence of wage labour, when referring to its existence in the export industry, is by no means conclusive.

Moving to Carmichael's critique, Macpherson was able successfully to refute one of its elements, relating to the existence of a universal opposition of powers in civil society. For Hobbes to have suggested anything else would have been odd, given that he wanted to demonstrate to all individuals the need for an absolute sovereign. Yet, Macpherson was unable to demolish Carmichael's central intuition. Hobbes' *text* did not show that his postulated opposition of powers was reducible and explicable in terms of competitive exchange relations and the corollary notion that he was attempting to ensure the peaceful invasion of each other's powers. This of course this may have been an *effect* of what he was suggesting, but Macpherson would have been on safer ground if he had argued his earlier position of 1945. This held that market-induced scarcity was the key problem, not the assuring of the peaceful invasion of powers, although obviously this can be seen as a consequence of the function of the state in defending private property. While one can agree that a partial shift in definition of powers occurs in chapters 10–11 of the *Leviathan*, the explanation does not have to be cast in terms of a possessive market society, of an actual market in competitive exchanges. Rather this move from self-direction to zero-sum can be explained by scarcity, albeit derived from the breakdown of medieval society, in which work and consumption were authoritatively allocated. Scarcity became individuated. Macpherson read into these chapters a move in definitions of power which led from self-direction to conflict, which supposedly required the introduction of social postulates not initially evident. There is no reason to suppose that his initial physiogical postulate did not incorporate not merely desire for con-tinued motion, but unlimited appetites, that is motion maximisation. Of course, this desire for motion maximisation as well as the anxiety at the pros-pect of its reduction could easily have been a reflection of a possessive market society, that is socially derived. With exchange regulating the social division of labour through a process of supply and demand, the individual is constantly invited to consume more, but is also faced continually with the prospect of a fall in demand for his or her labour or goods.[115] Hobbes, then, was not addressing the problem of ensuring the peaceful invasion of powers as directly as Macpherson interpreted.

– The viability of the possessive market society model –

This brings us to a third area of criticism, to do with Macpherson's derivation and use of a possessive market society model in accounting for Hobbes' social assumptions. Logical and empirical objections were mounted. In terms of logic, Macpherson, in offering only three models of society (customary, simple market society and possessive market society), was hardly providing an exhaust-ive list, which could also include democratic socialist or mixed economies. Letwin argued that, in having such a limited range of models, Macpherson was forced to deduce that England must have been a possessive market society.[116] Moreover, the features of the possessive market model, such as differences of energy, skills and possessions, and of some men wanting more powers and utilities than others, occurred in all societies.[117] In any case even if present society was characterised as a possessive market, most people were not com-petitive or acquisitive. There was also the more obvious question as to whether seventeenth-century England was actually a possessive market society, or signi-ficantly so in an innovative sense. There were severe restrictions on the alienation of land.[118] England was 'a mixture of status, custom, and innova-tion, of freedom and restraint, of efficiency and carelessness.'[119] Following Thomas, David Miller argued that England was a transitional society, and that it was neither feudal nor market between 1600 and 1800, and its 'ideology likewise'.[120] And Berlin maintained that it was 'still heavy with the landed and hierarchical past'.[121] Further, Letwin held that even if England was a con-tractual society and possessed a class of wage labourers in the seventeenth century this was hardly something new.[122] Indeed, Macpherson's point that Hobbes had ignored the possibility that the bourgeoisie was a cohesive class, and therefore needed no absolute sovereign, was empirically faulty. For it was not bound together by common interests.[123]

Shapiro in particular held that the possessive model was ahistorical and obscured Hobbes' importance as a transitional thinker, as between feudalism and capitalism, and for the subsequent liberal tradition.[124] Macpherson, because he assumed that the model had already established itself as dominant, failed to note the role of the state in promoting market relations at this time, especially through the revolutions in public and private law which were supported by Hobbes.[125] Macpherson was 'hoodwinked by the myth of the minimal state'.[126] And Hobbes' thought could not be reduced to a possessive model. For example, Hobbes did not see people as unequal in energy, skill and possessions, but as equally vulnerable in a physical sense.[127] Hobbes' significance for the later liberal tradition was that this postulated equality served to 'gloss' over inequality derived from capitalist exploitation.[128] Similarly, the possessive model misled Macpherson into assuming that Hobbes had a modern notion of utility and power. For Hobbes, power was not only for the maximisation of utilities, but stemmed from fear arising from physical vulnerability. Hobbes' theory, unlike modern utilitarianism contained not only a notion of subjective preferences, but also of objective interests, arising from natural law. Nevertheless, Shapiro did concede that 'at the heart of Hobbes' writing' was the possessive individual.[129]

Macpherson's reply and commentary

In replying to Letwin, Macpherson denied that he had employed a circular argument in deducing that seventeenth-century England must have been a possessive market society, because his two other models – status and simple market – did not fit. His characterisation had empirical support: wage labour was significant, as was the market in land. And although the phenomenon of wage labour may have existed before the seventeenth century, it had now become prevalent. Further, while he admitted that factual inequality and inequality of desire existed in other, non-capitalist societies, they only became significant in bourgeois society, when they were combined with labour as a commodity, with land and other resources becoming marketable. Then these inequalities became 'operative factors in the development of the new society'.[130] On the issue of whether Hobbes was working with a capitalist model in mind, whether Macpherson had taken quotations from Hobbes out of context, Letwin had ignored Hobbes' rejection of distributive justice, his views on taxation and his analysis of a changing English society in *Behemoth*. Finally, on the question of why Hobbes' argument for an absolute sovereign, based upon ignoring class cohesion, was unpopular among the bourgeoisie, Macpherson merely reiterated his point that they would not have objected to such a body provided that they were this body.

To evaluate the arguments posed by the choice of explanatory models, the first thing to note is that critics often committed a category mistake in denying the significance of capitalism in this period by confusing it with 'laissez-faire'[131] or 'industrialism' or an 'advanced economy'[132], or assuming that it was inconsistent with mercantilism or a 'landed' 'hierarchical form of society'.[133] Yet the defining mark of capitalism is in its production relations, in the prevalence of wage labour. Although Shapiro did not commit this error, he came close in proposing that Macpherson assumed that Hobbes advocated a minimal state. We have already seen that in his last piece on Hobbes, in *RFEJ* Macpherson recognised that his 'political economy' involved a positive role by the state in the promotion of private economic activity and the creation of a post-feudal property framework.[134] But even if England was more transitional than Macpherson supposed, ultimately the question does not turn on whether seventeenth-century England was completely a possessive market society, but only significantly so. As Macpherson admitted his possessive model was a 'post-Hobbesian construction',[135] although he thought that Hobbes registered an awareness of some of its most important facets, especially the commodification of labour and the acceptability of a market conception of justice. And there is no reason why Hobbes could not have been picking out economic and social *tendencies* he deemed as significant in his own society. After all, was not the seventeenth century a vital period in which the basis was laid for England (along with Holland) to become the first obviously capitalist power in the whole of human history? Thus Macpherson's argument does not have to rest on England as a fully fledged capitalist economy in this period. Moreover, in seeing his model as a 'post-Hobbesian construction' Macpherson was using it for heuristic purposes, to discover the extent to which Hobbes' thought correlated with this model in order establish his contribution to a possessive market ideology.

On this issue Shapiro claims that Macpherson missed Hobbes' significance in not highlighting his contribution of formal equality stemming from equal physical vulnerability, which obscured substantive inequality. Yet Macpherson noted what he believed to be a key characteristic of Hobbes' model, namely that political obligation could be derived from his factual, materialist postulates, 'the equality of need for continued motion, and equal insecurity because of equal liability to invasion by others through the market.'[136] Although his statement is uncharacteristically unclear, some notion of equal physical vulnerability can be deduced from it. Moreover, as already stated, Shapiro agreed with Macpherson that Hobbes' ontology was possessive individualist, all of which suggests that perhaps they were saying the same thing, merely in different ways. If not, their views on the importance of possessive individualism for the liberal tradition could still be construed as compatible. Similarly, even if Macpherson was slightly anachronistic about Hobbes having a modern conception of utility and power, the differences are more a matter of degree than principle in the sense that the British utilitarian tradition in reality consisted of a compound of objective interests and subjective preferences (see for example J. S. Mill). And if Hobbes reflected this, his stature within and influence on this tradition is not thereby diminished.

Ultimately Macpherson's critics, in order to demonstrate that his use of the possessive market model was ill-conceived, had to demonstrate that there was no significant correlation between it and the observations Hobbes made about the behaviour and practices of his contemporaries. The working assumption of these critics was that Hobbes had to be fully aware of what he was doing through the promotion of such a model, whereas Mapherson was asking a slightly different question which was about the compatibility between this model and Hobbes' 'political economy'. In other words, he was seeking to understand the objective, historical significance of Hobbes' *Leviathan* as a contribution to liberal ideology in its possessive mode.

– CONCLUSION –

The avalanche of criticism dented Macpherson's hypothesis about Hobbes. The question is whether the hypothesis has become so unsustainable that it should be jettisoned, which is what these critics were in effect implying, because apart from Shapiro none attempted to offer a modified, more defensible position. Critics were at their weakest when proposing that Macpherson characterised Hobbes as a protagonist of a rising bourgeois class. They therefore ignored Macpherson's aim which was not primarily concerned with Hobbes' motives or intentions, but with identifying certain semi-conscious or unstated social assumptions and their implications. In particular he wanted to tease out the *logic* of what Hobbes was saying in order to understand his contribution to the possessive market model: if a universal competition of powers is postulated, then for it to proceed peacefully, and for society to continue, a state must guarantee exchange.[137] They were on much stronger ground when evaluating the *textual* evidence supposedly demonstrating the pervasiveness of market assumptions in Hobbes' thought. Although critics found it hard to refute his market notion of justice, they found it easier to show that he did not necessarily assume a market in powers, especially a well developed labour market ready for capitalist exploitation, with the state ensuring the peaceful invasion of these powers. This may, however, have been the *effect* of what he was saying, as Macpherson argued. Yet in terms of textual fidelity his earlier interpretation, which attached far more importance to the role of market-induced individuated scarcity was more convincing. The model of an atomised, competitive society, upon which this scarcity rests, could easily be seen as the product of the market, even if Hobbes was not fully aware of this. Macpherson's notion in *PI* that Hobbes' state existed to

guarantee the 'peaceful' invasion of powers presupposed that Hobbes implicitly held a Marxist theory of exploitation. However, given that he had already
attributed to Hobbes a market conception of justice, there would seem little
reason to suppose that he thought of market relations as invasive. Significantly, Macpherson constantly came back to this Hobbesian-inspired notion
of scarcity in his later writings.

Critics also plausibly demonstrated that Hobbes' concerns were with the
hegemonic capacities of the aristocracy rather than the bourgeoisie. Although
we are here moving into the area of Hobbes' intentions, we may nevertheless
conclude that if, contra Macpherson, Hobbes' writings were not quite so
transparently 'of' a market society, they were definitely *for* a market society.
Whether he was conscious of it or not, he wrote for a modern, capitalist world
in which a centralised and ultimately secular state secured the conditions for a
realm of private economic activity based upon exchange, that is for a civil
society. But above all this, his model of 'man' was pre-eminently suited for the
market. However much he admired, and wished to sustain, aristocratic virtues
of honour, courage and magnanimity, perhaps essential to a ruling class, such
expectations were not for ordinary men. They could not transcend the
sovereignty of desire, the triumph of instrumental reason and want over
need, except for physical survival. These men could not banish from their
minds an anxiety arising from an individuated notion of scarcity, the product
of a *felicific calculus*. This was the Hobbes upon whom Bentham built.

— NOTES —

1. C. B. Macpherson, 'Hobbes Today', *Canadian Journal of Economics and Political Science*, 11, 1945, pp. 524–34, reprinted as 'Hobbes' Bourgeois Man' in *DT*, pp. 238–50.
2. L. Strauss, *The Political Philosophy of Hobbes* (Chicago: University of Chicago Press, [1936] 1952), pp. 118–28.
3. Ibid., p. 119, p. 120.
4. Ibid., p. 121.
5. *DT*, p. 241.
6. Ibid., pp. 241–2.
7. Ibid., p. 242.
8. Ibid., p. 246.
9. C. B. Macpherson, 'The Deceptive Task of Political Theory', *Cambridge Journal*, 7, 1954, pp. 560–8, reprinted *DT*, pp. 195–203.
10. *PI*, p. 2.
11. Ibid., p. 3.
12. Ibid., pp. 14–15.
13. Ibid., p. 19.

14. Ibid., p. 22.
15. Ibid., p. 69.
16. Quoted Ibid., p. 23.
17. Ibid., p. 23.
18. Ibid., p. 23.
19. Ibid., p. 24.
20. Ibid., p. 24.
21. Ibid., p. 29.
22. Quoted, Ibid., p. 35.
23. Quoted Ibid., p. 35.
24. T. Hobbes, *Leviathan* [1651] (Harmondsworth: Penguin, 1968), ch. 10, *passim*.
25. Quoted *PI*, p. 37.
26. Quoted Ibid., p. 38.
27. Ibid., p. 39.
28. Ibid., p. 59.
29. Ibid., p. 62.
30. Quoted Ibid., p. 62.
31. Ibid., p. 63.
32. Quoted, Ibid., p. 63.
33. Ibid., pp. 64-6.
34. Ibid., p. 67.
35. Ibid., p. 67.
36. Ibid., p. 77, p. 78.
37. Ibid., p. 78.
38. Ibid., p. 87
39. Ibid., p. 87.
40. Ibid., p. 80.
41. Ibid., pp. 85-7.
42. Ibid., p. 87.
43. Ibid., p. 88.
44. Ibid., p. 105.
45. A couple of critics did, however, query Macpherson's claim that Hobbes had effectively 'cracked' the fact/value problem in political theory: L. J. Macfarlane, *Modern Political Theory* (London: Nelson, 1970), p. 179; D. Miller, 'The Macpherson Version', *Political Studies*, 30/1, 1982, p. 122. While in strict logical terms they may be right, Macpherson's overall point was to emphasise Hobbes' modernity in basing his theory on the observable facts of human nature rather than relying on metaphysical postulates.
46. I. Berlin, 'Hobbes, Locke and Professor Macpherson', *Political Quarterly*, 35/4, 1964, p. 445.
47. R. Tuck, *Hobbes* (Oxford: Oxford University Press, 1989), p. 103.
48. A. Ryan, 'Hobbes and Individualism', in G. A. J. Rogers and A. Ryan (eds), *Perspectives on Thomas Hobbes* (Oxford: Clarendon Press, 1988), p. 101.
49. In K. C. Brown (ed.), *Hobbes Studies* (Oxford: Blackwell, 1965).

50. Ibid., p. 187.
51. Ibid., p. 189.
52. Ibid., p. 235.
53. Ibid., p. 232.
54. Ibid., p. 222.
55. Ibid., p. 228.
56. Ibid., pp. 228-9.
57. Ibid., p. 223.
58. Ibid., p. 229.
59. Ibid., p. 229.
60. Ibid., p. 230.
61. Ibid., p. 231.
62. Ibid., p. 236.
63. J. P. Sommerville, *Thomas Hobbes: Political Ideas in Historical Context* (London: Macmillan, 1992), p. 180 footnote, I. Berlin, 'Hobbes, Locke ...', p. 452; W. Letwin, 'The Economic Foundations of Hobbes' Politics', in M. Cranston and R. Peters (eds), *Hobbes and Rousseau* (New York: Anchor, 1972), p. 157; L. J. Macfarlane, *Modern Political Theory*, p. 182, D. Miller, 'The Macpherson Version', p. 123.
64. D. D. Raphael, *Hobbes: Morals and Politics* (London: Allen & Unwin, 1977), p. 93; D. Miller, 'Macpherson Version', p. 123, A. Ryan, 'Hobbes and Individualism', p. 101.
65. N. Wood, 'Thomas Hobbes and the Crisis of the English Aristocracy', *History of Political Thought*, 1/3, 1980, p. 451.
66. Miller, 'Macpherson Version', p. 123.
67. Tuck, *Hobbes*, p. 103, L. J. Macfarlane, *Modern Political Thought*, p. 182.
68. Tuck, *Hobbes*, p. 103; Macfarlane, *Modern Political Thought*, p. 182; Ryan, 'Hobbes and Individualism', p. 101.
69. Macfarlane, *Modern Political Thought*, p. 183, Berlin, 'Hobbes, Locke ...', p. 455.
70. Ryan, 'Hobbes and Individualism', p. 101.
71. Ibid., p. 100.
72. Raphael, *Hobbes*, p. 93.
73. Berlin, 'Hobbes, Locke ...', p. 459, p. 449. See also, Letwin, 'The Economic Foundations ...', p. 157.
74. Berlin, Hobbes, Locke ...', p. 447.
75. Ryan, 'Hobbes and Individualism', p. 102.
76. Tuck, *Hobbes*, p. 103.
77. J. Tully, 'The Possessive Individualism Thesis: A Reconsideration in the Light of Recent Scholarship', in J. Carens (ed.), *Democracy and Possessive Individualism: The Intellectual Legacy of C. B. Macpherson* (New York: State University of New York Press, 1993), p. 29.
78. C. B. Macpherson, 'Introduction' to Hobbes, *Leviathan* (Harmondsworth: Penguin, 1968), p. 12, p. 52.
79. *RFEJ*, p. 136.
80. Macpherson, 'Introduction', p. 50.

81. Ibid., p. 52.
82. *RFEJ*, p. 136.
83. See also *PI*, pp. 1415.
84. *RFEJ*, p. 136.
85. D. Baumgold, *Hobbes's Political Theory* (Cambridge: Cambridge University Press, 1988), p. 81, p. 87.
86. For example, Ryan, 'Hobbes and Individualism', pp. 100-1.
87. Raphael, *Hobbes*, p. 93, and Miller, 'Macpherson Version', p. 123.
88. See also M. Lessnoff, *Social Contract* (London: Macmillan, 1986), p. 108.
89. Raphael, *Hobbes*, p. 93, J. Viner, ' "Possessive Individualism" as Original Sin', *Canadian Journal of Economics and Political Science*, 29, 1963, p. 552, Berlin, 'Hobbes, Locke . . .', p. 451, W. Letwin, 'The Economic Foundations . . .', p. 157.
90. Viner, 'Possessive Individualism . . .', p. 552.
91. Raphael, *Hobbes*, p. 93.
92. Letwin, 'The Economic Foundations . . .', p. 154.
93. Ibid., p. 156.
94. Berlin, 'Hobbes, Locke . . .', p. 447.
95. Ibid., p. 458.
96. D. J. C. Carmichael, 'C. B. Macpherson's "Hobbes": A Critique', *Canadian Journal of Political Science*, 16/1, 1983, pp. 61-80.
97. M. M. Goldsmith, *Hobbes' Science of Politics* (New York: Columbia University Press, 1966), p. 68, footnote.
98. Carmichael, 'C. B. Macpherson . . .', p. 70.
99. Ibid., p. 80.
100. *RFEJ*, pp. 137-41.
101. Ibid., p. 136.
102. Ibid., p. 137, emphasis in original.
103. Quoted Ibid., p. 142.
104. Quoted Ibid., p. 142.
105. Quoted Ibid., p. 142.
106. Ibid., p. 146.
107. C. B. Macpherson, 'Leviathan Restored: A Reply to Carmichael', *Canadian Journal of Political Science*, 16/4, 1983, pp. 795-805.
108. Ibid., p. 802.
109. Ibid., p. 804.
110 Lessnoff, *Social Contract*, p. 108.
111. Quoted *PI*, p. 24.
112. For example, Raphael, Viner and Berlin.
113. For example, Thomas and Letwin.
114. See, for example, R. Peters, *Hobbes* (Harmondsworth: Penguin, 1956), pp. 25-6.
115. In a later discussion, Macpherson acknowledged that in a market society most people were motivated by a 'mixture of hope of getting more and fear of getting less': 'Currency of Values', *Transactions of the Royal Society of Canada*, 9/4, 1971, p. 32.

116. Letwin, 'The Economic Foundations ...', p. 145.
117. Ibid., pp. 146-8.
118. Ibid., p. 152.
119. Ibid.
120. Miller, 'Macpherson Version', p. 126, See also Wood, 'Hobbes ...', p. 438, J. Shapiro, *The Evolution of Rights in Liberal Theory* (Cambridge: Cambridge University Press, 1986), p. 70.
121. Berlin, 'Hobbes, Locke ...', p. 452.
122. Letwin, 'The Economic Foundations ...', pp. 151-2.
123. Ibid., p. 159.
124. Shapiro, *The Evolution of Rights in Liberal Theory*, p. 69.
125. Ibid., pp. 75-6.
126. Ibid., p. 72.
127. Ibid., p. 72.
128. Ibid., p. 73.
129. Ibid., p. 69.
130. C. B. Macpherson, 'Review of *Hobbes and Rousseau: A Collection of Critical Essays*', *American Political Science Review*, 68, 1974, p. 1731.
131. Berlin and Ryan.
132. Thomas.
133. Berlin.
134. *RFEJ*, pp. 141-2.
135. *PI*, p. 61.
136. Ibid., p. 265.
137. See, for example, Macpherson, 'Introduction' to the *Leviathan*, pp. 38-9.

CHAPTER 3

LOCKE AS POSSESSIVE INDIVIDUALIST

Macpherson's portrait of Locke, the patron saint of Western liberalism, as a possessive individualist aroused even more controversy than his picture of Hobbes. His detailed textual analysis of Locke's *Second Treatise of Government*, demonstrating that Locke's fundamental contradictions could be explained by social assumptions closely entwined with a nascent capitalism, was more than his critics could stomach, at least initially. His unflattering account of Locke invited both refutation and the need to offer an alternative interpretation. Yet after the dust settled most grudgingly accepted that there existed some kind of link between Locke and capitalism. The net effect of the debate surrounding Macpherson's interpretation was to tie Locke even more closely to an emergent capitalism. As in the argument over Hobbes, this debate contained the small irony that critics mistakenly thought that Macpherson had misread Locke's intentions. Their concern with authorial intention did not extend to a proper acknowledgement of Macpherson's purposes.

Just as Macpherson had built on Strauss's portrait of Hobbes, so he did of Locke. Strauss had judged Locke's theory of property as 'the classic doctrine of the "spirit of capitalism"'.[1] Locke's civil society, consequent upon the introduction of money in the state of nature, created 'the conditions under which the individuals can pursue their productive-acquisitive activity without obstruction.'[2] As we shall see, Macpherson among other things developed this argument in greater detail. More obviously than Strauss he did not focus primarily on Locke's intentions. As with his approach to Hobbes, he employed a 'logical' and 'historical' analysis. He looked at Locke's 'unstated [social] assumptions', derived from his own society, which he 'carried into' his own political theory.[3] And as with Hobbes this mainly 'assumptive' analysis, he claimed, helped solve numerous unresolved problems in Lockean interpretation, namely, problems of an all-inclusive theory of obligation in a 'joint stock company' (Stephen, Laski, Vaughan, Tawney), of individual obligation if Locke is perceived as a majoritarian democrat (Kendall), and of attempting to effect a compromise between the individualist and collectivist elements in Locke's theory (Gough). These interpretations ignored or left 'unexplained' the 'contradictions and ambiguities' in Locke, in particular that he sometimes saw men as on the whole rational, and most of them not, and that the state of nature is 'rational, peaceable and social, and it is not.'[4] The point of Macpherson's analysis was to explain these contradictions and ambiguities by showing how Locke 'read back into the nature of men and society certain preconceptions about the nature of seventeenth-century man and society which he generalized quite unhistorically, and compounded, rather unsystematically, with traditional conceptions such as those to which he assented in his frequent invocations of Hooker.'[5]

— MACPHERSON'S LOCKE —

Macpherson's starting point was to demonstrate that Locke, especially in chapter five of the Second Treatise, in effect legitimated the unlimited accumulation of capital. Locke's 'astonishing achievement was to base the property right on natural right and natural law, and then to remove all the natural law limits from the property right.'[6] Briefly stated, he sought to show how Locke justified unlimited appropriation after initially positing a state of nature where individual rights to appropriate the fruits of the earth and the earth itself were subject to limitations, in accordance with natural law. The first limitation was that 'enough, and as good' had to be left for others, that is a sufficiency limitation. Secondly, no one should accumulate so much that it spoils, that is a spoilage limitation. Thirdly, an individual was entitled only to that with which they mixed their labour, that is a labour limitation. Locke then argued that the first two limitations could be legitimately transcended through the invention of money, which occurred because men tacitly agreed to put a value on gold and silver as media of exchange. Money did not spoil, and Macpherson deduced that the purpose of accumulating money was not primarily to increase consumption but to increase capital, although this was identified in mercantilist terms with national rather than individual wealth.[7] The invention of money also enabled the sufficiency limitation in land to be overcome because agricultural surpluses could be exchanged for money. This encouraged the enclosure of land, because there was an incentive to produce for the market, and furthermore there was an inducement to increase productivity. Locke argued that even the landless were better off because of this productivity. The day labourer was better 'clad' than a 'king' in America, where land had not been enclosed. Hence, subsistence no longer had to be identified with land ownership. Thus private land ownership, which created a landless proletariat, worked within the spirit, if not the letter, of the sufficiency limitation, which guaranteed self-preservation. Further, the land owner by enclosing, by more efficiently utilising the land and making it more productive, was in effect 'giving' land to mankind.

As for the labour limitation, Locke, according to Macpherson, merely assumed it away by presupposing that wage labour existed in the state of nature. Locke assumed that the 'turfs' that a servant had cut were the property of the master, because it was the master's 'labour'.[8] It could only be so if there existed a prior wage labour contract, entitling the master to claim ownership of the labourer's labour. Macpherson concluded that Locke laid 'the moral foundation for bourgeois appropriation'.[9] For he had insisted that a man's labour, which was his own, was contractually alienable for which he owed nothing to society, once the two other limitations had been removed. Labour could be 'infinitely' purchased by the 'master'. No longer did labour and property necessarily entail social functions and obligations.

Locke provided a 'moral basis' for capitalist society in another way. He justified 'as natural, a class differential in rights and in rationality'. Macpherson sought to demonstrate that labourers for Locke were not 'full members of the body politic and had no claim to be so' and that they cannot live a 'fully rational life'.[10] Locke took 'these propositions for granted'.[11] Locke advocated the harsh treatment of able-bodied unemployed in workhouses, because their unemployment was due to their moral depravity, and so in effect did not see them as 'full or free members of the political community'.[12] His attitude towards employed workers was hardly different. They lived at subsistence level, from 'hand to mouth'. And if they revolted, this was due to 'mismanaged government'.[13] Given that they were incapable of rational political action, it was unlikely that he extended to them the right of revolution. Their lack of a developed rationality was further evinced by the need to instil obedience in the labouring classes through inculcating the Christian doctrine of divine rewards and punishments. 'The greatest part cannot know, and therefore they must believe.'[14]

These differentials in political rights and rationality, derived from his own society, Locke read back into the nature of man and society in general. Although initially in the *Second Treatise* there was no assumption of class differentiation, with the stress on the equality of natural rights, in the chapter on property this was transformed into differential natural rights, so that individuals no longer had a natural right to landed property and to be free from the jurisdiction of another. The 'industrious and rational' could rightfully acquire all the land, leaving the rest the only option to stay alive by selling their labour. This differentiation of property was according to Locke natural, taking place outside the 'bounds of Societie'. And clearly the non-property owners Locke recognised were dependent upon the property owners and therefore subject to their jurisdiction, that is they lost their self-proprietorship.[15] Civil society was established to protect these unequal possessions and rights. What Locke took to be natural differential rights were derived from assumptions he made about his own society. Nevertheless, Locke still held to the initial assumption of equality, as all individuals were proprietors of their own persons and capacities, while assuming a *de facto* inequality, as a result of workers having to sell their capacity to labour.[16] As for differential rationality, this occurred with the introduction of money, which separated labouring from appropriating through differential land ownership. Full rationality went with the appropriating landowner, who could improve his land and use it as capital, not with the landless labourer. Locke had assumed that the activity of accumulation was morally and expediently rational *per se*, although it had been checked in the initial stage of the state of nature by the absence of money and markets. And paradoxically, although he was opposed to covetousness, he assumed this human trait did not become generalised until after the introduction of money. And significantly he did not object to the covetousness of the rational accumulator, but of those who would invade his appropriation.[17]

Macpherson then sought to account for Locke's ambiguous state of nature, in which all men were rational and yet there were two different classes of rationality, and where all had natural rights yet where different orders of natural rights holders existed. Equally, sometimes the state of nature was inhabited by social and rational human beings, living peacefully under the law of nature; yet at other times it took a Hobbesian turn, in which the state of war was normal. Locke's 'central contradiction' was to posit the state of nature as sometimes 'opposite to the state of war, sometimes identical with it.'[18] This contradiction could be explained by his contradictory social assumptions, which stemmed from his own society. On the one hand he conceived of society as composed of 'equal undifferentiated beings', which derived from the Christian natural law tradition combined with seventeenth-century atomistic materialism. He also assumed equality because all men were equally capable of 'shifting for themselves', in terms of looking after themselves. Thus one conception of society was premised upon the bourgeois and Christian natural law view that men were rational and peaceable. The alternative view, which was also bourgeois, was that some – the men of property – were more rational than others – the men without property. The propertyless were less rational because of their economic position resulting from the free alienation of their labour, and required the discipline of supernatural sanctions as well as legal ones. Locke's contradictory conception Macpherson attributed to the 'ambivalence of an emerging bourgeois society which demanded formal equality but required substantive inequality of rights.'[19]

This ambiguity was mirrored in his account of the formation of civil society. The object was the protection of property. Yet property in Locke had a broad and a narrow definition. Broadly defined as 'Lives, Liberties and Estates', everyone had an interest in the creation of civil society and was clearly capable of entering it. Yet he sometimes referred to it as consisting only of goods or land. Citizens without these were in and not in civil society, because although they had property in the broadest sense, they did not have it in the narrow sense and were therefore not entitled to full membership. Only those with property in the narrow sense were full members, because only they had a full interest in the preservation of property and possessed full rationality enabling them to be voluntarily obligated to the law of reason, essential to full participation in civil society. This differential membership was revealed in Locke's distinction between express and tacit consent. All, by virtue of their ability to derive some advantage from living in civil society, gave their tacit consent. But only those who gave their express consent were entitled to become full members, and they were the land owners and those who expected to inherit land.[20] Locke only ascribed full membership to those who gave their express consent in establishing political society, and the only example he gave of express consent was the inheritance of land (11: 120).[21]

This notion of a class state based on equal natural rights was not deliberate on Locke's part. His natural rights assumptions were 'honestly held'. But they included the right to the unlimited accumulation of property, leading logically to differential class rights and the legitimation of a class state. He was unaware of this contradiction, derived from the equal natural right to unlimited property, because he 'simply read into the realm of right (or the state of nature) a social relation which he accepted as normal in civilized society.'[22] The 'source of the contradictions in his theory is his attempt to state in universal (non-class) terms, rights and obligations which necessarily had a class content.'[23]

Finally, Macpherson urged that his perspective on Locke helped resolve some outstanding interpretive problems. The 'joint stock' problem was solved because the state could be seen to consist of the property owners and the rest of the labouring population. Although workers were part of the company, they were not to take part in the decision-making process. The problem about the contradiction between majority rule and individual property right, especially if the majority consisted of the propertyless, was also cleared up. Locke assumed that only those with property were full members of society, and therefore constituted the majority. Similarly, the conflict between the principle of majority rule and the need for individual consent in relation to taxation was resolved once full citizenship consisted of property owners, who ultimately had one joint interest: the protection of their property. By the same token, the 'individualism vs. collectivism' problem disappeared, because handing over rights to the state, including possessions and land (2: 120), was not a problem if civil society was controlled by men of property.

In historical terms, Macpherson concluded that the greatness of Locke's liberalism lay in its 'assertion of the free rational individual as the criterion of the good society'. Its 'tragedy was that this very assertion was necessarily a denial of individualism to half the nation'.[24]

— MACPHERSON'S CRITICS —

Many criticisms followed the same pattern as those which challenged Macpherson's account of Hobbes: Locke could have been no champion or apologist of capitalism because this was not his intention. Critics also sought to show that, whatever his intentions, Locke's state was not built on narrow class foundations: there were no differential rights founded upon a differential rationality, determined by class. And one critical intervention by Tully sought to sever altogether the link between Locke and capitalism.

— Locke as capitalist apologist —

The presumption that Macpherson was attempting to portray Locke as an apologist for capitalism was evident in the earliest criticisms of his thesis. Laslett was unconvinced by the proposition that Locke's 'object could only have been "to provide the ideological support for capitalism"',[25] that he was 'deliberately justifying the acquisition of capital.'[26] Macpherson was 'ideological' and a 'dogmatic, economic sociologist of a familiar, but refined, Marxist cast.'[27] According to Dunn, he painted Locke as a 'self-conscious and dedicated ideologist of the rising bourgeoisie.'[28] Ryan asserted that, in Macpherson's account, 'Locke intends to supply the moral basis of ... the dictatorship of the bourgeoisie.'[29] Yet, in reality Locke offered 'no ruthless, dictatorial programme of class domination.'[30] Ashcraft assumed that Macpherson interpreted Locke's *Two Treatises* and *The Reasonableness of Christianity* as 'written to express the ideas or the interests of a propertied oligarchy.'[31] Finally, Skinner proposed that Macpherson ascribed to Locke a 'particular intention' of defending the rationality of unlimited capital accumulation.[32]

Having defined Macpherson's line of inquiry in this way, the critical task became simple: to demonstrate that Locke did not consciously advocate capitalism. Laslett, one of Macpherson's earliest critics, rejected his suggestion that Locke even acknowledged the existence of wage labour. Rather, Locke talked of a servant as selling a 'service' rather than labour. He also denied that Locke aimed to legitimate unlimited acquisitiveness, because he advocated 'regulating' property, condemned *amor sceleratus habendi*, evil Concupiscence'

(2: 111) and wanted to make society subject to the laws of nature (2: 135).[33] As we shall see, Tully developed this line of critical response to Macpherson.

The clearest evidence for critics that Locke was not a bourgeois apologist stemmed from his attitude towards charity. They pointed to his stipulation that the rich had obligations to those in 'extreme want' (1: 42).[34] This duty was perceived as the corollary to obeying the law of nature, which required self-preservation and the preservation of others. Critics moreover noted that Locke had maintained that virtue and prosperity did not necessarily go together.[35] Locke damned covetousness and 'evil concupiscence' associated with acquisitive behaviour.[36] Another form of supposed 'bourgeois behaviour' condemned by Locke was idleness, not merely among the labouring classes, but also among the leisured classes.[37] Macpherson failed to take seriously Locke's theological concerns, especially the Calvinist doctrine of a 'calling', necessary for individual salvation, which advocated diligence for individuals of whatever social background. Virtue was not the exclusive property of the propertied classes.[38] From this it could be inferred that no occupation was more privileged than any other, and there could be an enormous gulf between an existing social structure and the normative inferences to be drawn from God having given the world the 'industrious and rational'.[39] And finally, critics argued, Locke's religious concerns meant that he could not have espoused the possessive individualist doctrine of the rationality of unlimited desire. Rather, the rational individual was preoccupied with personal salvation.[40]

Macpherson's reply and commentary

This suggestion that Macpherson had portrayed Locke as *deliberately* providing a moral basis for capitalist domination completely missed the mark. Critics again committed a category mistake as they had over his interpretation of Hobbes. As already indicated, Macpherson had adverted that he was looking at Locke's 'unstated assumptions' rather than his intentions.[41]

More specifically, in *PI* he replied to Laslett, who had already criticised one of his original articles, 'Locke on Capitalist Appropriation'.[42] Macpherson maintained that in the turfs passage (2: 28) wage labour was clearly indicated by Locke's unequivocal statement that the labour performed by 'my' servant is 'the labour that was mine',[43] and that what was sold in a wage contract, whatever the task, was the future ability to work for a contracted period.[44] As for the false attribution of unlimited acquisitiveness to Locke, Macpherson indicated that he had demonstrated how Locke had overcome all the natural law limitations on property. Moreover, for Locke the regulation of property was not the same as restriction. Rather, it was required in order to secure property (2: 120). In making the laws of nature hold in society no restriction on accumulation was implied. He had already dealt with the question of Locke's opposition to covetousness in the main body of the text, holding that this referred to the quarrelsome and contentious in order that the industrious and rational could be protected.[45] Macpherson, in a letter to Laslett, made most of these points, as well as responding to his original objection that for Locke the regulation of property was for mercantilist purposes, and was therefore not capitalist. Macpherson pointed out that mercantilism was not inconsistent with unlimited accumulation and that Laslett confused capitalism with laissez-faire economic policies.[46]

Macpherson also briefly responded to Dunn's criticisms. Apart from stating that on the issue of differential rationality Dunn had not considered all his evidence, he argued that there was nothing antithetical in seeing Locke as both a Calvinist and a possessive individualist: for Locke unlimited appropriation and the maximisation of one's chances of salvation through the pursuit of a calling were both rational, and were two ways of saying the same thing.[47]

Discussion of the adequacy of Macpherson's reply to Laslett will be considered later, because it can be subsumed under Tully's critique of Macpherson, which in totally detaching Locke from capitalism built on Laslett's arguments. The only point to be made about his response to Dunn is that Locke's theology and economics can be reconciled, even leaving aside the question of a 'calling'.[48] Locke may have advocated charity, but it was an unenforceable obligation and would arise only in a limited number of instances because Locke blamed most poverty on idleness. Moreover, there is nothing inherently anti-capitalist about charity. The converse may be true: it can serve as a form of legitimation by focusing on immediate needs, rather than the structural causes of neediness. In any case, Macpherson repeatedly indicated the Christian roots of Locke's political philosophy. More plausibly, Locke can be interpreted as effecting an accommodation between Christianity and capitalism, because he also maintained that God had given the world the 'industrious and rational', who were entitled to prosper through their own efforts and would expect the chances of personal salvation to be good. And Locke also saw the enclosing and improving landlord as carrying out God's command to 'be fruitful, and multiply and replenish the earth and subdue it' (Genesis, 1: 28, 1: 23). Locke argued that such a landlord was in effect not merely 'giving' land to others, but as raising the living standards of the 'day labourer'. Thus, there was no necessary antithesis between selfishness and charity.[49] By the same token, on the question of covetousness, Macpherson noted that Locke was decrying not the covetousness of the rational accumulator, but of the quarrelsome and contentious, 'who sought to acquire possessions not by industry but by trespass.'[50]

– Locke's class state –

Whatever Locke's intentions, all his critics were agreed that the state he advocated was not designed to protect the interests of a particular, capitalist class, either in terms of its function or membership. They argued that Locke's state was far more universalistic in scope: the rights of non-property owners (defined in the narrow, conventional sense) were equally protected. And some critics maintained that Locke wanted equal rights to political participation. In other words there was no assumption of differential rights based along class lines. Underlying this criticism was the notion that Macpherson wrongly attributed to Locke an assumption of differential class rationality.

The reason why critics assumed that all (men) had the same rights was that when Locke argued that the job of the state was to protect the rights of property owners, he meant property defined in the broad sense of life, liberty and property, rather than in the narrow sense of material possessions. Locke's definition of property ultimately rested upon the idea that it was something which no one can be deprived of without their consent, which included life, liberty and possessions.[51] And even if property was defined in the narrow sense, all, apart from slaves and alms takers, had some property to protect, even if only 'clothes and tools'.[52]

Critics also objected to Macpherson's argument that Locke assumed differential membership based upon the distinction between express and tacit consent. Full membership, Macpherson claimed, went with landowner-ship because land owners were the only group that gave their express consent. The landless, and those who could not expect to inherit land, only gave their tacit consent. Therefore, they were 'in and not in' political society. Dunn challenged this view on a number of counts. First, Locke may have conceived of other 'motives' for joining political society apart from the protection of landed property, given the existence of the landless rich and poor.[53] Secondly, Locke was addressing the issue of becoming incorporated when political society was first established, and did not discuss the problem of who gave express consent in later generations. Where Locke did discuss becoming a member of an existing society and cited express consent being given upon the inheritance of land, he was attempting to avoid the destruction of the terri-torial integrity of state.[54] Finally, when Locke discussed tacit consent it was in relation to foreigners. There was the question of how the landless natives could be identified as actual subjects. This implied that there had to be some form of swearing of allegiance, since Locke had argued that express consent was necessary for membership. However, he did not bother to specify the form it would take.[55]

The part of Macpherson's argument which attracted the greatest volume of criticism was his claim that Locke assumed differential rationality along class lines. In part Macpherson inadvertently weakened his case by being slightly ambiguous on the subject. He initially stated that the labouring classes were in too low a position to be 'capable of a rational life', that is capable of leading a moral life based upon reason.[56] He attributed to Locke what can be termed an 'absolutist' position. Yet he seemed to qualify this by saying that they were not capable of living a '*fully* rational life', that is a relativist position.[57] Many critics then took Macpherson's first assertion to be what he meant. Workers according to Macpherson 'had lost their rationality',[58] or were 'not rational'.[59] Undermining Macpherson's thesis then became simple: to show that Locke attributed *some* rationality to them, if only by implication. Locke for example, held that rationality was associated with adulthood (11: 58, 61),[60] and that only 'lunaticks and Ideots' and 'madmen' were irrational (11: 60).[61] And all were free by virtue of their rationality.[62] Political society was founded in order to protect property in the broadest sense, and accordingly all adult males as possessors of property could be expected to give their consent rationally.[63] Indeed, Locke's political philosophy contained a 'moral egalitarianism' and therefore an opportunity for all to be rational.[64] According to Dunn, for Locke both the rich and the poor had in effect an equal responsibility to exercise their 'calling', to be realised in productive activity.[65] And if the poor were irrational, Locke could on occasion blame the upper classes for this failing.[66]

Critics did, however, explore Macpherson's contention that rationality was differentially distributed on class lines. They indicated for example that Locke saw individuals who were either rich or poor as irrational, in the sense that they could be idle, that is not industrious,[67] and this was the reason why he was so insistent upon moral reform of all classes through education. Locke clearly supported the idea of individual social mobility through industriousness.[68] Conversely, rationality and industriousness existed in all classes.[69]

The last major doubt critics had concerning the differential rationality hypothesis lay in Macpherson's interpretation of *The Reasonableness of Christianity*. He argued that Locke advocated a simplified Christianity for the labouring classes, who could not 'know', and must therefore 'believe'. This work was not, according to at least one critic, about social control but about the salvation of the labouring classes.[70] Locke was a deeply religious thinker who took their salvation seriously, for its own sake. And what they 'cannot know' is 'the full deductive system of the obligatory law of nature', which no non-Christian, however intelligent, maybe including Locke himself, would understand.[71] Another critic questioned Macpherson's account of Locke's intention in writing *Reasonableness* to bring the labouring classes to obedience. Rather it was an attack on the presumptuousness of philosophers and the clergy who 'arrogated to themselves the authority to instruct mankind in matters for which they have neither the authority nor adequate knowledge, and who had forgotten that Christianity was intended as a religion for the poor.'[72] In essence, the virtue of Christianity was as a rationalist ethic built on divine revelation, which the poor could 'believe' with a minimum of reasoning. Locke was not criticising the masses for their lack of rationality, rather the 'superfine distinctions of the schools', which impeded the development of Christianity among them.[73]

Although critics rejected the tacit/express consent distinction and the differential rationality hypotheses as determining unequal political rights, very few were prepared to advance the view of Locke as a political (male) egalitarian.[74] Richard Ashcraft was one of the few exceptions.[75] He claimed that Locke was essentially a Leveller, that Locke intended that all adult males had a 'presumptive claim to be part of the legislative power' in society.[76] In interpreting paragraph 2: 140 on the relation between representation and taxation, since all paid taxes of some kind, all this meant was that those who owned more wealth should pay more taxes and all tax payers had the right to vote.[77] As for paragraphs 2: 157 and 2: 158 concerning Locke's demand for fair representation of under-represented areas in Parliament, such representation was not to be based on wealth alone but on the number of inhabitants.[78]

Macpherson's reply and commentary

His only reply to the question of whether Locke advocated a class state consisted of a riposte to Jacob Viner, who thought that he had not sufficiently emphasised Locke's use of the broad concept of property implying a broad conception of citizenship. Macpherson emphasised that he was attempting to understand the contradictions in Locke's writings, including these two definitions of property, and had acknowledged that 'Locke's attachment to private property was not exclusive: he was also attached to life and liberty and Christian morality.'[79]

Critics seem to have partially misunderstood his interpretation of Locke's idea of citizenship. They suggested that all adult (males) must have been citizens, because all had some property to protect in its wider meaning of lives, liberties and estates. However, Macpherson's intention was to explain his contradictory attitude towards citizenship. He noted the significance of the broad definition. This is what gave all citizens an interest to be 'in' civil society.[80] His point was that those without possessions, especially land, were also not 'in' civil society. They did not have the same political rights as 'full members', that is those with possessions, because they could not be so rational, and did not have the same interest in the preservation of property in the narrow sense.

Critics nevertheless hit on a weakness in Macpherson's hypothesis that full membership coincided with land ownership as a condition of express consent. Locke's question was whether, contra Filmer, an individual was ever free to form a new state (11: 113). He answered in the affirmative, unless it led to the physical dismemberment of an existing state. This meant in effect that one could start a new one in a 'free and unpossessed' territory (11: 121), provided one had not given one's express consent upon the coming of age to an existing government (11: 117). Tacit consent merely expressed the need to obey the laws of a country because of a derived benefit, whether owning land or travelling in its roads, and so on (11: 119). It could not establish an individual as a member of a political community. Only express consent could do so (11: 121). However, there are some queries that can be made against the nature of these criticisms. First, the fact that Locke did not bother to specify how the landless were to incorporate themselves merely confirms that he was concerned almost exclusively with the allegiances of those with landed property. Second, Macpherson was well aware that Locke could also posit other reasons for becoming a member of a state when he defined property in the broad sense of life, liberty and estate. His point was that Locke in many crucial passages used property in the narrow sense of estates, and hence the ambiguity and differential *membership*.[81] What his critics seemed to miss was an even greater problem with this line of argument, which is that no notion of differential *political rights* can be drawn from this passage. Locke is only dealing with the question of who are 'subjects or members' of a 'commonwealth' (11: 122). And elsewhere, as in his proposed constitution of Carolina, he stated that those over seventeen years old and who had estates or possessions or derived protection and benefit from the law had to swear allegiances. Property was not a condition of membership, and the propertyless were expected to give their express consent.[82] Macpherson in introducing the notion of 'full membership' only confused the issue, because Locke was merely addressing the question of formal membership and was not even by implication raising the question of differential political rights.

However, there is much scope for speculation because Locke was so silent on the specific issue of who was entitled to vote. Ashcraft was not able to demonstrate textually that Locke advocated universal manhood suffrage. And even if it were possible to show a difficulty in using evidence that Locke favoured a restricted franchise, this does entail the corollary notion that all adult males had a 'presumptive claim'. Moreover, Locke did not specify what being 'part of the legislative' meant, because representation was not necessarily the same as democratic accountability through a universal (male) voting system. Further, the passage 2: 158 is about the need to establish 'new corporations' so that the legislative became more truly representative. Precisely how representatives from these corporations were selected and elected was not specified in the text. Becker has plausibly shown that Locke made an intentional distinction between 'freemen' (for example, 2: 99) and 'free men' (for example, 2: 62) the former being entitled to vote and the latter, such as servants, not, because they were in some way dependent for their livelihoods on others.[83]

As for whether Locke assumed that since taxation carried with it the right to vote, and since all adult males paid taxes of some kind and were therefore entitled to vote, there are at least a couple of objections. As Ellen Wood has noted the debates over the relation between the franchise and taxation were not related to indirect taxes but to property taxes,[84] and one could not assume that in Locke's day the right to be represented was synonymous with the right to vote.[85] Sociologically, the 'people' that Locke probably had in mind included not only the land owners, but also certain sections of a growing urban population, including 'alienated intellectuals', merchants, artisans, tradesmen and leaders of 'commerce'.[86]

In broader terms, that Locke could have been a closet Leveller seems counter-intuitive. For example, he recommended for the colony of Carolina hereditary serfdom.[87] And generally his attitude towards the poor, the unemployed and the labouring classes was such that it would seem odd that he secretly championed their political rights. 'The ignorant ... confused multitude' was an 'untamed beast'.[88] Labourers lived a 'hand to mouth existence', were 'always superstitious and therefore empty-headed'.[89] Ashcraft's position appears to be counter-intuitive because of Locke's dim view of the reasoning abilities of the labouring classes owing to the nature of their work, and his intended audience which was clearly not the labouring classes. More important, historically great significance was attached to the franchise. Political equality and economic equality were seen as interlinked until the mid-nineteenth century, so that one of the great objects of political equality was to achieve economic equality. Given this widely held assumption, and Locke's defence of economic inequality, it would have been illogical on Locke's part to have advocated political equality. Only historical experience has demonstrated that the rich can live with universal suffrage, because it has not had a significant levelling effect, and indeed may contribute to all-round political and social stability. That Locke was a Leveller would be strange for another reason. As McNally has indicated, the Levellers saw poverty as a result of the activities of the rich rather than as a product of the moral defects of the poor, and in his economic policies Locke clearly gave greatest consideration to landed wealth.[90]

Thus, on the issue of differential political rights, on balance a good case can be made in Macpherson's favour. There is little firm evidence to assume that Locke adopted a Leveller position. His general attitude to the lower classes would seem to strongly count against such a claim. Putting the question rhetorically, given his unequivocal belief in the virtues of unlimited accumulation, which side would Locke have been on in the Putney Debates? The knowledge that we have in the twentieth century, that the granting of the franchise makes fundamentally little difference to the shaping of economic relations, was not available to him. From the ancient Greeks to his own times democracy was seen strongly in class terms, having vital implications for property relations and the distribution of wealth. Macpherson was genuinely attempting to locate Locke within his times: to present him as a modern-day liberal democrat on the grounds that he was a Leveller or a medieval natural law thinker would be to fall into the trap of some kind of anachronism. Moreover, critics failed to historicise capitalism in so far as they understood it, by falsely attributing to Macpherson a well developed model.[91] Failure to appreciate how Macpherson related Locke's thought to the prevailing economic and ideological background meant that they captured neither its complexity nor its internal tensions. Of course, if the question of intention is introduced, then a richer account can be given, allowing for the fact that he was attempting to build up a political alliance in favour of the 'Glorious Revolution', especially between the Whig aristocracy and London radicals, which entailed the use of anti-paternalist arguments, without promising the masses an equal political voice that would threaten property (in the narrow sense).[92]

The issue of differential rationality is also a complicated one. Macpherson could be construed at one level as attributing to Locke two notions of rationality, one absolute, the other relative, thereby making himself an easy target. That Locke endowed the labouring classes with some rationality, certainly in terms of individual potentiality, was clear. Indeed, the absolute notion was not consistent with Macpherson's own thesis which was in part to explain Locke's ambiguities, and why the working class was in and not in civil society. He saw the lower orders as both rational and not rational. If unemployed, they were morally defective (and implicitly irrational because they were not listening to God's commands), and if employed they were short on reasoning capacities because they lived 'from hand to mouth'. Macpherson acknowledged that Locke could see all as morally equal as children of God, and capable of 'shifting for themselves'.[93] More importantly, the possessive individualist assumption that all citizens were equally proprietors of their persons and capacities was central to his defence of the inequality of outcomes because capacities were alienable through exchange.[94] The explanation of this ambiguity according to Macpherson was that he used Christian natural law arguments, especially from Hooker, concerning equal rationality, to counteract Filmer's paternalism, which he combined with observations derived from his own society of a differential (bourgeois) rationality and read them back into the state of nature.[95] A general point can be made here: critics often failed to note that Macpherson was trying to account for many of Locke's known ambiguities, displayed in his analysis of the state of nature, civil society and property. The question then arises as to whether these critics actually agreed with Macpherson that these ambiguities existed in Locke's thought and had to be explained. If so, they should have sought to provide a better explanation for them, or if not, established an argument holding that ambiguities were insignificant.

Nevertheless, putting these ambiguities to one side, an argument can be made that Locke did see rationality along class lines. And some critics agreed with Macpherson on this.[96] Locke treated an idle beggar or an unemployed worker differently from an idle, drunken landlord. For the latter sanctions in the hereafter would have seemed appropriate, while for the former the secular sanction of the workhouse was more suitable. Moreover, as Macpherson implicitly noted,[97] Locke patently thought little of the reasoning capacities of workers, given their toil and the lack of leisure required to develop them. Locke did not see workers as inherently stupid. Rather, they did not have the opportunity to develop their rationality.[98] This, as Dunn has indicated, was of some concern to Locke.[99] Yet, the notion of labour-saving technology which could significantly reduce the working day was not available to Locke. And although Locke assumed that members of all classes could be industrious, and allowed for social mobility, this applied to individuals and not classes. Generally, for Locke as for other members of the ruling elite the industriousness of the working class was problematic.[100] In addition, the notion that individuals could be socially successful through hard work – as was Locke himself – could be viewed as strengthening Macpherson's argument. It legitimated the idea of an opportunity state and the notion that poverty was the product of individual failings rather than of the social economic structure. And as for Dunn's point that Locke blamed the upper classes for the irrational behaviour of the labouring classes, this merely confirms Macpherson's argument that if they revolted this was due to their 'male-administration'.[101] Workers were merely the objects of state policy.

A final issue about differential rationality concerns how Macpherson used evidence from *The Reasonableness of Christianity*. While Locke in his own mind may have genuinely sought the salvation of the labouring classes, there is no reason to suppose that personal salvation and social control have to be antithetical, especially in the light of his Protestant notion that salvation and industriousness go hand in hand. And in a historical sense the ethic of hard work was crucial to an emerging capitalist economy, where toil was no longer determined by the rhythms of nature but those of the market. On the question of whether those who could not 'know' and therefore must 'believe' referred to virtually the whole of humanity, including Locke himself, thereby implying that intelligence was not class-based, Locke must have presumed that he was as close as anyone to understanding the 'full deductive system of the obligatory law of nature'. Was not this at the base of his whole philosophical and literary enterprise, to demonstrate the inseparability of revelation and reason? Presumably he thought that his own efforts would not be comprehended by the masses, and that a simplified kind of Christianity was appropriate. Although, as Ashcraft suggested, *Reasonableness* may well have been an attack on philosophers and theologians for whom the faithlessness of the masses seemed to be of little concern, and Locke may well have wanted to remind his readers that Christianity was originally conceived of as a religion for the poor, this does not detract from Macpherson's point. Labourers, owing to the nature of their work, had limited reasoning capacities and in making Christianity accessible to them a minimum of reasoned argument had to be employed.[102] This work does not have to be seen as *either* an attack on the 'schools' *or* as a call to bring the masses to 'obedience'. It can be both.

– Tully's alternative –

Most critics rejected Macpherson's specific reading of Locke, but conceded that *some* connection existed between Locke and the rise of capitalism.[103] Yet James Tully, following Laslett's lead in his introduction to Locke's *Two Treatises*,[104] attempted to dissociate Locke completely from capitalism. As he said somewhat later, as a result of his experience as a Cambridge postgraduate, he wanted to break free of the 'tyranny' of the question of seeing Locke's thought as a justification for capitalism.[105] Tully boldly asserted: 'The capitalist not only never appears in the *Two Treatises*; there is no place for him to appear.'[106] Tully firmly placed Locke within the natural law tradition as developed by Aquinas, Suarez, Grotius, Puffendorf, Hooker, Cumberland and others, and put individual property rights on a clearly communalistic footing. The grounding ethic of property was informed by a 'workmanship model' of the relation between man and God, which manifested itself in two ways. First, it imposed a duty on all individuals because they had been made by God and were His property, to ensure their own and others' preservation. This entailed not merely respecting the life and possessions of others, but also transforming nature through labour for subsistence and comfort. Secondly, such labour was a duty because in its creative dimension it imitated God's endeavours.[107]

In applying this model, Locke's anti-capitalism revealed itself in four ways. First, Locke's famous chapter V in the *Second Treatise* on property was not a recipe for unlimited individual accumulation of landed property. Instead, its purpose (2: 25) was merely to 'show that particularization of the natural common is possible'.[108] Locke's 'model' of 'particularization' or 'individuation' was the English Common, where the English yeoman, or 'tenant in common' possessed the right of usufruct. Property rights were inclusive rather than exclusive. He was therefore entitled to as much land as he could make use of and its produce, although the land itself was still communally owned (2: 28).[109] Thus, his right to land was conditional upon its use, and not absolute. In other words there should be no fixed property in land. Tully argued that it was Locke's opponents such as Filmer that advocated the unlimited right to private property. Rather than supporting existing property relations, Locke was in essence a Leveller. As a result of the widespread use of money, covetousness and unequal land holdings had arisen in the state of nature. Government was required to constitute 'a new order of social relations that will bring the actions of men once again in line with God's intentions' through the civil law of a 'positive community' (2: 135, 2: 50).[110] Natural individual property entitlements were now replaced by conventional ones. The individual subjected his property to the jurisdiction and regulation of the community (2: 120).[111] His possessions now belonged to the community. Property now had to be 'regulated' to promote the 'public good', which significantly included the principles of distributive justice. This consisted of allowing to each the products of their honest industry (2: 3, 2: 42),[112] and where this was not possible, to each according to need or from inheritance. These principles entailed the duty of charity to those in need, where individuals had surplus goods, in order to preserve mankind, God's workmanship (1: 42, 2: 6, 2: 37).[113] More significantly, land had to be distributed in order for people to exercise their honest industry, which involved undermining the legitimacy of 'larger possessions' (2: 50)[114] on the basis of usufruct. And if land was unused it returned to the common.[115] Finally, because he favoured communal (individuated) property, he opposed primogeniture.[116]

Secondly, Tully urged, the landless proletarian made no appearance in Locke's writings either, because he made no reference to a capitalist wage labour relation. Indeed, Locke's account of this relation was a 'fetter to the development of capitalism'.[117] The turf-cutting servant and the turf-owning master depicted by Macpherson as symptomatic of Locke's unconscious recognition of such a relation harked back to a pre-capitalist era. Work was performed according to the workmanship model, in which a servant sold a complete service to the master rather than his labour power, and was not subject to detailed supervision (2: 85).[118] Thus, the product of labour rather than labour itself was alienated. Moreover, the servant was not compelled to work for the master – this would be tantamount to slavery. It was a voluntary relation. Thirdly, Locke had no concept of capital either in money or land. Locke's justification of land appropriation on the basis that it increased productivity was so that more land would be left for others (2: 37).[119] Further-more, only the products of land could be exchanged, not the land itself (2: 46, 2: 50).[120] In addition, Tully challenged Macpherson's argument that for Locke the increased productivity of enclosed land more than made up for lack of land available to others.[121] Rather, 2: 37 referred to less land being needed by individuals for their comfort and subsistence, leaving more for others.

As for money, Tully suggested that it was not reinvested to make more money. Rather it was hoarded, and Locke saw it as 'the root of all evil' as a source of human corruption.[122] Thus Locke, far from advocating capitalist acquisitiveness through the unlimited accumulation of property, decried covetousness and championed liberality and charity.[123]

Commentary

First we can note that Tully's interpretation had a number of critics. Although they did not necessarily think they were defending Macpherson, their reading of Locke in effect lent support to Macpherson's account of Locke's theory of property as favourable to capitalism. They established that for Locke the state's powers to 'regulate', 'determine', and 'settle' property did not entail the possibility of its wholesale redistribution.[124] Rather these terms referred to its power to adjudicate between different claims and protect existing acquisi-tions, as implied in the 'preservation' of property.[125] And in attempting to use the English Common as paradigmatic of inclusive property rights, Tully failed to distinguish between land which had already been individually appropriated to which the above terms applied when government was established, and that which was still unappropriated (for example, the English Common) which was regulated by agreement. Put another way, according to Locke, the Common was established by compact, whereas individual holdings did not require express consent.[126] Also, a compact-created Common only entitled one to its fruits, not the actual land, unlike the situation pertaining in the state of nature.[127] In addition, the submitting of possessions to the community, along with one's person (2: 120), could not have meant that Locke was advocating slavery (that is, ownership of the person by the community), and in any case these possessions were submitted on the condition that they could not be taken without individual consent (2: 138-40).[128] The individual's person and possessions merely become subject to criminal and civil law. Submission of land to the community merely meant that land could not be withdrawn from its jurisdiction.[129]

Secondly, Tully's critics effectively demonstrated that property ownership carried with it minimal social obligations. The duty to preserve others meant not to harm their life, liberty or possessions.[130] Sustenance, for Locke, only became an issue for those unable to work, which would be few in number since Locke believed that most poverty was the product of idleness.[131] In any case the duty of charity was not enforced by the government.[132]

On the question of whether Locke either recognised or espoused capitalism, in the case of land as alienable for the market, while Locke did not mention this, he at least saw it as disposable through gift or inheritance.[133] And as for whether Locke intended that others were to benefit directly from someone who had made their land more productive, because such a person would not need so much land for subsistence, Wood pointed out that most agrarian improvers at the time assumed that larger land holding increased productivity and that this generally improved living standards.[134] Whether money was perceived as capital, Locke clearly saw the benefits of hoarding money as a stimulus to agricultural improvement.[135] More can be said here: whether he had a *concept* of capital is beside the point. His attitude towards money was not that it was just a medium of exchange (in Marx's terms C-M-C) of simple commodity production. It was also used in a way characteristic of capitalist commodity production (M-C-M1). Money provided the link between rationality and industriousness, because industriousness after the introduction of money made better sense. Extra effort would not be spoiled but rationally registered through the acquisition of durable objects. Thus, we can see in Locke a clear utilitarian message: the private vice of hoarding can have beneficial 'public' consequences.

As to whether Locke was opposed to primogeniture thereby implicitly favouring a more collectivist approach to property, that he was not opposed to it in principle could also be demonstrated. He merely rejected Filmer's assertion that it was God's law.[136] Locke recognised that the father could dispose of property as he wished subject to civil law, and he never questioned existing laws of inheritance which favoured primogeniture. Related to this issue, whether or not Locke noted and commended a market in land was not decisive. Usufruct in land was not antithetical to capitalism, because the basis of agrarian capitalism in seventeenth-century England was the tenant farmer, who cultivated land owned by others but produced for the market.[137]

On the issue of Locke's recognition of capitalist wage labour, Tully's critics showed that his turf cutter's example did not rule it out. Locke was fully aware that servants sold their labour for a specific period of time and not just a service *per se* (2: 85).[138] And he acknowledged elsewhere that labour could legitimately be drudgery rather than expressive in a way analogous to the workmanship model (2: 24).[139] Furthermore, Tully misunderstood the nature of labour under capitalism. In a significant sense, it was juridically voluntary and not tantamount to slavery as he suggested. Coercion arose because the worker was compelled to work for an employer, even if he or she could choose which employer and negotiate the terms of employment. And Locke acknowledged that wage contracts were not quite as voluntary as Tully suggested. He maintained the legitimacy of master–servant contracts, even where the hunger of the servant was involved, and believed in the necessity for there to be servants (2: 77).[140] Finally, Tully did not understand the evolution of wage labour under capitalism from formal subsumption of its pre-industrial phase, which entailed craftsmanship, to real subsumption in its industrial phase, when tasks became fragmented and subject to detailed supervision.[141] Tully, however, in a later work did admit that his view of the master–servant relation was 'mistaken'. Unfortunately, he did not respond to the criticisms advanced above, although most were available to him.[142]

However, more than a *de facto* defence of Macpherson can be offered. First, evidence of Tully's tendentious use of texts is reinforced at a symbolic and symptomatic level. The sentence of his first quotation from chapter V (2: 25) on the first page of the first chapter is truncated without acknowledgement.[143] Tully suggests that Locke was endeavouring to show that although the earth had been given to mankind in common, individual entitlements were legitimate. The rest of the sentence reads 'and that without any express Compact of all the Commoners.' To have included this would have posed questions at the outset for Tully's portrayal of Locke as wanting the state to pursue welfare policies involving redistribution. Locke's whole intent was to resist Filmer's interpretation, which suggested that since the world had been given to Adam, it was his private property. Therefore, Filmer argued, Adam's male (king) descendants necessarily had absolute political rights over their subjects. In contrast Locke emphasised the communal origins of property against Filmer, yet wanted to establish the fact that the community had minimal control over it once it had been enclosed and had labour mixed with it. Thus, a king could not arbitrarily tax his subjects in the name of the common interest. Not merely did Locke avoid express, communal consent through the mixing of labour entitlement, later in chapter V he did so equally through the notion of *tacit* consent in relation to money.

Secondly, Tully seems to have had problems with reading not only Locke's text, but also Macpherson's, just as Laslett had done before him. So, in relation to covetousness, which supposedly revealed Locke's opposition to acquisitiveness, Macpherson had indicated that the covetousness to which Locke objected was not the accumulating activities of the industrious and rational, but of the 'quarrelsome and contentious'.[144] In addition, Macpherson did not attribute to Locke a notion that he was an advocate of modern consumerism.[145] Rather he noted that Locke's views on property fitted in well with the accumulating activities of landed proprietors. As already indicated, Locke held that their hoarding activities had beneficial effects in stimulating the productivity of the soil.

Thirdly, Macpherson's understanding of capitalism was more nuanced than Tully implied, because he saw it as subject to a developmental process, as having a history and assuming different forms.[146] He never purported to demonstrate that England was a well developed capitalist economy by the seventeenth century, and that Locke was aware of all its features and commended them.[147] Rather, Macpherson registered how capitalism was developing and breaking down medieval economic practices and value systems. Whether or not, for example, there was a market in land at the stage of what Marxists have called 'primitive accumulation' is not a telling argument. We can see with hindsight that the Enclosure movement, as well as for example the dispossession of the Amerindians, marked the beginning of the development of capitalism, albeit in an agrarian form. And even if Locke did not see or advocate a market in land, he saw land as capital, to be improved, owing to the existence of markets, thereby increasing the landowner's wealth. Elsewhere Tully refers to Locke's attitude towards workhouses as indicating that no free labour market existed – again this is attributable to the specific stage of capitalism. As Hundert and others have noted, in this period a problem of labour discipline existed as a result of economic changes. Ironically, to present Locke, as Tully does, as portraying labour as unalienating and voluntary runs directly counter to his recognition that for some the coercive measures of the workhouse were necessary. Locke seemed to have had few qualms about the use of force and did not entertain a strategy that would demonstrate to the poor and unemployed the rewarding nature of work at least in an intrinsic sense. As Tully himself later commented, the labourer was viewed by Locke as a 'resource' who can be 'reformed by repetition and practice to be a productive and utile part of a strategy to increase the strength of the nation vis-à-vis other states.'[148]

The fact that capitalism was in this emergent phase also helps to explain Locke's attitude towards money, which, we have already seen, was ambivalent. Although it may have the power to corrupt, it also had the great power to stimulate industriousness, and therefore the possibility of land improvement, enabling it to support a greater population as commanded by God, in going forth and multiplying (1: 33).[149] If Tully is correct, then Locke's attempt to unite contemporary economic practice with the scriptures would make no sense. While there may have been moral costs attendant upon the introduction of money, this was outweighed in Locke's mind by the enormous increase in the productivity of the soil. This meant that the earth, through market driven enclosure, not only could support a larger population, but also provide higher living standards, even for the dispossessed. As Leo Strauss remarked about Locke's argument, 'Unlimited appropriation without concern for the need of others is true charity.'[150] What Tully's interpretation fails to do is to capture Locke's ambiguity, of using the language of the natural law tradition, while adopting a reasoning process well fitted for the market ethic.

To perceive Locke's chapter on property solely in abstract market terms does little to capture the historical specificity of his background assumptions. Here Neal Wood has convincingly demonstrated that Locke has to been seen as part of a movement concerned with agricultural improvement. As Wood states, 'Locke's language [in chapter V] is similar to that of the seventeenth century agricultural reformers for whom God's injunction in Genesis ['Be fruitful, and multiply, and replenish the Earth'] was a favourite justification in their call for enclosure and utilization of waste land.'[151] Nevertheless, Macpherson was not necessarily a market reductionist. Rather, he was attempting to correlate Locke's thought with the *rise* of the market, thereby allowing for other non-market influences, and in this case Hooker. This chapter was in a sense a manifesto for the improving landlord and market oriented tenant farmer utilising the services of the agricultural day labourer. A significant motif of the *Second Treatise* was not the celebration, as Tully would have it, of the creatively (and spiritually) fulfilling *homo faber*. In truth Locke sets the stage for *homo economicus* in the form of the 'industrious and rational' agrarian capitalist to make his triumphal entry.

— CONCLUSION —

The thrust of this discussion is that critics misread into Macpherson a concern with Locke's purposes. While in certain respects Macpherson could not avoid discussing them, he was not aiming to show that Locke had a capitalist Master Plan, merely that he was responding to, and intervening in, a changing economic and social environment, which we can see with hindsight was becoming significantly capitalist. Critics also seemed to ignore Macpherson's intention to explain Locke's contradictions and were unwilling to enter into this debate. Further, they were not able to disprove the possibility that Locke restricted full political participation, that is voting rights, to only those with property in the narrow sense. They were on stronger ground in showing that full citizenship did not turn on the express/tacit consent distinction. Macpherson did not convincingly demonstrate that express consent was given only by property owners. However, a plausible case can be made for Macpherson's attribution to Locke of differential class rationality in the relative sense. This was not an issue of whether the working class was innately less rational, but one of circumstance – this was the logic of Locke's empiricist epistemology. Neither did critics manage successfully to rebut Macpherson's reading of chapter V of the *Second Treatise*, which amounted to a justification of unlimited accumulation. The *effect* and *significance* of the argument in this chapter is plain: capitalism without apologies, albeit of an undeveloped, agrarian sort. Furthermore, his Calvinism can be combined with what was in effect a bourgeois outlook. Nearly all Macpherson's critics apart from Laslett and Tully, whatever their reservations over particular arguments, saw an indissoluble tie between Locke's *arguments* in the *Two Treatises* and the legitimation of capitalism.

Nevertheless, there is a difficulty with Macpherson's rendition of Locke. Although evidence shows that Locke cast the reasoning abilities of the labouring classes in a poor light, this does not mean that we can draw an inference that this provided 'a moral basis for capitalist society', since he justified 'as natural, a class differential in rights and in rationality'.[152] Macpherson had based his case on what he detected as Locke's 'ontologising' process that he had also perceived in Hobbes, namely that contemporary human characteristics that Locke saw around him were read back into the state of nature and therefore became natural. The problem is that such a justification has little in common with characteristic capitalist legitimation, which stresses individual formal economic *and* political equality, especially in the procedural sense. Here, Macpherson's interpretation of capitalist legitimation had a far too Platonic ring. As a couple of commentators have correctly indicated a differential rationality is not an essential component of bourgeois ideology.[153] Macpherson himself appeared to contradict himself because he later recognised that Locke did not see this differential rationality as inherent, but 'socially acquired by virtue of different economic positions.'[154]

Macpherson seemed to be running two discrete tasks together, (1) showing how Locke contributed to providing the moral basis for bourgeois ideology, (2) explaining Locke's ambiguous assumptions implicit in his conception of differential political rights and rationality in terms of the social and ideological transitions occurring in seventeenth-century England. The attempt to explain Locke's contradictions and ambiguities should either have been separated from the question of his contributing a moral basis to capitalist society, or it should have been shown that differential rationality and rights constituted a moral basis in the early period of its development. It could be argued that Locke's differential rationality and rights demonstrate his *limitations* as a bourgeois thinker due to the specific societal and ideological context. Locke would have done better, from Macpherson's point of view, if he had at least by implication proposed equal political rights. Perhaps the reason why Macpherson was so keen to establish his 'differential' argument was that he claimed that the enfranchisement of the British (male) working class in the nineteenth century created a problem of political obligation, which could be construed à la Macpherson as undermining the moral basis of capitalist society. It did not make sense for the working class to obey a state that supported the capitalist order once they were enfranchised due to the mismatch between political and substantive economic equality.[155] Yet, it could be argued that at an ideological level the moral basis of capitalist society has been deepened in extending formal political recognition. In his later work, he clearly acknowledged this fact.[156]

Macpherson could have made this task easier here if he had made the simpler point: that his possessive individualist interpretation of Locke – who put the (broad and narrow) property owning individual at the centre of his concerns – demonstrated how the state was formed by freely consenting, contractually minded individuals. These individuals wished to protect exchange relationships and acquisitions already created in a state of nature.[157] This kind of individualism served to either conceal or legitimate a capitalist class structure. At the same time, he would have strengthened the historical side of his interpretation if he had clearly stated that Locke's contradictions were not essential to bourgeois ideology, but were an expression of the times in which he was living, of early capitalism. In other words, Macpherson elided two types of contradiction. The first, characteristic of modern bourgeois ideology, was between formal and substantive equality, and Macpherson certainly noted its presence in Locke.[158] The second, more specific to early capitalism and manifest Locke, was between different conceptions of legal and political rights, and rationality, so that the labouring classes were full legal subjects without political rights. At the same time Macpherson could have strengthened his case by acknowledging more clearly the dynamic, critical edge to Locke's liberalism, which although it supported an existing *system* of property relations, did not necessarily endorse the social status quo. Whether for Calvinistic, mercantilist, geopolitical or utilitarian reasons, his writings zealously emphasised 'improvement' and 'industriousness', whether in relation to moral and intellectual capacities, or to the productivity of labour or the soil. These suggestions still work within the hypothesis established by Macpherson which firmly linked Locke's political philosophy with the rise of capitalism. The results of the debate he stimulated perhaps correlate Locke even more closely with its rise.

— POSSESSIVE INDIVIDUALISM AS METHOD AND INTELLECTUAL HISTORY —

These two chapters conclude with a brief discussion of various methodological issues that arose, and of two general critiques by David Miller and James Tully of Macpherson's use of the possessive model to understand the origins of liberal thought in the early modern period (1600–1800). To take the methodological issues first: as already indicated at the outset of these two chapters, Macpherson was asking a variety of questions within the possessive individualist 'paradigm'. The one question that did not command his attention was authorial intention, which has been the preoccupation, along with linguistic context, of the so-called 'Cambridge School' of Skinner, Pocock and Dunn, and subsequent generations such as Tuck and Tully. While the question of authorial intention was largely absent in his treatment of Hobbes but crept into his discussion of Locke, for example when citing *The Reasonableness of Christianity*, Macpherson's aim was to uncover Locke's unstated social assumptions, particularly his attitude towards the labouring classes.[159] As Macpherson stated, his line of inquiry was largely 'logical' and 'historical'. As such, his research was prompted by questions which sought to understand the historical significance of Hobbes and Locke for the contemporary dominant, liberal ideology by looking at the logical, but unintended, consequences of their arguments, that is irrespective of whether both thinkers were fully aware of what they were doing. Thus, according to Macpherson, the 'logic' of Hobbes' philosophy legitimated the peaceful 'invasion' of individual powers necessary for a market society, and the 'logic' of Locke's transcendence of the natural law limits of property ownership legitimated unlimited capital accumulation. In other words, Macpherson was asking how successful these philosophers were in contributing to the construction of a possessive market ideology. Although Macpherson did not say so, perhaps Hobbes' laid the basis for the image of 'man' as 'infinite consumer', and Locke of 'man' as 'infinite appropriator'. There were also more strictly historical questions asked about how their thought correlated with an emergent capitalism. Yet again, the question of authorial intention is not paramount. Of course, how successful Macpherson was in this enterprise is open to debate.

Nevertheless, the crucial point is that a certain type of methodology flows from the kind of questions asked. Macpherson's methodology can be summed up as 'realist', in the sense that 'real' speech acts are defined independently of the beliefs of agents. So, for example, as Shapiro argues, an individual in accepting a job or an offer of marriage may be unaware of the significance of these speech acts for human production and reproduction. An 'external', 'realist' perspective is required to understand the full meaning of such speech acts, because certain kinds of 'objective' description might not be available to agents in this context. By the same token, an analysis of 'internal' authorial intention would not, for example, help answer the question about a thinker's contribution to, or replication of, an ideology that facilitates the reproduction of the social world.[160] Macpherson was particularly interested in Hobbes' and Locke's contributions to the possessive market ideology that legitimates capitalist relations of production and reproduction. Equally, a more historical question may be asked, which again suggests an 'external' standpoint, where only with hindsight can the full meaning of an 'illocutionary act' be obtained, because a plausible desciption was not available to the agent.[161] The argument is not whether one methodology is better than another, but which is appropriate to the type of question asked. Indeed, critics hostile to his project have grudgingly accepted the possibility of a plurality of approaches to the history of political thought that can include a Macphersonian line of interrogation. The choice of approach may involve 'no necessary intellectual disagreement, but reflect, rather, more or less sharp divergences of taste and interest'.[162] A fault with many of Macpherson's critics was that their own concern with authorial intention did not allow for methodological pluralism.

We now turn to the general critiques of Miller and Tully. Although they had specific criticisms of Macpherson's treatment of particular thinkers, they concluded that his whole account of the intellectual history of the early modern period was deeply flawed. Here again, as we shall see, they did not sufficiently appreciate the fact that Macpherson was pursuing particular lines of inquiry. Miller and Tully both sought to minimise this 'rise of capitalism' thesis as a significant figuration. Tully effectively agreed with Miller's general conclusion that English society in this period 'should be regarded as *sui generis*, neither feudal nor market, and its ideology likewise.'[163] Their argumentative strategy was to demonstrate that the thought of the early modern period (1600–1800) was not explicable in terms of a possessive market society, especially a full-blown one. More specifically Miller, after a discussion of Hobbes, Locke, the Levellers, Harrington and Hume, made four generalisations. First, unlimited consumption was not endorsed, although charity was. Second, although property rights were defended against state encroachment, they were not 'necessarily' unlimited ones and carried with them obligations to the needy, and were 'broadly' defined (to cover lives, liberties and estates). Third, society was acknowledged by these thinkers to be a mixture of status, based on land ownership, and market. Fourth, these thinkers were preeminently 'political' and not economic, preoccupied with 'political stability in the face of uncertainty'. Hence, they advocated the suppression of economic interests whenever they threatened to undermine the security of the state.[164] With these considerations in mind, Miller then criticised Macpherson's account of Burke on the grounds that although his economic thought was 'bourgeois', his social views both reflected and supported a landed hierarchy. There existed, however, a congruence between his economic and social views because landowners were 'often in the forefront of industrial innovation'.[165] Miller, although he conceded that Macpherson had not claimed that Burke's thought could be explained *in toto* by the possessive individualist model, maintained that Macpherson had destroyed his case by admitting that England in the mid-eighteenth century was primarily a status society, that contract was dependent upon status and that therefore it was not a capitalist society.[166]

Tully's critique carried on where Miller's left off. Tully argued that many studies of this early modern period in British, and indeed European, thought demonstrated the irrelevance of the possessive individualist explanatory model. First, thinkers in this period focused on the nature of 'political (not economic) power'. Thus the Grotius-inspired concept of self-ownership in Hobbes, the Levellers and Locke was juridical as well as 'moral, political and military, not economic', and was concerned not with the alienation of labour power, but with political power, especially the right of self-defence, 'with preservation, not consumption'.[167] Second, Hobbes and Locke were mercantilists. Thus labour power and property were to be regulated by the state in order to preserve and strengthen it.[168] Hobbes' and Locke's political economy was concerned with the state supervision of 'improvement' of the productivity of labour and the soil. And most patently in Locke's vision a free labour market was not extolled: rather, the authoritative allocation of labour in the workhouse. This was the era of the 'utilizable individual'. Thirdly, the possessive individualist model did not capture the importance of the republican tradition, epitomised in the thought of James Harrington, which maintained that landed property was the basis of citizenship. Out of this tradition in the eighteenth century there arose a disquiet about the rise of 'commercial society' and the growth of moveable, non-landed property which had a corrosive impact on civic virtue. And these developing market relations were not only condemned but also legitimated in the language of republicanism. Indeed, Scottish political economists and neo-Harringtonians were 'ambivalent' about the achievements of 'commercial society'.[169] As for the allocation of labour, these eighteenth century thinkers thought themselves unique in not advocating its government regulation.[170] Lastly, they were concerned not merely with the economic matters of a market society, but also with representative institutions, civil and religious liberties and the 'problematic military complex'.[171]

To a large extent both Miller and Tully's criticisms rest on various misunderstandings of the relevance of the possessive individualism thesis for Macpherson's project as a whole. Although as we have seen, especially in his treatment of Hobbes, he could exaggerate the significance of market relations, and with Locke he could stray slightly into the question of intentionality, his purpose was not to give a straightforward history of the intellectual thought of this period. Rather, it was to unearth possessive individualist social and ontological assumptions of major thinkers, held unconsciously or semi-consciously, which would prove significant for later liberal thought. The point of his historical narrative was part of his argument that the possessive individualist side of liberalism, which had served a historical function in promoting and legitimating a capitalist market economy, was becoming played out in the twentieth century. Put at its starkest, the material conditions which fostered this pro-market ontology, which began to crystallise in the seventeenth century, were in the process of changing so as to make it redundant: with the onset of abundance the scarcity-induced psychology of infinite consumption could no longer act as an incentive to production. Macpherson therefore hypothesised that some correlation existed between the rise of the capitalist market and proto-liberal and liberal political philosophers.

We have already noted the tendency for Macpherson and his critics to be at cross purposes. What critics saw lurking behind his thesis was an attempt to reduce thinkers to class interests, thereby inviting questions of intentionality and motive. Miller and Tully likewise assume that these thinkers according to the 'Macpherson version' *wanted* to make 'the world safe for capitalism'.[172] The question of intention therefore became central to their reading, and not surprisingly Macpherson's narrative seemed totally implausible. Furthermore, because Macpherson was pursuing a specific 'assumptive' line of inquiry he was not concerned to explain the totality of a particular political philosopher's thoughts. So whether, for example, Hume's or Burke's thinking is explicable in terms of possessive individualism is beside the point. That their thought manifested possessive individualist elements is, however, relevant, and this Miller admitted.[173] In addition, because intentionality is not the issue, a thinker's attitude towards the market is not relevant. The fact that Harrington and the Scottish political economists were 'ambivalent' about it, as Tully argues, is hardly decisive. As already noted, Macpherson did not regard Hobbes' 'excoriation' of the merchants as problematic for his thesis.[174] Equally, he would not have argued with the contention that all thinkers in his period were concerned with 'political stability in the face of uncertainty'.[175] It is hard to think of any great political philosopher who was not. His concern, to repeat, was with the social and ontological assumptions they made in their arguments in so far as they reflected an emerging capitalism.

The misunderstandings run a little deeper. Both Miller and Tully assume that Macpherson had (mistakenly) argued that thinkers in this early modern period were working with a full-blown market model. So, for example, Tully imputed that Macpherson's Hobbes was concerned about the 'economic competition among self-interested consumers',[176] and Miller suggested that Macpherson portrayed all thinkers in this period as regarding men as 'infinitely desirous consumers of utilities'.[177] Nowhere does Macpherson offer such an anachronistic reading. Although he noticed infinite desire in Hobbes, Macpherson's stress when discussing markets in Hobbes' work was on the commodification of labour and the marketisation of the concept of justice. Of course, the *logic* of Hobbes' ontology is highly appropriate for a market society, but Macpherson did not attempt to show that he was conscious of this connection, or that it was his central concern. And the implication of Locke's theory of property was 'infinite' appropriation rather than consumption. Macpherson was aware of the fact that England in the seventeenth century was in the transition to capitalism.[178] Thus Miller, in claiming that the period 1600–1800 was 'sui generis', neither feudal nor capitalist (he means neither totally feudal nor totally capitalist), is not saying anything significantly different from Macpherson.

One more misunderstanding, again stemming from the assumption that Macpherson was working with a notion of a fully developed capitalist economy in this period, concerns Tully's use of Locke's advocacy of the workhouse system. This supposedly demonstrated the non-capitalist nature of government policy, of an 'authoritative allocation' of labour. Yet, such a system could be viewed as needed to inculcate labour discipline, either by threat or example, required by the rhythms of capital accumulation, rather than of the seasons, and was understandable for a society in transition to capitalism. Moreover, the supposed need for a workhouse system is inexplicable in the absence of a market context, which generated surplus labour. Again on the question of charity, although the concept itself is clearly *pre*-capitalist in origin, there is nothing essentially *anti*-capitalist about it, and its practice can serve as a socially stabilising function. Both Hobbes and Locke in recommending charity could be interpreted as truly representative figures in capitalist transition in the sense that they clung onto the vestigial notion of economic justice, while simultaneously recognising the growing autonomous sphere of market relations which were unstoppable and in which medieval notions of justice were deemed inappropriate. Tully himself recognised that by the mid to late eighteenth century the Scottish political economists had fully noted this development, thereby in effect marking the full decline of 'economic justice'. We have already seen in these two chapters that Hobbes and Locke could be interpreted, as indeed Macpherson did, as harbingers of this process.

Mixed up with the question of transition is that of the nature of capitalism itself. Although Miller gives a perfectly adequate definition of capitalism, he then equates it with commerce and manufacturing and juxtaposes it with 'landed society'.[179] There seems to be no room for 'agrarian capitalism' – to use Neal Wood's phrase – although he recognised that landowners could be at the 'forefront of *industrial* innovation.'[180] And Tully equates capitalism with laissez-faire economics, presuming mercantilist policies to be non-capitalist, and the early modern thinkers who advocated mercantilism to be likewise. On this point Tully had not read Macpherson closely. Even in *PI*, Macpherson had argued that mercantilism was consistent with the possessive market model, and may 'indeed be required at some early stages in the development of a possessive market society'.[181] And in his last work, he boldly asserted that mercantilism *was* capitalism.[182] Such policies were used either to promote industry and trade or to protect society against market fluctuations.[183] Thus whether pro- or anti-capitalist, governments were dealing with the *fact* of the market. Historically the role of the state has been crucial in developing capitalism, as can be seen by its role in nineteenth-century Germany, France and Japan, all of which should be seen as no surprise if economic and political elites are seen as intertwined.

Another misunderstanding surrounding the link between the 'political' and the 'economic' is that Tully, following Miller, wanted to stress the *political* nature of early modern political thought. Macpherson would not have denied this. He merely wanted to highlight a neglected side, which impacted upon later liberal thinkers, namely its *political economy*, or as he said 'the economic penetration of political theory'.[184] Tully in emphasising the notion that self-proprietorship was political, juridical, military and moral goes too far in asserting that it is 'not economic'.[185] Leaving the 'military' aspect aside, while the origins of the concept may lie with Roman Law, Locke's broad notion of property included 'estates', and his ('economic') labour theory of acquisition is morally grounded upon a notion of self-ownership (God-willed self-preservation), which requires legal and political recognition. In other words, Tully is separating out the economic, political, juridical and moral, when in fact they should be seen as interconnected.

Perhaps Miller, Tully and his other critics were a little too eager to find fault with Macpherson, and did not fully acknowledge the specific lines of inquiry he was pursuing which required a distinct methodology. He was not always successful, but his critics, if they wished to reject his account of the early modern period, ought to have begun with a greater appreciation of where Macpherson was starting from and the compass he was using.

— NOTES —

1. L. Strauss, *Natural Right and History* (Chicago: University of Chicago Press, [1950] 1974), p. 246.
2. Ibid.
3. *PI*, p. 194.
4. Ibid., pp. 196–7.
5. Ibid., p. 197.
6. Ibid., p. 199.
7. Ibid., p. 207.
8. Ibid., p. 215.
9. Ibid., p. 221.
10. Ibid., p. 222.
11. Ibid.
12. Ibid., p. 223.

13. Quoted, Ibid., p. 223.
14. Quoted, Ibid., p. 225.
15. Ibid., p. 231.
16. Ibid., p. 232.
17. Ibid., pp. 236-7.
18. Ibid., p. 241.
19. Ibid., p. 247.
20. Ibid., p. 249.
21. This means the *Second Treatise of Government*, section 120.
22. *PI*, p. 251.
23. Ibid., p. 251; see also p. 261.
24. Ibid., p. 262.
25. P. Laslett, 'Market Society and Political Theory', *Historical Journal*, 7/1, 1964, pp. 152-3.
26. Ibid., p. 153.
27. Ibid., p. 154.
28. J. Dunn, *The Political Theory of John Locke* (Cambridge: Cambridge University Press, 1969) (hereafter *PTJL*), p. 5.
29. A. Ryan, 'Locke and the Dictatorship of the Bourgeoisie', *Political Studies*, 12, 1965, p. 219.
30. Ibid., p. 229. See also I. Berlin, 'Hobbes, Locke and Professor Macpherson', *Political Quarterly*, 34/4, 1964 p. 462; K. I. Vaughn, *John Locke, Economist and Social Scientist* (Chicago: University of Chicago Press, 1980), p. 106.
31. R. Ashcraft, *Locke's Two Treatises of Government* (London: Unwin Hyman, 1987), p. 259.
32. J. Tully (ed.), *Meaning and Context; Quentin Skinner and his Critics* (Oxford: Polity, 1988), p. 78.
33. P. Laslett (ed.), J. Locke, *Two Treatises of Government* (Cambridge: Cambridge University Press, [1960] 1988), pp. 105-6.
34. J. Dunn, 'Justice and the Interpretation of Locke's Political Theory', *Political Studies*, 161, 1968, pp. 68-87, p. 69, p. 73; J. Dunn, *PTJL*, p. 217; J. Tully, *A Discourse on Property: John Locke and his Adversaries* (Cambridge: Cambridge University Press, 1980) (hereafter *DP*), p. 131.
35. Dunn, *PTJL*, pp. 217-18; P. Marshall, 'John Locke: Between God and Mammon', *Canadian Journal of Political Science*, 12/1, 1979, p. 80.
36. S. Buckle, *Natural Law and the Theory of Property* (Oxford: Clarendon, 1991), p. 152; Marshall, 'Between God and Mammon ...', p. 77.
37. I. Hampsher-Monk, *A History of Modern Political Thought* (Oxford: Blackwell, 1992), p. 93; Dunn, *PTJL*, p. 227, p. 232.
38. Dunn, *PTJL*, p. 222, p. 227.
39. Ibid., p. 233.
40. Ibid., p. 262.
41. *PI*, p. 194.
42. *Western Political Quarterly*, 4, 1951, pp. 550-66.

43. *PI* , p. 215, footnote 4.
44. Ibid., p. 298.
45. Ibid., p. 232.
46. Macpherson to Laslett, 7 November 1961. See also *PI*, p. 298.
47. Macpherson, 'Progress in the Locke Industry', *Canadian Journal of Political Science*, 3/2, 1970, pp. 324-5.
48. See also Marshall, 'Between God and Mammon', p. 84, and J. R. Jacob, 'Locke's Two Treatises and the Revolution of 1688-9: The State of the Argument', *Annals of Scholarship*, 5/3, 1988, p. 315.
49. See also E. Andrew, *Shylock's Rights: A Grammar of Lockian Claims* (Toronto: University of Toronto Press, 1988), p. 63.
50. *PI*, p. 237.
51. Ryan, 'Locke ...', p. 226. See also Berlin, 'Hobbes, Locke ...', p. 463, p. 467; J. Richards, L. Mulligan and J. K. Graham, '"Property" and "People": Political Usages of Locke and Some Contemporaries', *Journal of the History of Ideas*, 42/1, 1981, p. 39; J. Viner, '"Possessive Individualism" as Original Sin', *Canadian Journal of Economics and Political Science*, 29, 1963, p. 556.
52. Laslett, 'Market Society ...', p. 153.
53. Dunn, *PTJL*, p. 166; Dunn, 'Consent in the Political Theory of John Locke', *Historical Journal*, 10/2, 1967, p. 166; G. Parry, *John Locke* (London: Allen & Unwin, 1978), pp. 104-6.
54. Dunn, *PTJL*, p. 135.
55. Dunn, 'Consent ...', p. 168; Parry, *John Locke*, p. 107.
56. *PI*, p. 224.
57. Ibid., p. 226, emphasis added.
58. Ashcraft, *Locke's Two Treatises of Government*, p. 170.
59. Marshall, 'Between God and Mammon', p. 80. or 'non-rational' Ryan, 'Locke ...', p. 223. J. Cohen, 'Structure, Choice, and Legitimacy: Locke's Theory of the State', *Philosophy and Public Affairs*, 15/4, 1986, pp. 301-24, also takes this view.
60. Ashcraft, *Locke's Two Treatises of Government*, p. 168; Ryan, 'Locke ...', p. 23.
61. Ryan, 'Locke ...', p. 23
62. Laslett, 'Market Society ...', p. 153.
63. Ashcraft, *Locke's Two Treatises of Government*, pp. 172-4.
64. Ibid., p. 250.
65. Dunn, *PTJL*, pp. 233-4.
66. Ibid., pp. 235-6.
67. N. J. Mitchell, 'John Locke and the Rise of Capitalism', *History of Political Economy*, 18/2, 1986, p. 301; E. J.Hundert, 'The Making of Homo Faber: John Locke between Ideology and History', *Journal of the History of Ideas*, 30/1, 1972, p. 19. See also Jacob, 'Locke's Two Treatises ...', p. 330.
68. Hundert, 'The Making of Homo Faber', pp. 19-20.
69. Dunn, *PTJL*, p. 233.
70. Ibid., p. 234. See also, Marshall, 'Between God and Mammon', p. 83.

71. Ibid., *PTJL*, pp. 234–5.

72. Ashcraft, *Locke's Two Treatises of Government*, p. 253.

73. Ibid., p. 257.

74. Critics who recognised Locke as politically inegalitarian, Dunn, *PTJL*, p. 146, Parry, *John Locke*, p. 107, M. Seliger, *The Liberal Politics of John Locke* (London: Allen & Unwin, 1968), p. 288. Although Seliger suggests (p. 290) all may have the right to revolt, Locke certainly did not want the labouring classes to revolt in an autonomous way. These critics seemed to recognise that for Locke membership of a political community entitled all (men) to the *civil* rights of life, liberty and property but did not entail corollary *political* rights. See E. Wood's powerfully argued defence of this distinction, 'Locke against Democracy: Consent, Representation and Suffrage in the *Two Treatises*', *History of Political Thought*, 12/ 4, 1992, p. 679, and 'Radicalism, Capitalism and Historical Contexts: Not Only a Reply to Richard Ashcraft on John Locke', *History of Political Thought*, 15/3, 1994, p. 323, and J. Cohen, 'Structure, Choice and Legitimacy', p. 303.

75. See also Tully, *Meaning and Context*, p. 173; Richards et al., 'Property and People ...', p. 39.

76. Tully, *Meaning and Context*, p. 175.

77. Ibid., p. 177. See M. Hughes, 'Locke on Taxation and Suffrage', *History of Political Thought*, 11/3, 1980, pp. 423–42.

78. Tully, *Meaning and Context*, p. 177.

79. Macpherson, 'Scholars and Spectres: A Rejoinder to Viner', *Canadian Journal of Economics and Political Science*, 29/4, 1963, p. 561.

80. *PI*, p. 248.

81. Ibid., p. 248.

82. D. Wootton, *John Locke, Political Writings* (Harmondsworth: Penguin, 1993), pp. 231–2, articles 116–19.

83. R. Becker, 'The Ideological Commitment of Locke: Freemen and Servants in the *Two Treatises of Government*', *History of Political Thought*, 12/4, 1992, p. 641. See also David Wootton who has argued that it would be reasonable to assume that only freeholders had the right to vote. 'John Locke and Richard Ashcraft's *Revolutionary Politics*', *Political Studies*, 40, 1992, p. 96.

84. E. Wood, 'Locke against Democracy', p. 675, footnote 39.

85. Ibid., pp. 674–5. See also Hughes' reply 'Locke, Taxation and Reform: A Reply to Wood', *History of Political Thought*, 12/4, 1992, pp. 691–702, where he does not directly respond to these points.

86. G. J. Schochet, 'Radical Politics and Ashcraft's Treatise on Locke', *Journal of the History of Ideas*, 50/3, 1989, p. 505.

87. Wootton, 'John Locke and Richard Ashcraft', p. 85.

88. Quoted Becker, 'The Ideological Commitment of Locke', p. 654.

89. Quoted N. Wood, *John Locke and Agrarian Capitalism* (Los Angeles: University of California Press, 1984), p. 43.

90. D. McNally, 'Locke, Levellers and Liberty: Property and Democracy in the Thought of the First Whigs', *History of Political Thought*, 10/1, 1989, p. 32.

91. Even Hundert, a sympathetic critic, does this: 'The Making of Homo Faber . . .', p. 17.
92. See, for example, McNally, 'Locke, Levellers . . .', pp. 37–8, and N. and E. M. Wood, *A Trumpet of Sedition* (London: Pluto Press, 1997), pp. 119–22.
93. *PI*, p. 244.
94. Ibid., p. 231.
95. Ibid., pp. 243–6, p. 269.
96. E. J. Hundert, 'Market Society and Meaning in Locke's Political Philosophy', *Journal of the History of Philosophy*, 15, 1977, p. 42; Marshall, 'Between God and Mammon', p. 82.
97. *PI*, p. 246.
98. See *Essay Concerning Human Understanding*, quoted in R. R. Albritton, 'The Politics of Locke's Philosophy', *Political Studies*, 24/3, 1976, p. 256.
99. Dunn, *PTJL*, p. 235.
100. E. J. Hundert, 'Market Society . . .', p. 42.
101. *PI*, p. 223.
102. See *PI*, p. 299, note O for an example of Locke's estimation of the 'illiterate's' reasoning abilities.
103. See, for example, Ashcraft, who stated that in Locke's thought there existed a tension characteristic of liberalism 'as a social theory between its universalistic claims to moral and religious equality – liberty, equality and fraternity – and its instrumentalist treatment of human beings as part of the process of capital accumulation': *Locke's Two Treatises of Government*, p. 265. Indeed, it would seem that the real difference between Ashcraft and Macpherson had to do with the type of capitalist state that Locke recommended. See also Ryan, 'Locke . . .', p. 229: Dunn, *PTJL*, p. 216, p. 255. Dunn made this very clear in a review article of Neal Wood's *Politics of Locke's Philosophy*: 'What is entirely clear is that the cultural impress of his major work (and indeed his published thinking as a whole) was singularly propitious for and effective at forming a self-conscious and confident bourgeoisie in Britain over the century or so which succeeded his death': *Journal of Modern History*, 1985, 57/2, p. 344. See also Mitchell, 'John Locke . . .', pp. 304–5; I. Shapiro, *The Evolution of Rights in Liberal Theory* (Cambridge: Cambridge University Press, 1986), p. 139, p. 143. Even a hostile critic such as Dunn could accept Macpherson's reading of chapter five of the *Second Treatise*, and described it as 'probably the most brilliant piece of analysis of any part of Locke's text yet produced': *PTJL*, p. 215, footnote 9.
104. Laslett, 'Introduction' to J. Locke, *Two Treatises . . .* , pp. 105–6
105. Tully, *An Approach to Political Philosophy: Locke in Contexts* (Cambridge: Cambridge University Press, 1993), p. 126.
106. *DP*, p. 138.
107. Ibid., pp. 109–10, pp. 116–17.
108. Ibid., p. 2, p. 100.
109. Ibid., pp. 124–5.
110. Ibid., p. 154.

111. Ibid., p. 164.
112. Ibid., pp. 162–7.
113. Ibid., p. 131.
114. Ibid., p. 152.
115. Ibid., p. 124.
116. Ibid., p. 133.
117. Ibid., p. 136.
118. Ibid., pp. 136–42.
119. Ibid., p. 149.
120. Ibid., p. 149.
121. *PI*, p. 212.
122. *DP*, p. 150.
123. Ibid., p. 176.
124. G. A. Cohen, 'Marx and Locke on Land and Labour', *Proceedings of the British Academy*, 71, 1985, p. 387.
125. J. Waldron, 'Locke, Tully, and the Regulation of Property', *Political Studies*, 32/1, 1984, pp. 98–104; Waldron, *The Right to Private Property* (Oxford: Clarendon Press, 1988), p. 138, pp. 232–3; Cohen, 'Marx and Locke ...', p. 386; J. L. Mackie, 'Review of *A Discourse on Property*', *Philosophical Quarterly*, 23, 1982, p. 93.
126. G. den Hartogh, 'Tully's Locke', *Political Theory*, 18/4, 1990, p. 663; N. Wood, *John Locke and Agrarian Capitalism*, p. 82.
127. Cohen, 'Marx and Locke ...', p. 386.
128. Waldron, 'Locke, Tully ...', p. 105; den Hartogh, 'Tully's Locke', pp. 656–72, p. 667; Cohen, 'Marx and Locke ...', pp. 386–7; Mackie, 'Review', p. 93.
129. Den Hartogh, 'Tully's Locke', p. 668.
130. Cohen, 'Marx and Locke ...', p. 383.
131. Waldron, *The Right to Private Property*, p. 139.
132. Cohen, 'Marx and Locke ...', p. 384.
133. Waldron, *The Right to Private Property*, p. 220.
134. N. Wood, *John Locke and Agrarian Capitalism*, p. 83.
135. See also K. Vaughn, *John Locke*, p. 101 who held that for Locke it was merely a medium of exchange.
136. Wood, *John Locke and Agrarian Capitalism*, p. 80.
137. Ibid., p. 81.
138. J. Waldron, 'The Turfs My Servant Has Cut', *Locke Newsletter*, no. 13, ed. R. Hall, 1982, p. 16.
139. Waldron, *The Right to Private Property*, p. 229.
140. Wood, *John Locke and Agrarian Capitalism*, p. 90; Waldron, *The Right to Private Property*, p. 227.
141. Wood, *John Locke and Agrarian Capitalism*, p. 90.
142. J. Tully, *Locke in Contexts*, p. 132.
143. *DP*, p. 2.
144. *PI*, p. 237. See also N. Tarcov, *Locke's Education for Liberty* (Chicago: University of Chicago Press, 1984), pp. 143–4.

145. *DP*, p. 176.

146. See also Wood, *John Locke and Agrarian Capitalism*, p. 92.

147. See also Hundert, 'Market Society . . .', p. 40, who criticised Macpherson on the grounds that he 'claimed that England [was] a full "possessive market society"', because a free labour market did not exist.

148. Tully, *Locke in Contexts*, p. 66.

149. Waldron, *The Right to Private Property*, p. 221.

150. *Natural Right and History*, p. 243. See also P. Kelly, '"All things richly enjoy": Economics and Politics in Locke's Two Treatises of Government', *Political Studies*, 36/2, 1988, p. 287.

151. Wood, *John Locke and Agrarian Capitalism*, p. 57. Wood criticises Macpherson's method as being too philosophical and too ahistorical (pp. 7–9). However as already indicated Macpherson stated that he was attempting a 'historical' and 'logical' analysis. While Wood's account of Locke is far more fine-grained historically than Macpherson's, there is nothing wrong in principle with adopting this kind of approach, which is attempting to explore how an ideology, in this case liberalism, is formed. Here, logical analysis is often required to unearth unstated assumptions, especially occurring through a process of 'ontologising', that is of making specifically historically created human traits into natural ones. The question of how well Macpherson applied his own method is another question, and as already indicated in the previous chapter he was guilty of making his market assumptions do a little too much work in his analysis of Hobbes in *PI*.

152. *PI*, p. 221.

153. Shapiro, *Evolution of Liberal Rights*, p. 139; Mitchell, 'John Locke . . .', p. 304.

154. *PI*, p. 246.

155. Ibid., p. 273.

156. See *RWD*, p. 16. See also C. Pateman, *The Problem of Political Obligation. A Critique of Liberal Theory* (Cambridge: Cambridge University Press, 1979), p. 50.

157. See R. Poole, 'Locke and the Bourgeois State', *Political Studies*, 28/2, 1980, pp. 233-4; J. Isaac, 'Was Locke a Bourgeois Theorist? A Critical Appraisal of Macpherson and Tully', *Canadian Journal of Political and Social Theory*, 11/3, 1987, pp. 118–21; Mitchell, 'John Locke . . .', p. 304.

158. *PI*, p. 269.

159. Ibid., p. 224.

160. See I. Shapiro, 'Realism in the Study of Ideas', *History of Political Thought*, 3/3, 1982, p. 561.

161. See K. Graham, in Tully, *Meaning and Context*, p. 153. See also essays by J. Femia and J. Keane in this volume.

162. J. Dunn, *The History of Political Theory and Other Essays* (Cambridge: Cambridge University Press, 1996), p. 19. J. G. A. Pocock, another member of the 'Cambridge School', in *Virtue, Commerce and History* (Cambridge: Cambridge University Press, 1985), pp. 70-1, accepted the existence of the possessive individualist element in many early modern thinkers, but thought that

Macpherson's method was too undialectical in economic reductionist and historically teleological ('Whig') senses. Macpherson's approach only becomes undialectical if he was attempting to explain the intellectual history of the period solely in possessive individualist terms, but not if he was seeking to expose a neglected element in the thought of this period. Intriguingly, the question may be reversed: if the possessive individualism category is accepted, have Pocock *et al.* dialectically combined it with political, linguistic and cultural analysis?

163. D. Miller, 'The Macpherson Version', *Political Studies*, 30/1, 1982, p. 126.
164. Ibid., p. 125.
165. Ibid., p. 127.
166. Ibid.
167. Tully, 'The Possessive Individualism Thesis', p. 29.
168. Ibid., p. 31.
169. Ibid., p. 38.
170. Ibid.
171. Ibid., p. 39.
172. Miller, 'Macpherson Version', p. 125.
173. Ibid., pp. 125–6.
174. *RFEJ*, p. 136.
175. Miller, 'Macpherson Version', p. 125.
176. 'The Possessive Individualism Thesis', p. 29.
177. 'Macpherson Version', p. 123.
178. For example, *PI*, p. 193.
179. 'Macpherson Version', p. 127.
180. 'Macpherson Version', p. 127, emphasis added.
181. *PI*, p. 58.
182. *RFEJ*, p. 137.
183. *PI*, p. 62.
184. See *RFEJ*, ch. 9 *passim*.
185. 'Possessive Individualism Thesis', p. 29.

CHAPTER 4

RETRIEVING DEMOCRACY (1): LIBERAL, POSTMODERN, 'DELIBERATIVE DEMOCRATIC' AND ECOLOGICAL CRITICS

The next two chapters deal with the wide variety of responses to Macpherson's attempt to recover, with the help of Marx, an earlier type of Millian liberal democratic theory that had been forgotten, as noted in Chapter 1. The responses to Macpherson's project indicate the extent to which it serves as a barometer of academic fashion over the past thirty years. Indeed, the fashion factor in academia was something of which he was acutely aware.[1]

The first wave of criticism in the early 1960s came from liberals, whose thinking was in many respects shaped by the Cold War. Although they did not say so openly, they firmly resisted Macpherson's proposed marriage of Marx and Mill. Their hostility was in a sense understandable, given the Soviet Union's ideological domination of what constituted Marxism. Most Western academics took Marxism to be Marxist-Leninism. And they saw it as an ideology that justified totalitarian tyranny. A 'new left' of independent Marxists in the early 1960s was barely in existence, and few bothered to ask the question whether the Soviet and similar regimes actually corresponded to Marx's ideals, or if they did only to say that they were living demonstrations of just how pernicious these ideals were. Moreover, as noted in the first chapter, 'ideology' in this period was supposed to have ended, and the scholar was meant to pursue his or her inquiries in a value-free, disinterested way. They saw Macpherson's work as an attempt to subvert the protocol of impartiality.

The second wave of criticism came in the 1970s from independent Marxists, who grew out of the 1960s student movement. While Cold War liberals disliked Macpherson for his Marxist kinship, the 'new left' critics distanced themselves from what they perceived as his liberalism. At the same time and from another direction non-Marxist communitarians also saw his thought as vitiated by this vestigial liberalism. And finally the postmodern turn in the 1980s and 1990s promoted a new academic agenda concerned with issues raised by New Social Movements, of identity and difference, as well as humanity's relationship to nature. Again, as a result of these preoccupations, his project was found wanting.

In attempting to *explain* why various types of criticism were mounted against Macpherson, no implication is made that they are reducible to political preference and academic fashion – *ad hominem* – and therefore invalid. The issue is whether these criticisms were *justified*. Nor is there the suggestion that all criticisms of Macpherson were ideologically inspired. There are questions that can be asked according to the practice of scholarship, of rigour, methodology, consistency, accuracy, implications, assumptions and omissions that transcend implicit or explicit ideological preferences. As we shall see critics of different political persuasions came up with a number of similar objections, although the temptation to give them a particular 'spin' could prove irresistible.

Another caveat must be entered. For presentational reasons, not all of the critics neatly fit the labels to which they have been assigned. Those with different ideological persuasions often made similar objections but have been classified according to ideology rather than type of argument. And sincerely 'academic' critics with no ideological axe to grind have been classified here in ideological terms. Moreover, there are critics with ideological commitments who maybe have been falsely classified, as in the case of Leiss, as a 'liberal' as opposed to, say, a 'social democrat' on the grounds that the latter have a common concern with the former in wishing to defend some kind of market capitalism.

This chapter concentrates on Macpherson's liberal, postmodern, 'deliberative democratic' and ecological critics, who either implicitly or explicitly could not accept Macpherson's Marxist affinity. The next chapter will consider those critics who thought Macpherson to be too liberal.

— LIBERAL CRITICISM —

The liberal response to his work assumed a number of forms, although at bottom the effect was a distancing from his perceived Marxism. No constructive engagement with his work was attempted. Macpherson's liberal critics either directly or indirectly challenged his use of abstraction and teased out the implications of his lack of concreteness, his eschewal of empirical detail. Accordingly, they challenged his conception of human nature and its relation to capitalism. They saw it as fraught with totalitarian danger. They also defended the market, seeking to demonstrate that in reality it did not stunt the development of human powers as suggested by Macpherson. In addition, they rejected the core of his critique of capitalism: the net transfer of powers, along with the notion that capitalism was necessarily coercive and 'invasive'. Not surprisingly his critics resisted his proposed alternative to the market and his support for the Soviet Union and Third World regimes. Finally, they queried his account of the liberal tradition.

Minogue chided him for the way he used abstraction, how he sought to derive 'all the features of politics from a single principle' of democracy.[2] This manifested itself in two ways: first, he attempted to solve many specific, practical problems, for example, of accountability in democratic institutions, by moving them into the 'more manageable territory of conceptual coherence'.[3] Secondly, he eroded the context of the 'limited term' democracy, and then used a 'new context more amenable to the desired manipulation',[4] as when he defined democracy not only as a system of government, but also as a kind of society in which citizens had the 'equal effective right to live as fully humanly as he may wish.'[5] As we shall see below, Minogue charged Macpherson with the inappropriate use of abstraction in other ways, which mired his discussion of human powers and the market, and of the possibility of a non-contentious society.

As for his account of human nature, liberal critics attacked his developmental ontology and its attendant notions of human powers and freedom. First, Wand argued that there were logical difficulties surrounding Macpherson's concept of human essence, stemming from his attempt to combine descriptive and evaluative statements. So, he could describe the essence of man in market society from the seventeenth to the nineteenth centuries as 'factually accurate'.[6] Yet he also claimed that the essentialist postulate was an 'ontological', value postulate[7] and that some essences were more desirable than others. Not only did this constitute 'intellectual muddle', according to Wand,[8] it was implicitly totalitarian. The notion of a 'real' human essence could only be derived intuitively, and so there was no way in which one of two contrasting, 'metaphysical' intuitions could be rationally chosen. This allowed for the possibility that human nature could be changed through 'moral regeneration' as Macpherson proposed.[9] It also precluded the possibility of an open democratic discourse as to what human nature might be, because political practice merely required facilitating the unfolding of this desirable essence, and one set of political rules or goals was appropriate to this process. His concept of human nature was also queried by Wright, because it was unclear whether he was taking an essentialist line, or took it to be historically, socially and ideologically variable.[10] This point was developed by Morrice who held that although Macpherson opposed the idea of a fixed notion of human nature, he required one in order to argue that the market manipulated human needs.[11]

In terms of relating human fulfilment to the market, Minogue, again claiming that Macpherson was too abstract, rejected the assumption that the market necessarily prevented people from leading a 'fully human life'. There was, he argued, no necessary correlation between material provision and spiritual happiness. Hence, a 'pigeon-fancying mill worker in Lancashire or Montreal may well be recognizable as a more fully developed human being than some well-endowed urban stockbrokers or merchants',[12] although he admitted that malnutrition, illiteracy and unemployment constituted impediments to self-realisation. Minogue also argued that many people developed or exerted their capacities while working for a wage. For example, a coal miner developed 'cameraderie and solidarity' and the door-to-door salesman 'enjoys the outlet for extroversion'.[13] And contra Macpherson, performing even boring tasks in work did not necessarily inhibit developmental capacities outside work. In any case capitalists often developed the skills of the workforce. Further, work of a non-developmental kind had to be undertaken by individuals in whatever society, including socialist ones. And even in capitalist societies people preferred to work rather than be unemployed.[14] In addition, job satisfaction was 'essentially subjective', so that some employees were happy in their work and self-employed not. Accordingly, there was no necessary correlation between job satisfaction and ownership of the means of production.

Dunn maintained in fact that he conflated two sorts of power, when discussing the market, namely labour power and creative ability.[15] In reality, most human abilities that were developed were not offered for sale.[16] In any case, there was a problem, even if a list of desirable human powers could be agreed upon, as to what precisely their 'maximisation' meant, their sum, product or average?[17] Moreover, he did not consider other impediments to the development of capacities which arose from the social division of labour apart from private capital. Even where private capital had been eliminated, as in the Soviet Union, capacities were not fully developed.[18]

More fundamentally, Macpherson's liberal adversaries questioned his extractive/net transfer of power hypothesis entailed in the wage labour contract. Even if a transfer of powers hypothesis was accepted, this did not mean that owners of the means of production were exploiting non-owners. Rather, all members of market societies exploited each other when they purchased a commodity in the sense that its production involved a developmental opportunity cost on the part of the individual producer.[19] Minogue suggested that conceptual difficulties arose in his discussion of power because in his endeavour to reduce phenomena to a single principle and avoid the possibility of genuine moral conflict in a post-market society, he saw it in homogeneous, mechanical terms, of 'transfers' and 'impediments'. Thus, he stated he failed to understand Macpherson's distinction between 'ethical' and 'descriptive' concepts of power, since the question for Macpherson was a simple one of whether these powers were freely flowing or not.[20] Once these powers were flowing freely the ethical dimension would seem to be ruled out.

Wand also saw conceptual difficulties in Macpherson's notion of powers and their net transfer. These arose from his attempt to distinguish between a descriptive and an ethical concept of power. Such a distinction was unwarranted, first because the concept of power was neutral and could be applied to a horse as well as a man. Wand characterised power as an innate or acquired 'dispositional property'. And secondly human powers were not necessarily diminished in a capitalist market society through a process of transfer, merely their *exercise*, that is the conditions under which they may or may not be exercised. Thus individuals may be forced to exercise them in 'undesirable ways' in the market.[21] However, in practical terms, different solutions could be offered depending on what type of restriction and what type of ethical principle is invoked. Where an individual is prevented from using faculties to acquire power, then for example education has to be improved (equity). Or where an individual is prevented from exercising their powers by certain persons, for example restrictive employment practices, then these have to be removed by an appeal to the principle of freedom. And where there was a failure to reward a person properly for work done, then the principle of desert could be applied.[22]

Chapman took a different angle of attack in attempting to demonstrate that no unequal transfers of powers necessarily occurred under capitalism. In contrast to Minogue, he moved from the concrete to the abstract to demonstrate the possibility of developing a normatively satisfactory rationale for the market. Nevertheless, his aim was the same: to show that the capitalist market was not necessarily unjust. He constructed a 'non-invasive' model of the market, based upon Rawlsian principles, where the freedom of one (the capitalist) was not at the expense of the other (worker). This model consisted of a capital tax for free public services that was also in part invested, full equality of opportunity, unrestricted competition for 'owner', 'which is now rather that of manager'.[23] Inequalities of income had to be dictated by the requirements of 'economic rationality', that both workers and owners would receive their marginal value productivity and compensated for their disutility. And income from property would be an incentive to 'optimization and innovation'.[24] Chapman suggested that no invasive transfer of powers occurred because both owners and workers were getting the 'most out of their respective capacities, given the state of techniques and resources'.[25] Their 'economic freedom' was in this situation 'moral and collaborative.'[26] 'Invasiveness' he held to be historically and politically contingent, based upon some form of 'monopolistic and oligopolistic advantage'.[27] He accepted that a class system based upon private property disadvantaged the worker, but as the 'differentiation of economic and political processes' increased and constraints on equality of opportunity were eliminated and society became more 'just', so 'invasiveness' became less.[28] Class income differentials, which were not correlated to 'economic efficiency' declined as economies developed. Especially important was the role of education in generating occupational mobility, which increased personal independence and lessened 'inefficient' income differentials.[29]

Chapman concluded that within the framework of the market, the liberal doctrine of natural rights could be accommodated and serve to reconcile economic rationality, the claims of moral freedom and the principles of justice, even if they had not been in the past. Employing Rawls' 'difference principle', he argued that the doctrine of natural rights meant that all should benefit absolutely from inequality of whatever form, and from this moral equality could be derived because no one would be perceived as gaining at the expense of another. No one would be 'invaded'.[30]

William Leiss produced the most extended and sophisticated defence of the market in his intellectual biography of Macpherson. Leiss had a critical sympathy with Macpherson's project, yet felt that the only way to remain faithful to its spirit was through drastic revision. He wished to remain true to its teleological underpinnings, but the 'real' and the 'good' could only be reconciled through significant conceptual and empirical recasting. Macpherson's intellectual framework, he declared, suffered from a potentially grievous defect, possibly as a result of his experiences in the 1930s: he saw the world in terms of binary oppositions, of 'either/or choices', which led him to neglect the empirical dimension.[31] First, he falsely juxtaposed 'doing' and 'consuming'.[32] In an earlier article Leiss had expanded this criticism. Macpherson seemed to imply that consuming was somehow a 'lower', material form of activity, and 'doing' (developing) a higher non-material activity.[33] But in the modern world of 'universalized exchange relationships' most developmental attributes were bound up with the production of utilities. Moreover, consumption was not merely material. It possessed a 'symbolic' dimension, which interacted with the material. Leiss agreed that the developmental ideal could be undermined by capitalism, but only in a contingent sense through, for example, the payment of subsistence wages, authoritarian management, and gross social and economic inequality.[34] However, such market relations were in the process of being reformed. Hence, there was no necessary correlation between the market and the non-development of human powers. Equally important, Macpherson's binary approach led him to posit a choice between capitalism *or* socialism, either a capitalist market *or* a planned socialist economy.[35] Generally, Leiss argued, Macpherson condemned the market *per se*, indissolubly linking it to capitalism, thereby assuming that a market could not exist without capitalism, and so the choice became either the market or socialism.

His wholly negative attitude towards the market, Leiss maintained, blinded him from the fact that it was experienced beneficially by most people in the late twentieth century. Thus he was unable to develop a theory of 'positive market relations'. Macpherson, in focusing upon the meaninglessness of labour, did not examine the positive aspects of consumption, which could be a deeply enjoyable and creative activity.[36] The issue was not about false needs and consciousness as Macpherson assumed. Marketing and consumer research revealed that for the most part the consumer experiences 'genuine gratification of quite genuinely and deeply-felt needs'.[37] Consumer behaviour was based upon 'voluntary choice', which was 'stimulating and enjoyable'. Consumers liked being surrounded with 'layers of objects', which was a 'basic human trait'. Moreover, they liked the 'playful indulgence in the circulation of images attached to objects, to the point where every act of consumption appears to be only a fleeting expression of a purely evanescent order, a walk in the kingdom of fairies.' Thus consumption had a 'symbolic aspect'.[38]

As for the 'supply' side of the equation, job satisfaction, there was no huge demand for 'radical change in existing social institutions'.[39] Seeking satisfying work was 'just one of a series of interconnected goals, along with high income, leisure' and so on. No evidence existed that 'most persons in Canada' did not regard either 'existing market relations or their consumer behaviour as being inconsistent with their present utilization of their capacities.'[40] This was symptomatic of the fact that advanced economies, such as the Canadian and those in the OECD, were in reality not capitalist economies. Using a phrase borrowed from Macpherson, they were 'quasi-market societies', which were 'beyond' capitalism and socialism, and towards which the economies of Eastern Europe were also heading.[41] Indeed, they were an 'emerging social formation on a global scale',[42] and constituted the 'thoroughgoing politicization of property'.[43] Leiss defined a quasi market society as a 'full market society' which promoted market transactions yet simultaneously set limits on them through state regulation. In contrast to raw capitalism, such societies pursued policies of income redistribution through transfer payments and 'safety nets' and high government spending. The market was crucial in promoting an acceptable level of 'economic performance', that could not be achieved through centralised planning.[44] Leiss concluded by suggesting that the concept of the 'quasi-market society' satisfied Macpherson's aspiration that political theory should provide a 'principle of unity' in political science, in focusing on the 'interaction of political ideas and concrete political facts'.[45]

Critics were also dubious about any proposed alternative to the market, a society in which all members could develop their capacities harmoniously. Thus Dunn held that even if the market was seen as morally undesirable, Macpherson did not consider the possibility that people might be anxious about the efficacy of any alternative to it, presumably in the light of knowledge of non-market societies and in the absence of concrete proposals on Macpherson's part.[46] Minogue suggested that under socialism there was a far greater possibility for coercion because the state was a monopoly employer. Indeed, under socialism individual autonomy would be severely encroached upon because private property would be abolished. Such property was essential to secure an individual's independence, which was necessary to protect them from inhuman treatment by others. For Minogue contentiousness was inherent in human nature. Macpherson assumed that 'war, crime jealousy, malice and other human vices derive mediately or immediately from the use of extractive power.'[47] Property enabled people to be not dependent on others with such human vices. Furthermore, in a socialist society in which private property was eliminated along with money, crucial aspects of people's lives would be subject to collective decision-making, rather than individual choice. This socialist model assumed a homogeneity of tastes, energies, beliefs and desires, thereby enslaving the individual to society.[48]

Chapman also failed to see how Macpherson offered a viable alternative to the market 'so long as men remain as they are.'[49] Democratic planning would cost too much in terms of 'contemplated negotiations'. We would have to be 'much more deeply, and irrationally, political animals than we are to be willing to absorb the costs of Macpherson's vision of participatory democracy.'[50] Chapman also maintained that human goals and wants were too diverse and that people would therefore feel oppressed living under a democratic plan. And, moreover, Macpherson's 'incoherent moral psychology' does not 'tell us how' individual creativity and social solidarity could be combined.[51]

Finally, in order to avoid being impaled on the horns of an ontological dilemma – *either* utilitarianism with its consumerist and acquisitive implications *or* expressivism with its totalitarian implications – some liberals came up with another description of their tradition. There existed, they suggested a 'third' ontology. Seaman and Lewis argued that his developmental ontology contained an incipient vanguardism, because it led him to support vanguardist coercion needed to create institutions that did not dehumanise people.[52] They saw the 'central flaw' in his 'ontology of development' as justifying vanguard rule.[53] There existed even in the West a temptation for radical theorists influenced by such an ontology to be vanguardist, because the masses were imbued with a consumerist mentality.

Seaman and Lewis maintained that Macpherson's developmental ontology in concrete terms precluded the choice of whether or not an individual would wish to develop certain capacities. Individuals in the 'real world' may choose to accept capitalism and its inequalities because they preferred what they perceived to be the benefits of consumption, even at the expense of self-development. They may choose to be 'dignified' or 'undignified'.[54] This absence of choice in Macpherson's essentialist liberalism arose because he falsely pitted the consumerist/acquisitive ontology associated with the market against a developmentalist one within the liberal tradition. There existed a third, Lockean ontology of 'self-governance' within that tradition, which Macpherson in *PI*[55] hinted at. It was truly liberal because it was empirically grounded, allowing for concrete individual choices to be made. His developmental ontology on the other hand was abstract and moralistic, and did not allow for a legitimate inequality of rights through individual agreement, which could arise because of the perceived benefits from doing so. In a sense this was also part of Minogue's argument: people chose capitalism because it was an expression of human nature. He held that Macpherson ignored the fact that people found capitalism agreeable owing to its ability to innovate continually. Capitalism was 'in quite a large part a response to the characteristics of the people who live under it' and corresponded to the 'real dispositions of human beings'.[56]

Damico also proposed a third liberal ontology, of individuals as rights bearers with an 'equal capacity for autonomy or independence', which complemented the liberal ideal of the rule of law.[57] This ontology was distinct from its utilitarian variant, since government policy on this principle could not be grounded on the aggregation of individual preferences. The ideal of autonomy was equally distinct from any argument based upon a self-developmental ontology, which was 'dark and elusive', given the 'opacity of human nature'. Rather, such an ideal had to be based upon individual freedom of choice, political rights and the right to privacy.[58]

Common threads of criticism can be seen running through these liberal commentaries on Macpherson. Many of them noted the overly abstract tenor of his thought and attendant lack of empirical detail when criticising capitalism or when offering a non-market alternative to capitalism. They set their faces against his proposition that capitalism was inherently unjust and as impeding the free exercise and development of human powers. They also saw totalitarian dangers in his concept of human essence and in his inferred alternative to the market. Further, they sought to offer a more congenial portrait of liberalism, both of its tradition and as a defence of capitalism.

– Macpherson's reply and commentary –

Macpherson in his reply to his liberal critics rejected, first, Minogue's accusation that he had inappropriately handled abstraction. Given that all scientific endeavour proceeded by the use of abstraction, he took Minogue to mean that he had remained at this level. Yet he asserted that he did move from the abstract to the concrete through using his concepts of net transfer of powers and extractive and developmental powers to analyse real social, political and economic relations and their origins.[59] Minogue on the other hand was unable to transcend the realm of appearances. His focus on down-to-earth examples meant that he was unable to understand 'real underlying relations between people, or between things, or between people and things.'[60] As for having used abstraction illegitimately to define democracy as a form of society rather than as a form of government, he stated that he was in the good company not only of Marxists and Rousseauists in the Third World, but also of others such as Mill, Green, Hobhouse and Dewey, Woodrow Wilson and Whitman.[61] His point was that democracy had to be conceived normatively, in terms of the value of its human aims, not merely empirically and 'scientifically'.

He also defended his conception of human essence against Wand. He rebutted the charge that to conceive of it both descriptively and evaluatively was irrevocably problematic. Again, he claimed he was in good company, since all the ethical theorists in the Western tradition did.[62] These theorists not only sought to delineate human, as opposed to animal, characteristics verifiable through observation and self-examination, but to persuade others of such a definition in order that they accept their prescription for a better society. In other words, the notion of human essence was inseparably descriptive and evaluative. Moreover, in a technical sense, he believed he was in the good contemporary company of Corbett, Hart and Berlin, all of whom saw 'man' for the purposes of political philosophy as simultaneously descriptive and evaluative. The very structure of our thought makes it impossible to avoid endowing descriptive statements about human beings with a normative content.[63] We should of course remember that part of his project was to resist logical positivist fact/value distinction and the developing academic apartheid within the study of politics between so-called 'scientific', empirical theorists, and normative ones.

In retorting to Minogue's comments on the relation between human powers and the market and his argument that there existed no necessary correlation between wealth and spiritual happiness, Macpherson stated that he never made such a claim. He was merely asserting that a wage earner had less developmental power than he or she would otherwise have owing to the wage/capital relation.[64] As to whether developmental powers occurred in such a relation, the issue was the extent to which this *diminished* from a maximum potential. And responding to Minogue's comment that everyone exercised extractive power through the purchase of commodities, he remarked that Minogue had misunderstood the concept of extractive power: it applied to those who extracted benefit from the *control* of the use of another person's capacities. By the same token whether someone was employed or self-employed was a relevant difference in terms of extractive power, because in purchasing the services of the latter extractive power did not occur since skilled labour and working capital were not exchanged, while in purchasing the services of the former extractive power occurs because the employer gets a return on capital and gains some of the value added from the labourer.[65] Although in both cases developmental opportunity costs occur, this was inevitable as long as human beings had to labour on an external nature in order to survive.

As for the supposed conceptual difficulties in distinguishing between descriptive and ethical powers because his notion of power was mechanistic, he replied to Minogue that this was not so. The concept of ethical powers was based upon a value judgement about the nature of the human essence, of man as a doer and exerter rather than as a consumer. And the use of terms such as 'transfer' of powers was employed to make the concept more concrete by talking about quantities of developmental power.[66] He also denied that this notion of power prevented the appearance of any genuine moral conflict. His argument against this liberal view was that such conflict may not be inherent in the human condition but the product of a 'competitive society of scarcity', and that past failures to verify this proposition did not rule out the possibility of successful attempts in the future.[67] And he did not wish to 'construct an entire intellectual edifice to prevent genuine moral conflict making an appearance'.[68] To Wand's objection that the concept of power, defined as a 'dispositional property', was ethically neutral and that markets could not diminish powers but only their exercise, he retorted that it was not ethically neutral because liberal theorists such as Mill and Green held that the development of powers was desirable.[69] Wand had also confused powers with capacities. For Macpherson power also *included* the ability to use a capacity, especially access to the means of production. Thus, any restricted access constituted a diminution of powers, and not their restricted exercise as Wand suggested.

Macpherson also criticised Chapman's attempt to develop a non-invasive, morally legitimate model of the market, principally through some kind of tax on capital. If only part of the returns on capital were taxed, then a net transfer of powers still occurred with reference to the untaxed portion, offending the principle of justice, that is one person gaining at another's expense. And if it was wholly taxed, then 'economic rationality' would cease to operate, since rewards to capital would not be based upon marginal productivity.[70] Moreover, even in this case the principle of equal moral freedom, as defined by Chapman, would be infringed, because the game played, despite equality of opportunity to become owner, was still tendentially oligopolistic, undermining perfect competition and with marginal productivity determining 'efficient' investment. Further, in relation to employees, these owners would still determine the type of work and conditions non-owners must do, thereby rendering the ability of people to make the best of themselves unequal. Chapman's argument also assumed capitalist economic rationality when discussing distributive justice, that is the notion that inequalities are only justified if they work to everyone's advantage. He did not consider whether any other form of economic system could provide even greater distributive justice. Finally, he confused the two liberal concepts of man: when discussing equal moral freedom he assumed the developmental model, yet when discussing justice he talked primarily in terms of income distribution, using the utilitarian, consumerist model.[71] Thus he ignored the essential requirement of the developmental model, namely the individual's control over the exercise of their capacities.

Macpherson responded to another attempt, by Leiss, to defend the market. In a letter to Leiss he was prepared to admit that utility was not solely a physical property of material things, but his points of difference were, first, under capitalism the developmental and consumerist ontologies were in fact opposed because 'the development activities get no exercise during the working day.'[72] Secondly, Macpherson suggested an empirical difference existed between them, of 'when we should cease to have capitalism (or to call it) capitalism [owing to the growth of state regulation]'.[73] For him capitalism would only cease when private capital accumulation was no longer 'the main steam of the economy'.[74] On the question of whether he wanted to abolish the market altogether, he replied that he would not be prepared to rule out market socialism, as practised in Yugoslavia, because a centrally planned and administered socialist economy could use markets as a distributive mechanism, 'without permitting market incentives to determine investment or pricing decisions or the whole direction of the economy'.[75] The aim should be to use markets rather than be used by them.[76]

How successful was Macpherson's defence against his liberal critics? As we have seen, the complaint about his abstractness, echoed by critics from other schools of thought, he had in effect answered in a number of ways – that it was a crucial ingredient in any scientific method, that he attempted to combine abstractness with concreteness as in his concept of the net transfer of powers. Indeed, tables could be turned against his liberal critics: he could claim that his 'political economy' and historical approach to liberal democratic thought meant that he was rendering many abstract liberal concepts – the individual, rights, freedom, democracy – concrete, that all these concepts had to be understood against the backdrop of either an emerging or existing capitalist market system. In other words, Macpherson contextualised these concepts. One of his complaints against Berlin and other political theorists was that they remained at the abstract level:

They need to be brought a little further down to earth. They need to be judged in terms of actual impediments to liberty in concrete historical situations. And these, if my analysis of the implications of the maximizing of men's powers has any merit, are more specific than those Berlin has considered.[77]

And against Minogue's accusation that in reducing the world to a single abstract principle of democracy, he could not deal with its specific problems such as democratic accountability, he could argue that Minogue was guilty of abstracting a specific problem from its capitalist context, and was therefore unable to see that genuine democratic accountability was impossible under capitalism. Liberals such as Minogue in effect refused to concretise their conceptual vocabulary in any systematic fashion, which meant that it was 'ideological' and 'justificatory' of capitalism. Ironically, current liberal thought working within a paradigm established by Rawls suffers acutely from abstractness in its quest for cogency.

Macpherson obviously saw the need for some degree of concreteness, because his Marxist-inspired sensibilities led him to see the need to ground his abstract principles in historical reality. His optimistic, teleological approach to history required the ultimate coalescing of facts and values. Yet, although he admitted that empirical analysis was not his *métier*, there remains the question of whether the real and good are in fact coalescing, because if they are not then his abstract ethical principles are doomed to remain ahistorical. His views on transition will be considered more fully in the next chapter.

Another difficult objection to meet, adverted to by Minogue, is the *way* in which Macpherson used a certain kind of abstraction, especially defining the term 'democracy' either as a society, that is in substantive terms, *or* a form of government, that is in procedural terms. It allowed him to argue that, although he was aware of the absence of civil liberties, the tyrannies in the Second and Third Worlds were somehow democratic because they aimed at a 'democratic' society of equally developing human beings. Of course democracy can be justified in terms of promoting this objective, but the objective should not confused with the democratic (or undemocratic) means. In reality he was arguing for a socialist society, but presumably wanted it to include some notion of democracy as well as persuade Western liberal democrats to become more tolerant of the Second and Third Worlds. The problem was that he did not subject the ideologies of the Second and Third Worlds to a critical, 'political economy' analysis as he had done to the First World. He seemed to take the words of the leaders of these worlds on trust. His argument for a democratic society against the liberal, procedural, governmental definition would have been strengthened (although it would have weakened his defence of the Second and Third World states) if he had continued to define democracy procedurally, but had extended the scope of such procedures into society, so that power relations in the private realm of 'civil society' became equalised, that is if he had broadened the scope of the 'political'. Equally, he could have argued that if liberals took political equality seriously even in the limited parliamentary sense, then a classless society was necessary (but not sufficient) in order to promote equal political 'efficacy'.

The liberal critique of his concept of human essence, although it raises difficult philosophical problems and Macpherson in part relied on what we might call the 'good company' argument, is not necessarily unanswerable. True, as Wand indicated, there may be logical difficulties in viewing the human essence in factual and evaluative ways. But while there may be no strictly *logical* connection between factual and evaluative statements, Macpherson's reasoning can be seen to transcend this problem if MacIntyre's Aristotelian notion of 'functional concepts' is adopted.[78] Objects are defined according to their purposes, and can be evaluated according to the extent to which they fulfil these purposes. Thus, if the human essence's 'purpose' or *telos* is expressed in terms of the exertion, enjoyment and development of human capacities, then human institutions designed to promote these activities can be evaluated accordingly. Alternatively, if this type of reasoning is objected to on the logical grounds that the premise here ceases to be a strictly factual one, Macpherson's case does not suffer from the introduction of a 'middle term', of a 'hypothetical imperative' linking descriptive and evaluative statements,[79] if human flourishing as specified by him can be demonstrated as a universal need, albeit assuming different historic and cultural forms.

There is also the related objection raised by Wright, and even more so by Morrice, that Macpherson seemed to want it both ways in regarding human nature as both ontological and historical. Although difficult questions are posed, his position is not untenable. While more will be said on this question, if a little tangentially, in the concluding chapter, a number of arguments can be offered in his defence at this juncture. His refusal, following Marx,[80] to go down either the historical road or the ontological road was for a good reason. If he had merely an ontological conception, then he would have been open to the accusation of crude essentialism, with its conservative or totalitarian and anti-democratic implications; if only historical, then he would have been vulnerable to the charge of relativism, making a critical standpoint more difficult except from an 'immanent critique' perspective. There is of course nothing logically problematical about seeing human beings as simultaneously fixed and changeable: some elements in human make-up may be fixed, others not. The argument does not have to be either fixity or malleability.[81] More importantly, there are two related levels to Macpherson's argument. The first is ideological: he was concerned to demonstrate how the 'ontology' or essence of human beings, for example as infinite consumers and appropriators, was socially and historically constructed and was beneficial to capitalism. Such a discursive ontological construction was, in other words, an expression of unequal power relations within capitalism, and served to license economic growth as an overriding priority. The second level is philosophical: human beings have to be understood in terms of both their essence and existence.[82] Dialectically, how human beings exist may tell us something about their essence, and conversely what is essential about a human being, that is what properties are necessary for a human being to be defined as such may tell us something about human existence. The concepts of essence and existence, in other words, are interdependent.

What Macpherson wanted to say in Enlightenment fashion was that human civilisation in certain respects was progressing. Thus, although for instance Locke was an archetypical possessive individualist committed to the idea of self-ownership, his 'assertion of the free rational individual as the criterion of the good society' was historically progressive.[83] Put another way, the concept of self-proprietorship has both negative and positive attributes: negative because self-ownership through capitalist, market exchange led to a net transfer of powers; positive, because it included the ideal of being independent of the will of another (negative liberty!). As a result of changing material circumstances, especially manifested in the growing productivity of labour, as well as human reflection upon these circumstances, richer notions of freedom could be developed. These incorporated the Lockean idea while simultaneously recognising greater possibilities for meaningful individual autonomy. The ideological and philosophical levels are related in the sense that the Kantian end-in-themselves doctrine − an extension of negative liberty − becomes embedded in a positive, communist ideal once commodity fetishism of capitalist production relations has been exposed. The ideal of meaningful autonomy can only be achieved through human cooperation and the rejection of an atomistic ontology of commodity fetishism that renders the cooperative nature of production under capitalism invisible. Thus, Macpherson's ontology has freedom built into it, and provided him with a critical standpoint because knowledge of capitalist practice, of its production and ideology, meant that he could understand how it was both an impediment to, and a facilitator of, human freedom. Hence, a greater understanding of ontology and freedom does not require in analytical fashion the rejection of one form of ontology of freedom in favour of another, but an awareness that certain elements of these concepts may be retained and others transcended. So, for example, freedom can be seen as essential for what it means to be human and requires a 'negative' element, yet such a concept can be wedded to certain kinds of 'positive' freedom because it is this which either makes the concept richer or more meaningful.

The charge that his ontology was necessarily vanguardist and totalitarian as Wand, Seaman and Lewis suggested also invites a reply. That Macpherson seemed to adopt a vanguard stance when discussing the Soviet Union and the Third World can be conceded. But this position did not stem from his deduction about human nature, but from what he thought leaders in these societies were doing. And when he had greater knowledge of these societies and their leaders, his position clearly changed.[84] There were vanguards and there were vanguards. There were those such as Stalin's that peddled a 'perverted doctrine', and was attributable to the West's attempt to sabotage the Russian revolution,[85] claiming that only they could 'know'. Then there existed those that made it their 'business to develop grass roots democratic participation'.[86] Further, as we have already noted in RWD, he favoured democratically organised vanguards.[87] He did, however, admit that certain notions of human essence and of freedom were more amenable to totalitarian inflexion than others. Thus Hegel's and Green's highly rationalist accounts of human nature and freedom were obvious candidates.[88] But other notions of 'positive liberty', such as his own, aimed at encouraging the realisation of a diversity of human purposes through unimpeded access to the means of life and labour, were not so susceptible. And Macpherson's dialogic practice of engaging with his critics, in attempting to persuade them that his preferred means were the force of argument rather than the argument of force, meant that he was not so open to the charge of 'performative contradiction' (Habermas). Moreover, his postulate about the human essence was not 'metaphysical' and derived from intuition as Wand claimed. He maintained that it had to be 'verifiable broadly by observation and self-observation'.[89] Whether he had sufficiently anchored his own notion of human essence in empirical postulates is another matter. Further, his style of argument, based upon a Socratic, immanent critique, is in essence democratic in orientation. Whatever his earlier dalliance with vanguardism, towards the end of his life he seemed to exhibit a greater distrust of its role in bringing the desired social changes.[90]

Liberals' attempt to demonstrate that the market did not necessarily involve a diminution of human powers was not particularly successful. Macpherson stated that he made it 'a test of my critics understanding of my analysis whether or not they understand the concept of the net transfer of powers. Few do.'[91] In order to be persuasive they would have had to criticise Marx's theory of exploitation, because this was in essence the basis of his concept of the net transfer of powers, although Macpherson expanded it in an 'ethical', 'qualitative' direction to include the loss of control of productive activity and the effect that this had on an individual's 'extra-productive powers'.[92] Minogue, Dunn, Wand and Chapman in their different ways failed to come to grips with his concept, and made objections that were off target. Dunn's and Minogue's suggestion that there was no necessary correlation between individual self-development and the market was weak. They did not show that a *diminution* of developmental power had not occurred as a result of the labour/capital relation. The worker in selling his or her labour power lost out in terms of self-directed activity in the time working for an employer, and the kind of often mindless activity undertaken in the capitalist labour process was bound to impact upon the exercise, enjoyment and development of their extra-productive powers. Thus, a *net loss* of developmental power occurs. Whether some individuals are able to develop or exert various capacities outside the workplace, or even inside it as Minogue suggests, is irrelevant to Macpherson's hypothesis, which held that only if they had free and equal access to the means of production could developmental powers be *maximised*. Although as Dunn indicated there was a lack of precision about what maximisation meant – sum, product or average? – Macpherson's real point was that capitalism did not allow individuals to decide which kind of measurement was desirable.

Let us turn to Minogue's argument that all were in a sense exploited by the market because of developmental opportunity costs. Even if we assume that all socially necessary labour in capitalist and socialist economies represents the loss of developmental autonomy, under socialism the possibility of developmental autonomy would be increased because there would exist a democratically and collectively controlled definition over what constituted 'socially necessary labour' rather than one dictated by the needs of capital accumulation, which is indifferent to the developmental needs, both in its extent and how it is distributed between individuals. And in response to Dunn's argument that impediments to developmental powers caused by the social division of labour require more than the mere elimination of private capital, Macpherson could have responded that this would be a necessary but not sufficient condition, because there had to be genuine collective or 'common' (as opposed to state, as in the erstwhile Soviet Union) control over the means of production.

Wand also failed to grasp adequately the net transfer of powers concept by arguing that power was a neutral concept, and that merely its *exercise* raised disparate ethical problems requiring particular remedies based on the principles of equity, freedom and desert. Although Macpherson responded by noting Wand's failure to understand his definition of power, which included capacities *and* ability to exercise them, he could also have noted that Wand's solutions to the problem of 'unethical' exercise all presuppose the existence of a capitalist labour market. He did not challenge Macpherson on the question of whether there exists under capitalism an inherent *deficit* in developmental powers.

Chapman too in attempting to construct a non-invasive model of the market did not effectively challenge the net transfer of powers concept at a fundamental level. He assumed that invasiveness, where the capitalist bene-fitted at the worker's expense, was historically contingent, and that under perfect competition and with a capital tax for welfare services both worker and capitalist would freely collaborate for mutual advantage. Apart from the prob-lem raised by Macpherson, that perfect competition in the real world gives way to oligopoly and therefore injustice, Chapman's model assumes investors who need an incentive to encourage innovation. A system of a net transfer of powers is required in order to create this incentive. Thus there is an inherent difficulty in positing the possibility of a 'moral and collaborative' relationship between labour and capital, since production would still be driven by competi-tive capital accumulation which, using Macpherson's Marxist derived hypo-thesis, relies on a transfer of powers. And even if this hypothesis were rejected there would still be difficulties with the idea of 'moral and collaborative' rela-tionship, because Chapman accepted unquestioningly the marginal produc-tivity of labour theory, which even if true would not necessarily be morally acceptable to a worker whose needs might exceed his or her marginal value. Although Chapman built into his model the notion that workers also have to be compensated for the disutilities of work, this raises more problems than it solves, because compensation could act as a disincentive to work and result therefore in a loss of 'efficiency'. In any case such compensation may not necessarily enable a worker to meet his or her needs, especially if conceived in terms of the exercise, enjoyment and development of their capacities. More-over, Chapman's theory ignores the inherently asymmetrical power relations between capital and labour, which trade unions can ultimately only slightly modify. Workers' needs and resources put them in a weaker bargaining rela-tion with capital in a systematic fashion.

Similarly, Leiss's support for a 'quasi- (or 'full', or 'positive') market society' suffered from an unwillingness to see the significance of the net transfer of powers concept, because he did not attempt to demonstrate that a transfer of powers was not occurring. Unlike Chapman, rather than propose an abstract, non-invasive model of a market society, he argued, appealing to empirical evidence, that advanced capitalist economies had now reached a stage at which property had become 'thoroughly politicized' through the growth of the welfare state whose policies involved significant transfer payments, although he acknowledged the persistence of poverty. Thus most human wants and needs were satisfied through a state regulated market. He did not see the transfer of powers and the diminution of ethical powers as morally prob-lematic, because there was little evidence that job dissatisfaction was rife and, equally significantly, evidence showed that people were strongly wedded to consumption activity which was in fact creative. That he failed to understand Macpherson's notion of a transfer of powers can be seen in his empiricist method, which meant that unlike Macpherson he was not prepared to explore the essential relations of capitalism. Net transfers of power were the fuel for capital accumulation, and the 'quasi-market society' posited by Leiss was still capitalist. His empiricism also meant that he failed to recognise the inherent instability of capitalism, and just as he accused Macpherson of not transcending the 1930s, so he could be equally accused of doing likewise in relation to the postwar boom, assuming that it would go on for ever. Historical evidence demonstrates that capitalism is an economically unstable system, which when going into slump severely limits the possibility of redistributing wealth. Moreover, the growth of a global economy has also put severe limits on what states can do in making market interventions.

Another aspect of Leiss's empiricist method requires comment. He argued that, given the evidence, the relation between the market and individual self-development was essentially unproblematic. On the question of job satisfaction he in fact provided *no* evidence, and the survey data that he would have to employ would have to be extremely sophisticated. The sorts of issues and questions it would have to deal with are: How do we actually measure job satisfaction? Why was it an issue for employers in the 1950s and 1960s in a period of relatively full employment? Why do many people retire early, and why do people put such a great value on leisure time, if given the chance? How do we account for the widespread nature of hobbies? What degree of occupational choice do people really have? Are struggles over wages and conditions not also struggles about self-respect? Why do managements in many companies devote such large resources to industrial relations? Indeed, questions can be raised about Leiss's reference to the value of survey techniques on the consumption side of the equation, because findings are saturated by context and the question of context-choice is not addressed. Although consumer behaviour at one level could viewed as based on 'voluntary choice',[93] 'infinite' consumption activity may be a desired option, given the alienating nature of much work under capitalism, as a form of escapism. And the power of advertising to exploit people's hopes and fears and inadequacies within a capitalist context should not be underestimated. In other words, we do not know what consumer behaviour would be like in a non-market dominated world (based upon a non-Soviet model), where the allocation and quality of work and consumption was not mediated through capitalist market relations.

In addition, on the consumption side of the equation, Leiss offered little evidence that capitalism enables the *maximisation* of the creative utilisation of consumption goods. Macpherson certainly approved maximising such creativity: 'Utilities . . . must be . . . measured [from the possible maximum] as soon as men are seen as primarily doers, exerters, and enjoyers of their capacities, and only instrumentally as consumers.'[94] The question is whether capitalism maximises this desired end-state. A negative answer is most likely. The uneven distribution of utilities that can be creatively utilised and the often tiring nature of the labour process under capitalism, making leisure a form of rest rather than recreation, makes it so. Further, what is strikingly absent from Leiss's critique, also reflecting an unwillingness to take the transfer of powers concept seriously, is any moral criterion for evaluating his quasi-market society. He did not bother to invoke Macpherson's principle that a fully democratic society must enable the maximisation of *all* individual's powers, of autonomously chosen activities, an equal and effective right of all to make the best of themselves, that is one person's self-development should not be at another's expense. And even if the transfer of powers concept were not accepted, there is a difficulty in squaring Leiss's vision of a quasi-market society with Macpherson's ethical developmental principle of equal opportunities for all. Leiss described his quasi-market society as perpetuating 'severe inequalities in the distribution of income and wealth, while providing, by its welfare floor, sufficient resources to enable the poorest person to avoid absolute deprivation'.[95]

Finally, we can note Leiss's critique of Macpherson's methodology of presenting the world in terms of dichotomies. We have already seen that in his reply to Leiss, Macpherson stated that he was not proposing the market *or* socialism, but a capitalist market versus socialism.[96] In other words it was preferable to 'use' markets rather than be used by them. And he stated that humans as doers and consumers were not antithetical in the abstract, but were so under capitalism for the simple reason that developmental activities were not exercised during the working day for most people.[97] What he seemed to be saying was that, following Aristotle, money and exchange can either be a manifestation of human cooperation to achieve human ends, or they can be the organising principle of human cooperation, whereby ends and means are reversed and quantitative values (money and property) triumph over qualitative ones (the exercise and development of human capacities). Additionally, in suggesting that a quasi-market society was somehow mid-way between 'raw' capitalism and bureaucratic socialism, Leiss neglected to note that such a society is still dominated by an economy driven by the imperative of capital accumulation, whatever label may be used to describe it, which limits the scope of 'positive' state intervention.[98] Macpherson's point was that production relations themselves had to be changed: 'Welfare-state redistribution . . . is not enough: no matter how much it might reduce class inequalities of income it would not touch class inequalities of power.'[99] Finally, he ignored Macpherson's assertion that to reach a quasi-market society in which property was seen as an inclusive as opposed to an exclusive right would require 'partial breakdowns of the political order and partial breakthroughs of public consciousness'.[100] He had not demonstrated that this end had been achieved, or if it had been, that the kind of transition envisaged by Macpherson was unnecessary.

Leiss, then, was unable to show that he had provided a new 'principle of unity', that a quasi-market society constituted 'interaction of political ideas and concrete political facts'. On empirical and ethical grounds such a claim is vulnerable to criticism. Ironically, there is something *déjà vu* about Leiss's position. He seemed to be following in the footsteps of the Marxist revisionist Eduard Bernstein, who at the turn of the century in *The Preconditions of Socialism* [1899][101] also advertised the possibility of a harmonious capitalism using an empiricist method to demonstrate the historical unity of ethical principles and reality. Moreover, like Bernstein who declared an affinity to the spirit of Marx yet rejected all his key premises, Leiss in keeping loyal to the 'spirit' of Macpherson's project abandoned its basic categories and thereby subverted its emancipatory intentions.

Liberals, on the other hand, who held that Macpherson's principles would not allow him to be reconciled with any form of capitalism and queried his non-market alternative, were in a sense on stronger ground. As Dunn argued, Macpherson did not offer any clear blueprint, and therefore was less persuasive in convincing people that an alternative to the market was possible, especially given the experience of non-capitalist states which were highly authoritarian. Minogue suggested that a post-market society was necessarily coercive, because individual autonomy would be lost with the disappearance of private property and money. And for Chapman consumption choices would be governed by the dictat of the democratic plan. Against this, something can be said in Macpherson's defence. First: all he was seeking to do was suggest a number of *principles* upon which a non-exploitative society should be founded. Second, in keeping with Marx's opposition to the utopian socialists, such a new society would be founded by individuals acting freely for themselves rather than according to a plan formulated by an intellectual (or party). With good reason he was tentative in offering detailed specifications: he wanted to avoid the utopian dream becoming the totalitarian nightmare. And his proposals for participatory democracy contained an open-ended quality with different forms of representation and the possibility of multi-party competition. The absence of institutional detail was the logical consequence of his ontology of freedom: only those participating in the loosely defined democratic system he tentatively advocated should have the freedom to work out its detailed operation through to trial and error in a way that was consistent with that freedom. A similar argument can be made about economic institutions. He was fairly agnostic about their future shape provided they provided equal access to the means of life and labour, which meant for example that markets had to be subordinated to this principle.

In practical terms, while Dunn may be right about people fearing practical alternatives to market capitalism, the question is whether in *any* conceivable situation people would not struggle to find an alternative to it. Marx's and Macpherson's argument, given what they perceived to be the inherent limitations of capitalism as a productive system in providing prosperity for the world's population *ad infinitum*, was that in the event of its economic, social and political breakdown, people would search for ethically and practically satisfying alternatives. As for the question of whether such an alternative would be *necessarily* oppressive, this is in a sense a practical issue. Any alternative that *decreased* an individual's autonomy in exerting and developing their capacities according to their own choices would be ruled out in principle. Different types of democratic planning can either help or hinder consumption choices and be designed according to whether the costs in participatory time want to be minimised. The key point is that there would be collective control of the means of production, meaning that the structure and dynamic of the labour process was no longer subject the alien power and rhythms of capital but opened up to much greater choice of organisation and ends. And both these could change in the light of practical experience. By the same token, the issue of how to combine individual creativity and social solidarity, raised by Chapman, is a practical one, and being practical would be dealt with through trial and error within a participatory democratic context. The opportunity to attempt this is systematically denied by capitalism.

The question of effective individual or collective choice under capitalism arises in the last element in the liberal critique of Macpherson's overall thesis. As we have seen Seaman, Lewis and Damico rejected Macpherson's version of the liberal tradition as dichotomised into possessive individualist or ethical. They proposed a third 'ontology'. Whether it was seen as individuals as self-governing beings or as rights bearers, the point was to emphasise the importance of choice in the liberal tradition. They suggested that on Macpherson's account self-development was somehow obligatory and therefore open to totalitarian abuse. Seaman and Lewis also suggested that capitalism was the product of choice: to sell labour power, owing to perceived benefits in consumption and an acceptance of inequality. In response to Damico's suggestion of a rights-bearing ontology, as Macpherson himself replied, Mill was not only a negative libertarian, he also put a supreme value on the ontology of self-development.[102] Thus such an ontology had to be included in the liberal tradition since Mill is regarded as one of its central figures. In any case, Macpherson wholeheartedly supported the liberal ideal of maximising individual liberty.

The question was whether capitalism necessarily facilitated this ideal. His point was that capitalism, because it was grounded upon private property and denied equal access to the means of life and labour, could not generate equal 'effective' rights for all, because it created inequality and dependence: one person's freedom could be another's oppression. Democratic theory, Macpherson stated, must 'assert an equal effective right to use and develop ... human capacities'.[103] Hence, capitalism could not realise the values championed by Damico. As for ontology there was little that was 'dark and elusive' about it. Macpherson merely held that to be fully human, people had to be allowed to exert and develop fully their human powers in any way they saw fit, provided they did not usurp other people's effective autonomy. There is overwhelming evidence that capitalism does not have this as its prime object: individuals are treated as means to the end of capital accumulation, not as ends in themselves. Furthermore, Macpherson was not suggesting that developmental ontology was a categorical imperative or the dictat of a central committee. His concern was to ensure that people had the *right* to make the 'best of themselves'. He then assumed that people would want to exercise this right and find capitalism a major hindrance.

A similar argument can be levelled against Seaman and Lewis's self-governmental ontology. Macpherson was not opposed to it *in toto*. Rather, he was concerned with the conditions that would ensure that an effective autonomy was maximised to the full for all individuals, the conditions of which capitalism was unable to provide. The right to private ownership of society's productive assets – a manifestation of possessive individualism – had to be dispensed with. Two other issues arise in their critique of Macpherson. One is their coupling of a developmental ontology and vanguardism. We have already noted that Macpherson denied any necessary linkage in his critique of Berlin: self-mastery did not entail a rational self-mastery to a rational 'higher' self, which was the privilege of the few.[104] We have also noted that for Macpherson there were vanguards and vanguards, and that their corruption required historical explanation. They are not pre-ordained to be totalitarian. Moreover, although he did not fully make this link, his endorsement of party competition in his normative ideal in *LTLD*, suggests that he aimed to make vanguards accountable through procedural democracy. We should also register his discussion of the one-party states that ruled the recently independent nations in the 1960s. They could, he argued, claim to be democratic to the extent to which leaders were controlled by the rank and file, membership was open to all and party activity was not so arduous as to make membership difficult.[105]

The second issue, to which Repogle replied in defence of Macpherson, is whether people have freely chosen capitalism. One cannot deduce from the use of money or from the sale of labour power, as Seaman and Lewis do, that people have voluntarily chosen capitalism. 'One cannot infer from what people want to do within an institutional context that they want to be in that context.'[106] Within the context of capitalism the choice to use money or sell labour is virtually non-existent. This was the problem with Locke's theory of tacit consent as a justification for the unlimited accumulation of money. Therefore, we could deduce that people do not have a free choice to sell their labour power with its possibly attendant disutilities because of the perceived benefits of consumption. Repogle also makes the significant point that Macpherson's developmental ontology has liberty as its precondition: to follow one's own conscious plans, to exert, enjoy and develop one's capacities requires freedom. Thus Macpherson's ontological assumption tells us why individuals value freedom.[107] And we can add that capitalism, from Macpherson's stand-point, is built on the invasion of a majority's developmental and 'exertial' powers for the benefit of the capitalist minority. Over and above all this, what seems to be missing from Seaman and Lewis' analysis is any discussion of how and for whose benefit power and ideology are exercised in capitalist society, the way in which oppositional or potentially oppositional forces are marginalised, the way capitalism is legitimated (either deliberately or uncon-sciously through its everyday practices), the greater political efficacy of the economically and socially privileged, and so on. To put the point crudely: we only have to note the amount of time, energy, money and lives that were devoted to defeating Communism.

In sum, Macpherson's liberal critics raised important difficulties. Certain kinds of abstraction in his thought created problems, as they do for all those who wish to question radically the status quo, namely how plausible and desirable is the alternative to capitalism, and how do we concretely achieve it? Moreover, the way in which he defined democracy as a society of self-developers, rather than seeing self-development either as an aim or precon-dition (political efficacy) of democracy, was problematic, and a difficulty that will be returned to. However, other kinds of abstraction in his thought could be regarded as essential to any coherent emancipatory theory. First, there is the idea of emancipation itself, the goal of such theory. If capitalism is regarded as inherently exploitative and oppressive, then an alternative to it has to be imagined and justified, often by abstract argument. The value of this kind of abstract thinking becomes greater to the extent to which capitalism undergoes deep and sustained crises. Yet, a danger arises, of which Macpherson was well aware, that if a utopia is too detailed it contradicts the self-emancipatory ethic. Secondly, in analysing empirical reality, abstraction is often required in order to understand underlying features that are cognitively imperceptible. At this point we may note that liberals too engaged in abstrac-tion, and, as already indicated, Macpherson was fully aware of the danger of liberal concepts, grounded on the ontology of the abstract, 'possessive' individual, licensing the net transfer of powers. In other words, liberal rights of self-ownership rendered the assymetric power relations between worker and capitalist invisible. Indeed, liberal critics were not able convincingly and concretely to demonstrate that a net transfer of powers did not occur under capitalism. The argument, therefore, between Macpherson and his liberal critics should not be about abstraction *per se*, but about how well it is used, depending upon ethical, practical and cognitive criteria. Liberal critics also raised strong objections to his notion of human essence, but these were not unanswerable, especially if conceived in a more Aristotelian way allowing for a developmental dynamic and cultural diversity. Finally, although some of these critics suggested that Macpherson had ignored a rights based element of the liberal tradition, he could claim that his notion of human flourishing had much in common with that of its major theorist - Mill - and that this 'effective' individual developmental right was essential to what it meant to be human.

– POSTMODERN AND 'DELIBERATIVE DEMOCRATIC' CRITICS –

Postmodernist-inspired and 'deliberative democratic' critics in many respects echoed the liberal objections to his thesis.[108] Both schools of thought stressed the immutability of conflict in human life, and while the first saw democracy as a way of acknowledging that this antagonism was the result of fluid individual/collective identities, and therefore requiring some form of political representation and/or protection, the latter was more interested in the effects of the transformational properties of the deliberative process upon its participants. Both rejected in their different ways Macpherson's Marxist affinity with what they viewed as its structuralism and economic determinism, as well as his implicit perfectionism associated with the notions of social harmony, material abundance and abolition of the state. There could be no 'end' to politics because the problems of 'contingency', difference and identity and the finite nature of the planet's resources could not be remedied by what seemed to be Marxist medicine. They also held that his democratic vision was characterised by a lack of institutional thought.

Keane argued that Macpherson's failure to consider institutional processes in his normative vision stemmed from three things.[109] In the first place, he did not come to terms with 'ethical pluralism'. His emphasis on democracy as substantive and normative - rather than as procedural - presupposed that common agreement could be reached as to what constituted the good life. 'His theory of democracy yearned for a perfectly substantive democracy, unhindered by procedural matters.'[110] However, human rationality, moral judgement, aesthetic creation and contemplation and religious experience – all aspects of Macpherson's notion of the human essence – were in fact heterogeneous in form because we live in a world of ethical diversity, of 'ethical indeterminacy', of 'contingent' ethical standards. Thus, democracy could not be grounded upon a specific, determinate ethical vision with its totalitarian implications. 'Ethical pluralism' crucially required procedural democracy, which guarantees 'openness within and between state institutions and civil society and, therefore, ensures that individuals and groups can fairly defend their particular norms in relation to other, possibly incompatible, norms.'[111] Contra Macpherson, democracy was not synonymous with the 'withering away of social division and political conflict'.[112]

Furthermore, and this was the second reason why Macpherson did not pay much attention to institutions, he thought in Marxist fashion that the state would wither away with classes. Although his writings, especially *PI*, contained an 'unintended statism',[113] he did not take seriously the classic liberal concerns about restricting the power of the state – the state/civil society distinction – and reconciling the freedom of different individuals and groups. His ideal of social harmony had authoritarian implications because it invited measures to ensure that it was maintained.[114] Moreover, such an assumption meant that little thought was given to mechanisms regulating and organising production and consumption in a post-market, post-private property society. The third reason for the lack of an institutional dimension could be ascribed to his 'fairy tale' faith in technologically created abundance. Scarcity would always be part of the human condition because human needs were constantly changing over time. Therefore, distributive procedures would always be necessary. Moreover, in a post-market society, large-scale, undemocratic production methods might be preferable, in terms of productive efficiency. Additionally, Macpherson's faith in 'infinite progress in the mastery of nature' led him to ignore ecological problems.[115] Here again democratic procedures were essential to check the technocratic power of the expert, who takes decisions without fully taking into account environmental dangers.

Connelly criticised Macpherson along similar lines. While he had much sympathy with Macpherson's project, especially its insistence upon the necessity for some degree of social and economic equality for a healthy democracy, the ideal of social harmony based upon 'true' identities and norms did not accord with 'late modern' notions of democracy, which were 'ambiguated'. 'Identities and norms are ambiguous formations and ... a democratic ethos properly formed responds best to this ambiguity.'[116] Identity was 'a contingent, relational formation laced with dissonances and ambiguities'.[117] Thus, democratic politics was properly 'the site of a tension or productive ambiguity between governance and disturbance of naturalized identities'.[118] By implication Macpherson's notion of democracy diminishes the 'importance of contestation, disturbance, and denaturalization to late-modern life'.[119]

Mansbridge, from a 'deliberative' democratic direction, followed Keane in underlining the absence of institutional thought in Macpherson's writings. His neglect of 'the political' was due not only to his stress on social harmony in an economically egalitarian society. It arose because he did not consider adequately the need for coercive power among equals. Instead, he focused on power in a vertical sense, based on existing realities, rather than in a horizontal sense that would be required in an ideal community.[120] This defect was, moreover, a consequence of defining democracy more in societal terms, rather than as a system of government. Omitting 'the political' could also be attributed to his failure to acknowledge fully the beneficial effects of political participation on the individual, of 'political efficacy' to use Carol Pateman's phrase.[121] Although he did refer to something like it in *LTLD* (pp. 101–4), the participatory process was not deemed as central by him to the maximisation of human powers. Most crucially, he did not consider how political deliberation could transform individuals and their perceptions of themselves and their interests in order to promote social harmony.

– *Commentary* –

Macpherson's postmodern and 'deliberative' democratic critics had much in common with their liberal predecessors in charging Macpherson with having lost sight of the importance of procedural democracy. He had failed to consider 'ethical pluralism' (Keane), 'ambiguated' norms and identities (Connelly), or the need for coercion among equals and political efficacy (Mansbridge). Two questions are raised here: did Macpherson ignore the need for procedural democracy? And did he in fact have a richer theory of democracy because he saw that any democracy worthy of the name had to pay attention to *both* the procedural and to the substantive?

There is sufficient evidence to show that he did take procedural matters seriously, and that they were built into his ideal society. He stated:

> The liberal values I want to see maintained are civil and political liberties: freedom of speech, association, publication, etc.; freedom from arbitrary arrest and imprisonment; freedom to exert political pressures whether by vote or other ways, and in general, civil and political liberties at least of the degree that we have them now in the liberal-democratic states.[122]

Mansbridge by implication seems to assume that Macpherson envisaged a non-coercive, stateless society. Yet, in response to Levine's accusation that he shared with Rousseau and Kant the view that a state would be needed because human beings were inherently irrational, he had replied, 'I assume that a state will still be needed for the coordination of productive activities and probably for the adjudication of different individual interpretations of what rules and interference are necessary to maximize individual self development.'[123] The notion of adjudication implies a possible need for coercion among equals, if agreement with the state's decision is not accepted. He also appreciated Mill's point that democratic deliberation transforms individual capacities. It promoted, quoting Mill, 'the advancement of community . . . in intellect, in virtue, and in practical activity and efficiency'.[124] And against Keane's charge that his paucity of institutional thought could be attributed to his lack of 'ethical pluralism', his model of participatory democracy accepted the possibility of inter-party competition. He recognised that a competitive party system was 'either unavoidable, or actually desirable, in a non-exploitative, non-class-divided society'.[125] Thus, he seemed to accept the possibility of competing values. And also against Keane, in his critique of Berlin, Macpherson resisted the idea of a state enforcing collective harmony: 'It is *not* necessary for an advocate of positive liberty to assert or assume that there is a single universal harmonious pattern into which the ends of all rational beings must fit.'[126] And in reply to Connelly, although he did not use the language of contingency, identity and difference, there would seem to be plenty of scope for seeing democracy as the site of *some* antagonism. Macpherson was merely opposed to 'destructive contention'.[127] The question is whether there has to be any necessary limits to this antagonism, which will be discussed presently. One final oddity with these critics' assumptions is that they give the impression that Macpherson must have had the thinnest of 'thin' notions of democracy: its *raison d'être* would seem to be as a register of people's preferences which spontaneously coalesce. There is no evidence that he held such an assumption, rather the opposite. It is the only forum in which differences can be resolved in such a way as to enable equal enjoyment, exertion and development of human powers.

There is a more general point that can be made against his liberal, postmodern and deliberative critics. Macpherson's complaint against the Western liberal conception of democracy was not *because* it was procedural (democracy as a means) and not substantive (democracy as an end). Rather it was a *limited* conception of democracy. This was the problem. Western liberal democratic theorists divested democracy of its ethical content and were blind to a capitalist market society shaping its structure and function. And although he argued that Second and Third Worlds were democratic in the substantive sense, he still wanted their leaders to introduce procedural democracy, recognising, however, that certain preconditions were necessary, such as a genuine rapprochement with the West. And while in *RWD* and *DT* he implicitly believed that states where democratic procedures did not operate could still legitimately claim to be democratic, in his final work he insisted that without civil liberties 'democracy is a travesty'.[128]

We can now move to the second question, which is whether his proceduralist critics have in overemphasising their differences with Macpherson made themselves vulnerable by not taking on board Macpherson's preoccupations. First a conceptual point: there is a danger in making ethical pluralism or ethical indeterminacy so absolute that it undercuts procedural democracy, because certain values do not recognise the need for political equality and may contain within them certain kinds of exploitation or domination. So in this sense a democracy could not be based upon an 'anything goes' approach to ethical or cultural diversity. A second limitation to ethical pluralism is that the concept of democracy has to be based upon a prior 'monism', upon a more important value than 'difference'. That is to say, it is grounded upon the recognition of a common humanity, that differences do not exploit or oppress others, so that all have the equal right to exertial and developmental autonomy. The recognition of a common humanity entails a recognition that all individuals have common survival and health (including mental health) needs which to be met involves both cooperation and forbearance, if individual purposes are to be realised.[129] Only within a limiting, yet enabling, framework of a common humanity or common 'identity' and of a fundamental equal recognition that all human beings have to be treated as ends and not means can ethical diversity be developed in a way that is genuinely universalistic. Another problem which goes back to Rousseau is that if differences and antagonism are really deep, then we may not have one political community, one democracy, but a number of 'particular' wills. This of course is a basic problem for any democratic theory. Indeed, Macpherson's 'staggering assumption' of social harmony is relevant here in the sense that it rules out 'destructively contentious' human characteristics that lead to the exploitation and oppression, of an individual being treated as a means and not an end.[130]

There is a practical point too: if ethical values are so diverse or indeterminate, or identities so unstable, why would people from these diverse constituencies necessarily want democracy in the first place? The outcome of democratic deliberation may go against them, or they may lose their identity through incorporation. The significance of Macpherson's democratic theory lies in implicitly posing the question of why we should value democracy. We value it because it is essential to our common humanity. While there is in my view a definitional problem derived from his immanent strategy in criticising liberalism discussed above, the value of democracy has to cut into the substantive, ontological issue of what it means to be human. And from Macpherson's viewpoint capitalism and humanity are in the final analysis incompatible. Hence democracy has to deal with the question of class, that is with substantive questions. This substantive issue in turn feeds back into the procedural means loop because in a classless system not only would inter-party competition no longer blur class issues creating apathy as under capitalism, lower social echelons would no longer be discouraged from participation.[131] In a sense we have now turned full circle, because the proceduralists, while recognising – Connelly in particular – that substantive questions are important, do not demonstrate how they are systematically interrelated with procedural ones in an ontological and ethical sense.

– ECOLOGICAL CRITICS –

Ecological critics also saw Macpherson's Marxist affinity, especially its productivist gloss, as problematic, especially in environmental terms. His work lacked, they argued, any serious treatment of the growing global ecological crisis and its implications for his democratic theory. Jung attributed this to his 'scientism' or 'technologism', that is an assumption that science and technology were benign and beneficial because they enabled greater mastery over nature and thereby the overcoming of scarcity.[132] However, the earth's resources were finite, and the problem of scarcity would be enduring.[133] Therefore, it could not be transcended through technology, and thus basic needs would have to be defined and how they were to be fulfilled worked out, and then resources would have to be justly distributed on this basis. Leiss on the other hand ascribed Macpherson's ecological deficit to his binary vision of the world, of a world divided by the conflict of capitalism versus socialism, which he had first developed in the 1930s.[134] Such a vision was historically exhausted 'completely'. The pressing question was not how to master nature in order to produce unlimited goods, but how to avoid 'catastrophic environmental degradation'.[135] And the political problem was to discover 'an appropriate representation between humanity and nature'.[136]

– Commentary –

In evaluating the strength of these criticisms, sympathetic references to environmental questions in DT [137] and Macpherson's later works ought to be noted.[138] Significantly, he championed these issues before they became fashionable. The reason for environmental concern should be fairly obvious. His emphasis on production was for the satisfaction of human needs, not for its own sake as under capitalism. He strongly opposed 'infinite' consumption for its own sake. It would be illogical to suppose that he would have championed productivity to such an extent that the environment was so degraded that human needs could not be met. And although his idea of a technological 'fix' triumphing over scarcity could be construed as anti-environmentalist, the notion of 'abundance' to be inferred from Macpherson's viewpoint is not of the consumption of limitless 'wants' objects. He regarded scarcity as the product of capitalism itself, either contrived (the image of infinite consumption), or real for the poor.[139] His argument was that a post-capitalist society would be able to deal with these kinds of scarcity, especially because qualitative values would become more important than quantitative ones, as we changed our image of ourselves from infinite consumers to exerters and developers of our human capacities. His assumption was that technological development did not have to be compulsively directed at producing an ever increasing supply of material objects, but could reduce the amount of time needed to produce the means of subsistence, as biologically and culturally defined, thereby increasing the time available to exercise and develop human capacities. Although this would require material objects, the transformation of our ontological self-perception would mean that we would not longer be 'acting in order to get more to consume' but 'consuming in order to act'.[140] He was thus able to respond in positive fashion once ecological questions became significant, and in a political sense his concept of participatory, socialist democracy was potentially a far more appropriate political system to cope with ecological problems than liberal capitalist democracy.

− Conclusion −

We have seen that most of his liberal, postmodern, 'deliberative democratic' and ecological critics did not read Macpherson either closely or sympathetically and that their own preoccupations prevented them from entering into any constructive dialogue with him or his ideas. As we have seen in the two previous chapters, critics preferred to find fault with his work and implicitly suggest that his project ought to be abandoned. For liberals, if that was their aim, then a thorough-going critique of his net transfer of powers concept would have been required, as well as a demonstration that capitalism could at least in principle provide a framework for the equal effective right of all citizens to exert and develop their human powers. Only Chapman attempted to do so with an idealised *model* of capitalism creating a non-invasion of powers. Not only was this model unrealistic, his commitment to the 'justice' of 'economic rationality' of work and investment incentives meant implicitly that he could not also commit himself to an equal effective right to self-development. Leiss, on the other hand, although he presented an idealised portrait of *existing* capitalism, was not prepared to make an explicit claim that it could comprehensively live up to Macpherson's developmental ethic. And in both cases the coercive nature of capitalism was discounted. The postmodernist and deliberative democratic critics were, however, more appreciative of his project. Yet, they followed the liberals in wrongly assuming that Macpherson was not sensitive to the importance of procedural democracy. In their desire to avoid ontological questions which might yield determinate ethical implications, they could only come up with a 'thin' theory of democracy. Its central function was to cope with 'difference'. And finally his ecological critics again either ignored his environment friendly statements or wrongly assumed that what he did have to say was not compatible with their concerns. Nevertheless, neither a failure to read Macpherson closely nor an inability to undermine his net transfer of powers concept meant that these critics had in every case totally missed their target. Certainly there was a weakness in his move to define a democratic society in terms of self-development, opening him up to the charge of being too uncritical of totalitarianism, if detached from the procedural definition of democracy as in *RWD* and *DT*. Moreover, while Macpherson was on strong ground defending the need for abstraction in terms of societal analysis, there still remains the practical question of how and in what form his 'abstract' ideals can be concretely realised.

— NOTES —

1. See, for example, Macpherson's response to Wand, 'The Criticism of Concepts and the Concept of Criticism', *Canadian Journal of Political Science*, 5/1, p. 141, 1972.
2. K. R. Minogue, 'Humanist Democracy: The Political Thought of C. B. Macpherson', *Canadian Journal of Political Science*, 9/3, 1976, p. 378.
3. Ibid., p. 380.
4. Ibid.
5. *DT*, p. 51.
6. *PI*, p. 275. See also pp. 13, 71, 73.
7. *DT*, pp. 21819
8. B. Wand, 'C. B. Macpherson's Conceptual Apparatus', *Canadian Journal of Political Science*, 4/4, 1971, p. 526.
9. *RWD*, p. 19; 'Deceptive Task of Political Theory', *Cambridge Journal*, 7, 1954, p. 567.
10. A. Wright, 'C. B. Macpherson, Democracy and Possessive Individualism', in L. Tivey and A. Wright (eds), *Political Thought Since 1945, Philosophy, Science and Ideology* (Aldershot: Elgar, 1992), p. 166.
11. D. Morrice, 'C. B. Macpherson's Critique of Liberal Democracy and Capitalism', *Political Studies*, 42/4, 1994, pp. 656-7.
12. Minogue, 'Humanist Democracy', pp. 382-3.
13. Ibid., p. 384.
14. Ibid., p. 386.
15. J. Dunn, 'Democracy Unretrieved, or the Political Theory of Professor Macpherson', *British Journal of Political Science*, 4, 1974, p. 494.

16. Ibid., p. 495.
17. Ibid.
18. Ibid., p. 496.
19. Minogue, 'Humanist Democracy', p. 385.
20. Ibid., p. 393.
21. Wand, 'Macpherson's Conceptual Apparatus', p. 539.
22. Ibid., p. 540.
23. J. W. Chapman, 'Natural Rights and Justice in Liberalism', in D. D. Raphael (ed.), *Political Theory and the Rights of Man* (London: Macmillan, 1967), p. 29.
24. Ibid., p. 30.
25. Ibid.
26. Ibid.
27. Ibid., p. 34.
28. See also Minogue who queried the notion that capitalism was necessarily coercive. It may have been in the nineteenth century, but it was not in the twentieth, with rising wage rates, strong trade unions and competition among employers for labour. Minogue 'Humanist Democracy', p. 390.
29. Chapman, 'Natural Rights and Justice', p. 36.
30. Ibid., p. 42.
31. W. Leiss, *C. B. Macpherson: Dilemmas of Liberalism and Socialism* (New York: St. Martin's Press, 1988), p. 41.
32. Ibid., p. 108.
33. W. Leiss, 'Marx and Macpherson: Needs, Utilities, and Self-Development', in A. Kontos (ed.), *Powers, Possessions and Freedom* (Toronto: University of Toronto Press, 1979), p. 131.
34. Ibid., p. 134.
35. Although he was a little inconsistent on this because he could also say that the issue was one of emphasis in 'downgrading' the consumerist model and 'upgrading' the developmental one. Ibid., p. 133, quoting *LTLD*, p. 2. See also Leiss, *C. B. Macpherson*, p. 75, p. 88.
36. Ibid., p. 102.
37. Ibid., p. 140.
38. Ibid., p. 141.
39. Ibid., p. 139.
40. Ibid., p. 101.
41. Ibid., p. 119.
42. Ibid., p. 114, p. 127.
43. Ibid., p. 135.
44. Ibid., p. 137.
45. Ibid., p. 135.
46. Dunn, 'Democracy Unretrieved', pp. 496–7.
47. Minogue, 'Humanist Democracy', p. 393.
48. Ibid., p. 394. Not only did Minogue hold that private property was essential for individual autonomy, he also questioned Macpherson's argument that the

concept of property itself was subject to historical change (ibid., pp. 389–90). Specifically, he rejected Macpherson's argument that it was changing from a capitalist market-induced exclusive right to things, to a socialist inclusive right. According to Minogue, the concept itself was not changing, merely the conditions under which property was held, that is varying the conditions of exclusion, for example the abolition of entails. And even public property was still property, since public authorities were still able to exclude people, such as older children from using swings in public parks. However, even if we accept Minogue's argument, while the concept of property may have not changed in the sense of its meaning, its changing historical significance is underlined by the need to talk about it in terms of 'public' and 'private' or 'common' property. The need for these adjectives is required to give the concept a more specific, historical content In any case, Macpherson seeing property in terms of inclusivity and exclusivity, was not differing from Minogue in relating property to some kind of inclusion/exclusion continuum. Macpherson after all defined property merely as an 'enforceable claim of a person to some use or benefit of something' which historically may either mean the right to exclude others, or the right not to be excluded. *DT*, pp. 123–3.

49. Chapman, 'Natural Rights and Justice', p. 307.
50. Ibid., p. 308.
51. Ibid., p. 309.
52. For example, *RWD*, pp. 19–20; *DT*, p. 106.
53. J. W. Seaman and T. J. Lewis, 'On Retrieving Macpherson's Liberalism', *Canadian Journal of Political Science*, 17/4, 1984, p. 727.
54. Ibid., p. 722.
55. *PI*, pp. 263–4. cf. *DT*, p. 103.
56. Minogue, 'Humanist Democracy', p. 387.
57. A. Damico, 'Liberal Still: Notes on the Political Theory of C. B. Macpherson', *Canadian Journal of Political and Social Theory*, 8/3, 1984, p. 89.
58. Ibid., p. 91.
59. C. B. Macpherson, 'Humanist Democracy and Elusive Marxism: A Response to Minogue and Svacek', *Canadian Journal of Political Science*, 9/3, 1976, p. 426.
60. Ibid., p. 430.
61. Ibid., p. 427.
62. C. B. Macpherson, 'The Criticism of Concepts and the Concept of Criticism', *Canadian Journal of Political Science*, 5/1, 1972, p. 143.
63. Ibid., pp. 144–5.
64. Macpherson, 'Humanist Democracy and Elusive Marxism', p. 429.
65. Ibid., p. 430.
66. Ibid., p. 428.
67. Ibid., pp. 428–9.
68. Ibid., p. 428.
69. Macpherson, 'The Criticism of Concepts ...', p. 143.
70. *DT*, p. 84.

71. Ibid., p. 87.
72. Macpherson Papers, p. 1, 13 January 1980.
73. Ibid., p. 2.
74. Ibid.
75. Ibid.
76. This reply would also seem to contradict Lessnoff's suggestion that Macpherson was opposed to markets *per se*. M. Lessnoff, *Political Philosophers of the Twentieth Century* (Oxford: Blackwell, 1999), p. 107.
77. *DT*, p. 108.
78. A. MacIntyre, *After Virtue* (London: Duckworth, 1981), pp. 54-7, and Macpherson as heavily influenced by Aristotelian thinking would certainly have approved!
79. M. Ramsay, *Human Needs and the Market* (Aldershot: Avebury, 1992), pp. 36-8.
80. See N. Geras, *Marx and Human Nature: Refutation of a Legend* (London: Verso, 1983), ch. 4 *passim*.
81. Ibid., p. 90.
82. See p. Lindsay, *Creative Individualism, The Democratic Vision of C. B. Macpherson* (New York: State University of New York Press, 1998), pp. 26-8, although the argument developed here is slightly different.
83. *PI*, p. 262.
84. *DT*, p. 107.
85. Ibid., p. 115.
86. Ibid., p. 107.
87. *RWD*, p. 27.
88. *DT*, pp. 109-11.
89. Macpherson, 'The Criticism of Concepts ...', p. 144.
90. Interview, 'C. B. Macpherson on Marx', in F. Cunningham, *The Real World of Democracy Revisited* (Atlantic Highlands, NJ: Humanities Press, 1994), pp. 19-20.
91. Macpherson, 'Humanist Democracy and Elusive Marxism', p. 424.
92. *DT*, pp. 65-7.
93. Leiss, *C. B. Macpherson*, p. 141.
94. *DT*, p. 59.
95. Leiss, *C. B. Macpherson*, pp. 134-5.
96. See Lindsay's attempt to interpret Macpherson's project in a market-friendly fashion, in *Creative Individualism*, ch. 5.
97. See also, *DT*, p. 34.
98. Ibid., *DT*, p. 12.
99. *LTLD*, p. 111.
100. *DT*, p. 140.
101. H. Tudor (ed.), *The Preconditions of Socialism* (Cambridge: Cambridge University Press, 1993).
102. Macpherson, 'The Politics of Self-Development', *Canadian Journal of Social and Political Theory*, 8/3, 1984, p. 98.
103. *DT*, p. 51.

104. *DT*, p. 111, and *DT*, p. 54. See also R. Plant, *Modern Political Thought* (Oxford: Blackwell, 1991), pp. 249–50, in distinguishing between 'minimalist' (promoting diverse conceptions of the good) and 'maximalist' (potentially totalitarian) positive liberty.

105. *RWD*, p. 27.

106. R. Repogle, 'On Seaman and Lewis' Liberalism', *Canadian Journal of Political Science*, 17/2, 1985, p. 376.

107. Ibid., p. 378.

108. See the collection of essays edited by J. Carens, *Democracy and Possessive Individualism: The Intellectual Legacy of C. B. Macpherson* (New York: State University of New York Press, 1993). Apart from Carens' introductory essay, the spirit of many of these contributions is distinctly odd. While they began by praising Macpherson, suggesting that he was an important theorist, they quickly went on to distance themselves from his work with not particularly well-informed criticism and positing theories sharply at variance with his. The net effect is to render Macpherson's legacy minimal.

109. Mouffe in the same volume puts forward similar arguments in favour of a 'plural democracy' as a result of her worry that Macpherson's ideal is 'of a perfect consensus, of a harmonious collective will' (ibid., p. 178).

110. J. Keane, 'Stretching the Limits of the Democratic Imagination', in ibid., p. 123.

111. Ibid., p. 117.

112. Ibid., p. 118.

113. Ibid., p. 121.

114. Ibid., p. 123.

115. Ibid., p. 128.

116. W. E. Connelly, 'Democracy and Contingency', in ibid., p. 208.

117. Ibid.

118. Ibid.

119. Ibid., p. 211.

120. J. Mansbridge, 'Macpherson's Neglect of the Political', in ibid., pp. 158–9.

121. Ibid. p. 162.

122. Macpherson, 'C. B. Macpherson on Marx' in Cunningham, *The Real World of Democracy Revisited*, p. 17.

123. Macpherson, 'Individualist Socialism? A Reply to Levine and MacIntyre', *Canadian Journal of Philosophy*, 6/2, 1976, p. 197.

124. *LTLD*, p. 47. Incidentally, Mansbridge elsewhere, in her desire to distance herself from Macpherson, wrongly suggests that he wanted to 'excoriate political parties', seemingly not to have noticed his remark and argument in *LTLD* where he declared that they may be 'positively desirable' (p. 112). 'Using Power/Fighting Power: The Polity', in S. Benhabib (ed.), *Democracy and Difference: Contesting the Boundaries of the Political* (Princeton, NJ: Princeton University Press, 1996), p. 56.

125. *LTLD*, p. 113.

126. *DT*, p. 111.

127. Ibid., p. 55.
128. *RFEJ*, p. 53.
129. Ramsay, *Human Needs and the Market*, p. 205.
130. *DT*, p. 55.
131. *LTLD*, p. 111.
132. H. Y. Jung, 'Democratic Ontology and Technology: A Critique of C. B. Macpherson', *Polity*, 11/2, 1979, p. 260.
133. Ibid., p. 265.
134. Leiss, *C. B. Macpherson*, p. 263.
135. Ibid., p. 271.
136. Ibid., p. 272.
137. *DT*, p. 76.
138. *LTLD*, p. 102; *RFEJ*, p. 48.
139. *DT*, 139, footnote 19. See also *DT*, pp. 24–5, and Cunningham, *Real World of Democracy Revisited*, pp. 5–6.
140. Macpherson, 'The Currency of Values', *Transactions of the Royal Society of Canada*, 9/4, 1971, p. 29. See also *DT*, pp. 58–9, D. McNally, *Against the Market* (London: Verso, 1993), pp. 190–2, and J. Hughes, 'An Ecological Perspective on Marx's Theory of Needs', in A. Dobson and J. Stanyer (eds), *Contemporary Political Studies* (Nottingham: PSA, 1998), vol. 2, pp. 690–702. Thus he did not conceive of 'limited demand for economic production' as Lessnoff, in *Political Philosophers of the Twentieth Century*, p. 108, suggests. His point was that ecological problems would be easier to cope with because there would no longer be a profit-driven, economic system which made consumption an end in itself.

CHAPTER 5

RETRIEVING DEMOCRACY (2): COMMUNITARIAN, MARXIST AND FEMINIST CRITICS

The previous chapter considered critics who disliked Macpherson's Marxist inflection. This chapter shows how his communitarian, Marxist and feminist critics saw his project as mired by the other central strand of his thought: liberalism. Perhaps unwittingly they picked upon a danger in his immanent critique of liberalism. This attempted to expose its two contradictory ontologies and suggested that its possessive individualist one was becoming historically played out. He suggested that its 'retrieved' Millian, developmental ontology was now a genuine possibility. In adopting this strategy Macpherson, these critics argued, was seemingly unable to move off the liberal terrain, especially of abstract individualism.

— COMMUNITARIAN CRITICS —

MacIntyre was the first to give voice to the communitarian critique. For him essential human capacities were not only significantly manifest in the abilities of individuals, but 'above all in the formation and maintenance of certain types of relationships between individuals in certain types of community.'[1] Thus how certain capacities were manifest depended on the type of community. So, for example, art of different kinds in pre-modern times was a public expression rather than a private, individual property as in market societies. In other words, in non-market societies individual powers were expressed in a communal form. MacIntyre suggested that Macpherson, in discussing individual capacities, conceded too much to liberalism in making his starting point the individual rather than the community. Thus he underemphasised the social nature and significance of essential human capacities, especially language.

Lukes developed this line of critical reflection. Against Macpherson he firmly asserted the social nature of human beings and the socially constituted nature of individual powers and identity. He detected in Macpherson an abstract individualism rejected by Marx in the sixth of his *Theses on Feuerbach*: 'the essence of *man* is no abstraction inherent in each separate individual. In its reality it is the *ensemble* of social relations.'[2] Human activities and potentialities were structured by social relations and could not be conceived independently of them. Macpherson's abstract individualism – its abstractness and its individualism – created a number of difficulties, especially for his concept of human essence and powers. The first problem was that his developmental ontology, embodied in the notion that individuals 'had an equal right to make the best of themselves', entailed abstracting powers from concrete contexts in an arbitrary fashion, based upon an 'abstract, anti-utilitarian moral perfectionism'.[3] The lack of empirical grounding meant that another list of human powers could be drawn up, premised not on human harmony, but conflict. His list, Lukes suggested, was built on an ungrounded moral theory. Furthermore, even his own list of essentially human capacities was imprecise, for there remained the vexed question of what exactly constituted, for example, 'rational understanding' and 'moral judgement and action' given wide divergences of opinion about the nature of these qualities.[4]

Another difficulty stemming from his abstract individualism, of seeing 'man' 'abstractly as an atom whose nature ('capacities') is independent of the relations in which he is involved' was his failure to show how individual identities were socially constituted.[5] This meant that his account of impediments to the development of human powers was inadequate because they were perceived mainly as 'external', and not as significantly 'internal'. Whether or not individual capacities are developed can crucially depend on a socially engendered self-image, self-belief and expectations, that is on the nature and extent of internal impediments, to which Macpherson only gave passing reference.[6] Thus, whether an individual's capacities are blocked or facilitated will depend upon the nature of the social relations that generate this identity.

The final problem, according to Lukes, again arising from his lack of concreteness, was that he did not look in more detail at the relationship between the 'external' impediments created by the net transfer of powers under capitalism and the specific powers that were stunted. Although the effects of poverty and unemployment on human capacities could be easily demonstrated, after that there still remained the need for a 'detailed demonstration of what desirable and possible forms of relationship and activity are blocked by the central institutions of capitalism.'[7] Further, Macpherson was not clear about what he meant by the 'maximization of powers', whether those of present individuals, or future, 'morally regenerated' ones, and the relationship between the present and future maximisation of powers was complicated because somewhere a line had to be drawn between developing an individual's capacities and transforming that individual.[8] An allied problem was that he did not adequately specify present and future conditions which would foster their realisation.

Parekh, following in Lukes' footsteps, emphasised Macpherson's lack of concreteness and abstract individualist shortcomings to an even greater extent. First, his liberal individualism meant that all an individual needed was the necessary material resources to develop their capacities. 'He does not examine how such capacities as rational understanding, friendship, religious experience, love, curiosity and moral judgement are hindered by the lack of material means or by the transfer of powers.'[9] Furthermore, in stressing the importance of material means required for self-development, he ignored social relations. Thus he did not analyse such relations necessary for the capacities that he valued to flourish. Macpherson was too entrenched in liberalism. Not only did he employ the liberal language of 'maximisation' (if of powers rather than utilities), he did not fully escape from the charge of possessive individualism that he levelled against liberalism. Rights were couched in the language of individual property – the right to life, liberty, guaranteed income, access to the means of production.[10] For Macpherson, the individual develops freely chosen capacities, and needed liberty, not in order to cooperate with others 'in developing a common way of life', to 'complete one another' and 'help others to grow and flourish', but to live an autonomous existence of self-chosen purposes.[11] And if this was the goal of human development it was not clear why individuals would want to be non-contentious and cooperative. Finally, Macpherson's liberalism meant that he applied Marx's analysis to society, rather than to the individual. Consequently like Mill, he was more concerned with the 'injustice of exploitation and the unfair transfer of powers in capitalist society than the atomization of man and the corruption of human potential.'[12] Parekh concluded pithily that Macpherson seemed to want 'to create a socialist society in order to realize liberal man ... and he liberalizes Marxism but does not Marxianise liberalism.'[13]

In sum, communitarian criticisms picked up on the overly abstract nature of Macpherson's thought, especially his failure to appreciate the extent to which the individual was socially constituted, and the importance of social values, which often did, and should, take precedence over individual ones. They attributed this to his residual liberalism.

– Macpherson's reply and commentary –

In replying to his communitarian critics, he thanked MacIntyre for coining the phrase 'cooperative and creative individualism' to describe his position.[14] But contrary to MacIntyre's suggestion, he denied that any significant concessions to liberal individualism had been made. He had already stated in DT[15] that society helped develop human capacities and that they were socially derived; and in chapter six in *DT* that essential human capacities became individual property with the rise of capitalism; while in *PI*, and in chapter one of *DT*, that the possessive individualist image of human beings owing nothing to society for their capacities was created by theorists of market society (Hobbes to Bentham). Just in case communitarians did not get his message, he reiterated it: in a post-scarcity society where there was zero extractive power, people would live 'as social beings, getting their maximum satisfaction in living and acting with and through others; that it is only scarcity and the extractive market situation that have made people behave atomistically.'[16] Furthermore, he could not understand MacIntyre's insistence that language had to be made the distinguishing feature of humans as communal beings: 'it has been equally effective as a means of communication between the Hobbesian individuals of the capitalist world.'[17] Macpherson also replied to Lukes in a private letter. He would be unable 'to write another word without [his] strictures in mind', especially for neglecting the sixth of Marx's *Theses on Feuerbach*, although he baulked at the idea that it had to be the test of ideological purity. He further maintained that despite the difficulties he raised their overcoming did not have to entail the discarding of the 'Millian individualist concept of human essence'.[18]

Thus the thrust of the communitarian argument against Macpherson was that he was too liberal. He had not sufficiently distanced himself from that which he criticised, still retaining the premises and values of liberal individualism. At one level this was true. He subscribed to Mill's ideal of individual self-development. Yet there is a difficulty, for this ideal was not uniquely liberal. Mill had borrowed it from the German Romantic tradition which, accepting both the inevitability and advantages of modernity, in turn had borrowed it, in a revised individualistic form from the Greeks. Marx too subscribed to this ideal. His theory of alienation is an explanation of why capitalism cannot develop a rich individuality. For Marx, as for Macpherson, the capitalist market prevented the free development of human powers. Thus although Macpherson did not detail capitalism's stunting of human capacities as demanded by Lukes and Parekh, he could claim that he took this as a given, as a fundamental insight of the anti-capitalist, humanist tradition which began in the nineteenth century and required no further demonstration.[19] No doubt the many human powers that were stunted by capitalism apart from those caused by poverty and unemployment could be easily identified: the lack of creativity stemming from the division of labour, the anti-social behaviour of individuals arising from competitive, capitalist-induced atomisation, many work-related illnesses, loss of a sense of community due to the growing mobility of labour and the decline of Fordist production methods, and so on. And beyond all this Lukes and Parekh did not challenge Macpherson's working assumption that the labour process under capitalism severely limits the time and energy for self-chosen activities. And if poverty and unemployment are also included, as they should be, as impediments to the exercise and development of human powers, the indictment of capitalism becomes formidable. With physical survival becoming top priority, the powers developed and exercised become extremely limited.

Perhaps the greatest fault with the communitarians was that they exaggerated their position to make a point that is only superficially evident in Macpherson's work owing to his immanent critique of liberalism. This gave an impression that he accepted most liberal categories.[20] We should note that even before Lukes's and Parekh's criticisms, he argued that the participatory democratic mentality had to include a sense of community. Consumer satisfaction of the possessive individualist could be an autonomous affair – it did not require others, but participatory democracy brought with it a 'self-image' suffused with a 'sense of community', because the 'enjoyment and development of one's capacities is to be done for the most part in conjunction with others, in some relation of community.'[21]

Unsurprisingly, because of his communitarian sensibilities and sympathies, he had no qualms in emphasising them when challenged by his critics,[22] in contrast to his reaction to liberals, which usually saw him digging deeper. Macpherson much was closer to his communitarian critics than they seemed to believe, in seeing individuals and perceptions about individuals as socially constituted, and in wanting to maximise their satisfaction 'living and acting with and through others'.[23] Yet he would not have gone as far as Parekh who seemed to imply that Macpherson's liberal individualism would be ruled out in a socialist society.[24] Here Parekh himself could be accused of a lack of balance in that a flourishing 'common way of life' involves not merely participation in forms of collective activity, but also a recognition of an effective individual autonomy which in turn strengthens communal life. In other words some kind of dialectic of recognition has to occur between the individual and the collective, which necessitates the existence of specific boundaries between them, wherever they may be drawn. Thus it is not clear whether Parekh's form of liberal/Marxist synthesis is too asymmetric in a communitarian direction in not discussing the need for boundaries. Macpherson, even before he became subject to communitarian scrutiny, wanted some kind of individual/collective balance: in regarding the human essence in terms of individual self-direction, he immediately cautioned that this did not mean that an individual

> should refuse to acknowledge himself to be a social animal who can be fully human only as a member of society. It is rather to say that the rules by which he is bound should be only those that can be rationally demonstrated to be necessary to society,

and so to his humanity. Or it may be put that the rules society imposes should not infringe the principle that he should be treated not as a means to other's ends but as an end in himself.[25]

Can Macpherson be defended against Lukes' charge of abstract individualism? On the question of whether Macpherson paid enough attention to internal impediments, Lukes himself later in his essay acknowledged that Macpherson had in fact discussed them, but then explicitly proceeded to ignore them. Macpherson's argument was that he saw external impediments as more important, since they were prior to internal ones and were more analytically manageable.[26] Lukes, therefore, in effect conceded that Macpherson was not an abstract individualist, which assumed that individuals contained some kind of pre-social essence, because internal impediments were socially generated. Moreover, while it is true that Macpherson did not sufficiently analyse these impediments − instead he merely referred to a wealth of literature on the subject, from Rousseau to Marcuse − he saw their interaction with external impediments as part of a 'vicious circle'. Thus, in a sense, to prioritise analysis of external impediments was a strategic decision on Macpherson's part. As such it was not based upon a presumption that internal impediments were insignificant. Lukes in a sense seems to have realised this and swiftly came back to the charge of abstraction against Macpherson. His concept of the net transfer of powers lacked a detailed 'demonstration of what desirable and possible forms of relationship and activity are blocked by the central institutions of capitalism',[27] an objection also taken up by Parekh.[28] To this Macpherson may have replied that he was using abstraction to understand the essence of capitalism, a class system which visibly creates social and economic inequality, and severely limits effective autonomy for most people. Macpherson presumably thought that the effects on the human potential, in terms of the loss of freedom to exert and develop one's essence, by capitalism were so self-evident as to not warrant detailed demonstration. On this point he did not think he had to persuade the sceptic. Equally, his argument was necessarily abstract because he was discussing the ethics of capitalism: the absence of equal opportunity for individuals to realise their human potentials, and the development and exertion of some individuals' capacities at the expense of others; the fact that it promoted contentiousness and licensed 'infinite' consumption and appropriation. He was primarily a political philosopher, searching for the best social, economic and political principles that would promote human flourishing.

Macpherson could also reply to Lukes' criticism that his abstract approach meant that his list of human qualities to be exerted and developed were arbitrary, smacking of 'moral perfectionism', and indeed in themselves arguable.

First, he was engaged in an immanent critique of liberal democratic ideology, and attempted to debunk its claims to maximise uniquely human capacities as described by ethical liberals such as J. S. Mill and T. H. Green. This may account for his studied reluctance to draw up a comprehensive list of human attributes and prioritise them, which could be 'variously listed and assessed'[29] and 'extended or rearranged in many ways'.[30] In a sense he was looking at this list from the other end. He was more interested in ensuring that inhuman, contentious attributes were not included, because by definition this offered the possibility of some human beings flourishing at others' expense, thereby not maximising the potentials of everyone. Thus his list is arbitrary because it stemmed from his moral framework, and followed from liberal democratic claims to promote human flourishing. A non-contentious society was a minimal requirement. Macpherson may also have been reluctant to provide a comprehensive and definitive list precisely to avoid the charge of 'moral perfectionism' and indeed totalitarianism. A democratic society had to be free to work out its own principles that would promote human values, but from his point of view it could not claim to be democratic if it sanctioned the invasion of some people's powers by others. Thus Macpherson was not demanding individual, moral perfection, merely stipulating a minimal ethical requirement of a democratic society, as he defined it, if it is to live up to its name. On the question of whether his choice of human capacities was arbitrary as Lukes maintained, it was in a sense deliberately so, because Macpherson's ethical starting point was the principle of reciprocal freedom, which recognised the equal right of all to exercise and develop their human potentials in ways that do not prevent others from doing the same.[31] Within this framework individuals can exercise and develop their capacities as they think fit, once they were no longer possessed by consumerism and endless appropriation.[32] Again we come back to Macpherson's ontology of freedom. Furthermore his 'list' of human capacities was based upon what he thought liberal democratic theorists would include in their own lists.[33]

Finally, he could have rebutted Lukes' criticism that the meaning of what constituted 'rational understanding' and so on was itself arguable, by stating that he was listing these attributes in a formal sense, which were characteristic of all human beings. In this sense, few would disagree that human beings possess these capacities. How they are defined, exercised and developed and how they ought to be exercised and developed, that is their specific content, would be up to members living in a democratic society to judge. Macpherson, following Marx's reluctance to be specific about his utopia, would probably have been reluctant to make substantive stipulations beyond these formal ones, on the grounds that this would constrain by implication the freedom of these members. And in his letter to Lukes he stated:

I do *not* [Macpherson's emphasis] say there is only one correct account of what constitutes the full and free development of essential human capacities. Rather, I had in mind Marx's deserved scorn for Utopian specifications of an ideal society, based on his point that the requisite satisfaction of future human needs cannot now be stipulated in advance since the fully human society is one in which people (future generations) are free to choose.[34]

This could have been his response to Lukes' other reproaches concerning his unwillingness to specify which generation's powers were to be maximised and the relationship between developing capacities and changing individuals. To make specific recommendations would be to fall into the utopian/totalitarian trap.

In conclusion, communitarians made a meal of their differences with Macpherson. He may have inadvertently created the impression that his writings moved in a liberal direction because his strategy heavily rested on challenging liberals on their own ground through an internal critique of their key postulates. Even his earlier writings, *PI* and *DT*, contained communitarian sensibilities, and later these became even more pronounced, just in case these critics did not understand him first time round. He criticised the United Nations Charter for not including collective rights. This individualistic, 'truncated' concept of human rights ignored that fact that 'membership of a national or cultural community which has defined itself historically is part of what it means to be human, and is sometimes the most important part'.[35] Although he had obvious communitarian sympathies, this did not mean that he was prepared to junk what he considered to be the best of liberalism. A society for him to be fully human had to enable individuals to exert and develop their capacities in the way they wanted to, provided this in no way undercut the powers of others to do likewise. The realisation of this ideal was, however, more visible in Marx than Mill. Marx maintained that the price of effective human autonomy had to be paid in some form of human coopera-tion. Hence his communist ideal consisted of 'an association in which the free development of each is the condition for the free development of all.'[36] Macpherson's enterprise therefore rested on an awareness of both communi-tarian and individualist sensibilities.

— MARXIST CRITICS —

Marxist critics, like the communitarians, attacked Macpherson for his liberal proclivities and abstractness. The new wave of independent Marxists, who arose in the wake of the various upheavals in the 1960s and imbibed a Marxism they took to be its purest form, strongly felt that he ought to have gone the whole way in embracing Marxism. Their response, however, was far from uniform. They can be divided, to use a courtroom analogy, into judges and prosecutors. The latter, in condemning him for his liberal fixation, argued that Marxists had little to learn from him, whereas the former, in noting the extent to which he utilised Marxist ideas, were prepared to give him a conditional discharge (possibly on the grounds of diminished (historical) responsibility!).

Levine and Wood condemned him outright and saw his views as positively harmful to the progressive cause. Levine's central charge was that Macpherson, in talking about the 'retrieval' of its developmental ontology, still wanted to 'affiliate conceptually with liberalism'. And he failed to understand the conceptual unity of political and economic liberalism.[37] Like Proudhon he saw the 'good' and 'bad' sides of liberalism, rather than register a sharp break with it. His political aim was to preserve political unity with the 'dominant liberal practice of western capitalism'.[38] He remained on the liberal terrain, and feared proletarian revolution. He in effect affiliated to social democracy, that is a political force in the workers' movement that began as an attempt to replace capitalism, but ended up colluding with it. His social democratic stance was revealed in his attempt to persuade (that is collude with) leaders of the capitalist West to embrace his idea of developmental democracy in competition with the Soviet Union for the allegiance of the Third World as in DT.[39] Levine also rebuked him for not adequately theorising a society in which the non-extractive transfer of powers could operate. The abolition of private property as in the Soviet Union did not automatically guarantee equal access to the means of production. Indeed, the Soviet Union could be characterised as state capitalist.[40]

Wood's Marxist critique of Macpherson was more detailed and damning. She condemned not merely his politics, but his project in toto. Macpherson, by writing in the idiom of 'abstract' political philosophy, had been 'seduced' by the Anglo-US liberal tradition.[41] She castigated him even more forcefully for not breaking with liberalism. She built her general critique of Macpherson on an analysis of his LTLD. Macpherson's 'seduction' manifested itself in the contradiction between his analysis of capitalism and liberalism and their interrelation on the one hand, and his proposed ideal of participatory democracy on the other. First, Wood suggested that Macpherson gave an inadequate account of class and state, because he failed to understand the nature of capitalism. Although he successfully demonstrated how the earlier liberal democracy of James Mill, Bentham and John Stuart Mill were ideologies of a class divided society, he fell short when analysing the contemporary liberal model of 'equilibrium democracy' in the works of pluralists such as Schumpeter and Dahl. The reason for this was that Macpherson judged their model as a 'substantially accurate' account of the modern liberal democratic system. In so doing he obscured a most important fact: the liberal democratic state was the embodiment of class power in modern western society. Macpherson conceptualised out of existence both class and state by using terms such as 'elites' and 'political system', which implied that no 'dominant and consistent concentrations of power exist.'[42] By employing the analogy of the market, the equilibrium model implied that political inequalities were explicable in terms of inequalities of purchasing power. And social inequalities could be interpreted in terms of Weberian stratification theory, that saw them as the product of market competition for goods and services, to be explained in terms of marginal utility, rather than as the outcome of capitalist exploitation.[43] Consequently, because he analysed capitalism on 'its own terms', thereby effectively endorsing it, his own programmatic preference of participatory democracy stood in sharp contradiction, because it presupposed capitalism's supersession.[44]

Macpherson's second concession to liberalism, Wood argued, was to portray it as historically contingent in its relation to capitalism. He abstracted liberalism from its social foundations. This was implicit in his strategy of attempting to win over his liberal audience to socialism, especially in his argument that Mill's ethical, developmental liberalism could be shorn of its market assumptions. Macpherson treated the concept of self-development in a formal manner, with no social content. Such a strategy was an 'empty formula'.[45] Macpherson supposed that the liberal ideals freedom and equality were somehow antithetical to capitalism, and that socialism was an 'extension' of liberalism. In reality, as Marx indicated, these concepts in their juridical expression, were ground into the very fabric of market exchanges in which labour was a commodity, and which masked capitalist exploitation and domination.[46] Liberal democracy embodied the legal and political freedom and equality of capitalist production relations. The liberal (capitalist) state had to be viewed as an active agent in the resultant class struggle that these relations engendered. A monopoly of force was required to maintain production relations that derived from surplus labour extraction. Socialism and liberalism as a 'system of ideas' could only be conflated by voiding them of their social content.[47]

Wood concluded that Macpherson's failure to portray liberalism and the capitalist state in this light stemmed from the 'abstract formalism' of Anglo-American political philosophy. This approach to political philosophy, she stated in a later piece in response to Panitch's critique, was a reflection of the divorce between the economic and the political in liberal democratic, capitalist societies. Thus the 'concepts of "freedom", "equality" and "justice" are subjected to intricately formalistic analysis deliberately divorced from social implications.'[48] Political science was similarly compartmentalised, because political behaviour was devoid of social content. As a result his strategy was profoundly elitist, relying on the 'persuasive propositions' of ethical liberalism rather than explanation. This kind of elitism implied that socialism was 'a gift from a segment of the "educated" ruling class' and a rejection the central role of class struggle in bringing it about.[49] Thus, Macpherson's 'very choice of project and method rests on certain fundamental attitudes he shares with his liberal adversaries'.[50] Nevertheless, although Wood in her earlier piece had criticised Macpherson's form of argument and intellectual strategy as conceding too much to liberalism, she demonstrated handsomely the extent to which Marxists could learn from liberalism in ensuring that the state was subordinated to society under socialism in order to protect the individual.[51]

Other Marxist critics of Macpherson, however, were more even handed in their judgement of Macpherson. Panitch sensitively defended him against Wood's main charges. He demonstrated just how much Macpherson owed to Marxism, especially his concept of the net transfer of powers as well as his theory of class and the state. He also indicated that she failed to appreciate how Macpherson used Marxism to demonstrate how liberalism failed to live up to its own promise, how the equilibrium model of democracy formulated by Schumpeter and Dahl failed in its own terms and how liberal democracy blunted the class struggle.[52] Yet he agreed with Wood that Macpherson's strategy, if he had one, was Fabian, in its attempt to educate the ruling class into socialism,[53], entailing the abandonment of Marx's concept of class struggle in the transition to socialism.[54] He also agreed with her that certain liberal values and practices were essential to safeguard the individual from the state in a socialist society.[55] But his main charge was that Macpherson had failed in his 'responsibility' to develop Marxism. His attitude towards Marxist political theory was defensive and uncritical in relation to the transition between capitalism and socialism, revealed both in his discussion of the Soviet Union and the Third World.[56] Panitch held that Marxist theory and practice was snagged by a tension between the need to protect itself from internal and external forces of counter-revolution ('discipline') and to extend democracy ('consent').[57] Although Macpherson was aware of this problem he made little attempt to solve it, oscillating between a rigid economic determinism and extreme voluntarism. He swung between explaining Soviet authoritarianism in terms of material scarcity, capitalist encirclement and its revolutionary origins on the one hand, and the naive faith in a revolutionary vanguard party committed to political freedom in a transitional situation, irrespective of circumstances, on the other.[58] Here, he quoted Macpherson: 'Where there's a will, there's a way.'[59] He also took the humanistic aims of the leaders of the newly emerging African one-party states at face value. Unfortunately, when he discussed his own ideal of participatory democracy, the problem of the tension between 'discipline' and 'consent' in Marxist theory was not adequately addressed. He did not discuss the internal organisation of political parties in the pre-revolutionary period, their relation to the working class and presumably how they would promote his desired liberal democratic ethic. Nevertheless, Panitch was far more tolerant of Macpherson's weaknesses than Wood. He attempted to explain his defensiveness towards Marxism: the absence of a vibrant Marxist intellectual community and well developed socialist movement in Canada, coupled with the notion, in the period of the Cold War, that a critique of 'official' Soviet Marxism would be construed as 'anti-Soviet' and reactionary.[60] And the kind of critical revision contemplated would be an enormous one for any individual to undertake.

Svacek was perhaps Macpherson's most sympathetic Marxist critic. He showed in extensive detail the magnitude of Macpherson's Marxist affinity. His ethical postulate of equal development, class analysis, materialist epistemology and theory of history based upon changing forces and relations of production were all Marxist in inspiration. He was 'in' the Marxist tradition, but not 'of' it, in effect 'five-sixths' a Marxist.[61] The missing sixth consisted of not having a Marxist theory of transition, particularly the acceptance of revolutionary violence. He was 'not able to accept the ultimate historical act of coercion proclaimed by all in the Marxist tradition who yet accept the theory of revolution.'[62] This was because he endorsed the liberal theory of negative liberty, that is the absence of restraint. And even in a communist society, 'violence would always be a legitimate recourse to mediate anti-social behaviour.'[63]

Macpherson's Marxist critics therefore varied in their objections to his project. Levine and Wood impugned it outright because his political strategy seemed to consist of winning over liberals (academics) to socialism rather than fostering proletarian revolution. This defect they attributed to his theoretical postulates which were fundamentally liberal. Panitch and Svacek, while more sympathetic and less dismissive of the Marxist elements in his project, both saw a fundamental fault: he had no adequate theory of transition, either due to historical circumstances (Panitch) or his lingering liberalism (Svacek).

– Macpherson's reply and commentary –

He replied to Levine and Svacek. In response to Levine he contended that he did not assume that the abolition of private property would automatically eliminate extractive powers, merely that such an abolition was a necessary if not sufficient condition.[64] And he denied that he had adopted an untenable Proudhonist stance towards liberalism, separating its 'good' side from its 'bad' side owing to its political and economic conceptual unity. The burden of his whole argument had been to demonstrate that this unity no longer existed in the late twentieth century.[65] He also rejected Levine's accusation that he merely wanted to reform capitalism. He had insisted that extractive power was inherent in capitalism, and that equal individual self-development was only possible if abolished.[66] In replying to Svacek's criticism that he had a deficient, that is non-Marxist, view of revolutionary transition because he eschewed violence, he implied that the position was complicated. Even Marx had noted that 'circumstances alter cases.'[67] And in the present circumstances, one third of the world was Communist, the Third World was trying many experiments and 'the ability of the remaining capitalist economies to avoid breakdown is increasingly precarious'.[68] Moreover, there had been a decline in class consciousness in the affluent countries. Nevertheless, if this was reversed, as Marx suggested in the *Grundrisse*, a future proletariat would be a 'transformed class, more confident, more leisured, and perhaps more able to take over without destruction'.[69] He also stated that the kind of empirical study required to estimate accurately the possibilities of transition was not his '*métier*'.

To evaluate the force of his critics' arguments: many of Levine's criticisms, as Macpherson demonstrated in his reply, were misplaced, and revealed a lack of understanding of his work, although the strategic weakness remained. Wood's critique of Macpherson, focusing as it did on *LTLD* also seemed to reveal a lack of understanding of Macpherson's work as Panitch's response showed. And the extent of Macpherson's indebtedness to Marxism should have been clear in the light of Svacek's article and his reply to it, published two years previously. Macpherson's kinship with Marxism needs stressing. First, the principles and goals of his ideal society of free and equal interdependent development was Marxist as much as Millian, and in effect probably more so, whatever his declared Millian affiliation. Indeed, he saw his notion of human essence going back to Aristotle,[70] and Marx could be said to build in an egalitarian way on Aristotle (technology had replaced the slaves) and on the notion that the full development of individuality required the cooperation of others. Second, his view of history was broadly Marxist, if in a slightly 'productivist' sense. It was also so teleologically: the good society was only possible given certain conditions (abundance) which were being created by capitalism, although both saw the 'real' and the 'good' coalescing only through conscious human agency. Third, his analysis of capitalism was Marxist, along with his view of class and state. Fourth, his epistemology was Marxist: his analysis of the liberal tradition and of political philosophies generally was materialist in a non-deterministic way. Fifth, his method of immanent critique was classically Marxist, in focusing on the contradictions contained in the liberal tradition, especially between its utilitarian and developmental ontologies, and between the declarations of liberal democratic societies and their deeds. This method avoided the problem of having to rely heavily on utopian thinking, in demonstrating the superiority of one set of ideals over another. However, a visible difference with Marxism remained, namely over the revolutionary potential of the working class.[71]

Wood, however, raised some important issues. First, while Macpherson was not guilty of the charge of abstract, socially contentless philosophising, there is the question which she poses of whether such philosophising in the Anglo-American genre plays into the hands of the liberal 'enemy'. Although Marx also rubbished this kind of philosophising in the *Communist Manifesto*, there is, however, the danger of succumbing to *ad hominem* argument, of linking ways of thinking with class interests and thereby delegitimating them if these interests are deemed less than universal. This indeed is Wood's attitude towards liberalism: it is functional to capitalism. Contra Macpherson, she argued, it does not stand in a contingent relation to capitalism and can only be 'extended' into socialism through evacuating its social content. Macpherson's point was that the possessive individualist side of liberalism, as a '*system of ideas*' (Wood), as an ideology which espoused freedom and equality, was indeed functional to capitalism. But contained within the liberal *philosophical* tradition, as developed by Mill and Green, whose concept of human essence was derived from the 'pre-liberal (or pre-market) Western tradition',[72] was something more humanist. This ontology could be used to wean liberals away from possessive individualism. His point was that there existed an inherent contradiction between this noble liberal end and the capitalist market means. Far from being unaware of the social content of liberal political philosophy, he was indicating what kind of society was necessary to realise Mill's ideals. Central to Macpherson's project was the demonstration that abstract liberal philosophy *did* have a social content, not merely in legitimating capitalist production relations, but also in containing a contradiction between possessive and ethical sides, which could only be solved if invested with a new social content. That Macpherson could be interpreted as a liberal or as conceding too much to liberalism was, however, partly the product of his method of immanent critique, leaving him open to misinterpretation. This approach meant that Macpherson did not have to declare his socialist affinity, but say that he was merely being a consistent liberal. Broadly speaking Macpherson was arguing that socialism was an extension of a *kind* of liberalism. Even if this was so only in a presentational sense, strictly speaking his argument relied heavily on stipulative definition, describing Mill as a liberal and therefore defining his own ontology as liberal. Yet *in reality* Macpherson rejected the Millian distinction between higher and lower pleasures and refused to prioritise capacities, discussing them in terms of exertion, enjoyment and development, including laughter, playing sport and so on.[73] For Macpherson, pushpin was as good as poetry in so far as both were expressions of non-destructive human potentials. Thus he was ontologically closer to Marx than Mill, and in reality conceded little to the liberal 'enemy', except in so far as this 'enemy' had values in common with Marxism.

The value of Macpherson's intellectual strategy of engaging the 'enemy' on its own ground can be defended in another way. The power of ideas in the past two decades has been clearly evident in the neoliberal new right's rapid global ascendency. Merely to expose neoliberalism as a capitalist weapon in the class struggle without showing its intellectual weaknesses, of engaging it on its own ground, is politically disabling. While it is important to demystify ideas both by explaining their origins and revealing their implications (which Macpherson did in relation to liberalism in its possessive individualist mode), this should not rule out the need to demonstrate the incoherence or implausibility of these ideas. This, of course, is contained in the Marxist notion of 'critique'. Obviously, if this was regarded as the *only* strategy to defeat the new right, then Wood would certainly have a point. But the principles and theoretical agenda determining how a socialist intellectual should operate cannot have lapidary status. As Panitch indicated Macpherson's strategic stance was historically explicable. And it was somewhat detached from the class struggle, from a Marxist practice. Similarly, today's socialist intellectuals write for and argue with their academic peers for many contingent reasons (including the general downturn in the class struggle in the West and anti-intellectualist, dogmatic nature of Marxist groups). The strategic choices made by socialist intellectuals are dependent upon time and circumstance. And given the milieu in which Macpherson was operating, to subvert liberalism through immanent critique rather than rely heavily on arguments for an alternative socialist value system was understandable. This form of critique made it easier for him to engage with that milieu than declare himself a socialist and thus be written off on account of having an alien belief system. This of course is not not imply that Macpherson's liberal commitment was wholly strategic, merely that to convince the 'world' of your ideas means knowing where the 'world' is 'at'. That Wood, developing in a different political and intellectual environment which was more radical, should have found this strategy as conceding too much to the 'enemy' is also understandable. Nevertheless, his liberal critics certainly did not welcome his attentions, and he made no concessions to their criticisms. Liberals never saw him as one of their own and, as we saw in Chapter 1, he withstood the flattery of Berlin only to deliver one of the most damaging assaults on his theory of liberty, now largely ignored. The extent of Macpherson's commitment to a large variety of Marxist concepts should not be underestimated.

In fact, his two other Marxist critics, Panitch and Svacek, did not underestimate Macpherson's Marxist affinity. Panitch charged him with being too defensive about Marxism, and not taking 'responsibility' for developing it through a process of criticism.[74] In particular, Panitch claimed, apart from the question of transition, this meant that he oscillated between voluntarism and determinism, ending up as an apologist for the Soviet Union. While Macpherson had a problem with vanguardism, which will be discussed presently, whether this could be attributed to a difficulty in integrating determinism and voluntarism is another matter. True, in formal Marxist terms, following the third of Marx's *Theses on Feuerbach*, this can only be done through 'praxis', but generally, Macpherson was sensitive to both circumstances shaping ideas, and ideas shaping circumstances, and the quotation used by Panitch 'where there's a will, there's a way', if seen within the context of his argument against Friedman, does not show him lurching to the 'extreme of sheer voluntarism'.[75] His point against Friedman, who claimed that socialism *necessarily* denied political freedom because there would be no competitive labour market, was that this was, first, a question of whether a socialist state could *ever* have the 'will' to guarantee political freedom, and secondly, as Panitch himself quotes, of the 'circumstantial forces' shaping that will.[76] Thus, there is hardly any oscillation between 'extremes'. Panitch rightly poses the coercion/consent problem for Marxist theory and practice, and Macpherson certainly did not deal with it, or with the question of the internal organisation of vanguards, except to say that he favoured democratically organised ones. Nevertheless, as Macpherson stated, conditions are an important consideration in shaping the policies and behaviour of vanguards, but more than this, there is the question of the ideology of the vanguard. However democratic internally a vanguard might be, if its ideology is based upon the 'certainty' of history, then rival 'vanguards' are thereby delegitimated. Macpherson, if only in part dealing with this problem, suggested that in a socialist society there should not be a 'ubiquitous party' and that civil and political liberties had to be recognised.[77] And in *LTLD* his model of participatory democracy included inter-party competition.[78] Perhaps a better way of highlighting Macpherson's difficulty was not that he was too defensive of Marxism, but of the Soviet Union. Although the context in which Macpherson wrote may help explain this defensiveness, he did not subject the Soviet system to the same kind of immanent critique as he did the liberal democracies of the West. To do so might have suggested that there was some form of class state or class conflict existing within this system, rendering the realisation of the official ideology inherently problematic.

Turning to Svacek's criticism, that he did not have a theory of transition, Macpherson correctly replied that transitions were condition-dependent, and he did not hold to a theory of negative liberty, as Svacek suggested, that ruled out violence *tout court*. The extent to which force was used depended upon political, economic and social conditions. He could understand why force was used in the Soviet Union and elsewhere, but as already indicated in his reply to Svacek, in the future with a confident and leisured workforce this may not have to occur. However, can he be absolved from the charge of having adopted a Fabian style strategy in trying to persuade liberals to embrace socialism? At one level he cannot: that seemed to be the purpose of his immanent critique of liberalism, and he appealed to 'leaders in the West' to support or initiate a 'fundamental change in the liberal-democratic justifying theory'.[79] On the other hand he could see a transition in a more mass revolutionary way with 'a partial breakdown of the political order (national or international) of the market society' and a 'partial breakthrough of consciousness'.[80] And in *LTLD* he discussed the possibilities of a reaction against the 'concentration of corporate power to dominate our neighbourhoods, our jobs, our security, and the quality of life at work and at home', helping to establish his model of participatory democracy.[81] Macpherson, then, did not have a comprehensive and clear strategy for attaining the 'good' society. And as already noted, he had his doubts about the possibility of proletarian revolution owing to the decline of class consciousness in the West.[82] And as Wood noted, he used Marx's theory of exploitation, as interpreted as net transfers of power, not as explanatory theory of change through class struggle, but as an ethical theory, to demonstrate that one could not be committed to the Millian ideal of self-development and be simultaneously committed to the capitalist market. Yet against his Marxist critics he was on more solid empirical ground in questioning the hegemonic role of the proletariat as conceived in the classic Marxist texts. In a sense he could claim that in being open minded about precise strategy he was closer to Marx than some of the latter's followers would care to admit in declaring that it had to be condition-dependent (in reply to Svacek). Furthermore, it is one thing not to have *a* theory of transition (which he did not), and it is another to have a *good* theory, which is plausible, practical, consistent and genuinely emancipatory (which his critics did not, and who does?).

However, although his writings manifested much anti-elitism, certain kinds of elitist apologetics, as we have seen, crept in. For example, he talked about the need for 'moral regeneration' by vanguards in the Second and Third Worlds, and strategically in the First World he appealed to political elites to exercise 'moral leadership'. Why this inconsistency? It was probably attributable to a variety of factors: on the one hand, the lack of a mass progressive movement in the West visibly bringing about social change, the kind of teleological, scientific Marxism which was available to him in his formative years, his notion of the 'enlightening' role of the scholar and maybe an unconscious Millian elitism; and on the other hand, a strong liberal commitment to individual autonomy, which he might have seen at the heart of an 'ethical'

Marxism. More specifically, his inconsistent attitude towards the First World on the one hand and the Second and Third Worlds on the other which legitimated vanguardism can be explained in at least three ways. First, as a good 'Marxist' he chose not to fetishise the form of transition. Some might be more vanguardist in form than others, depending upon circumstance. As we have seen, whatever form it took, the ultimate ethical objective had to be the same: the maximisation of humanity's various powers. Secondly, in his desire to shake the faith of Westerners in their belief in the superiority of Western democracy, and encourage a far more tolerant and respectful attitude towards the political and economic systems of the Second and Third Worlds, he argued that the ethical objectives of these three worlds were similar. Thirdly, and related to this, was his distinction between democracy as a (procedural) means and as a (substantive) end in *RWD* and *DT*, and his separation of both in order to put the 'democracy' of the East and South on an equal footing with the West. This meant that he did not see them as organically related in these texts, although in his last work he patently did.[83]

All this may of course explain the tensions in his work, but it does not explain them away. How are values of freedom and democracy to be defined and realised? Through individual autonomy, or participatory democracy, or by intellectuals such as Macpherson? Some kind of argument can be developed that these are necessary tensions for anyone committed to the idea of genuine human freedom for all citizens within a society. These tensions do not have to be mutually destructive, but invite problems to be overcome rather than an allegiance to a particular way of defining and realising such values. The interrelation between these different ways of defining and realising the values of freedom and democracy can be demonstrated by showing that individual freedom for all members in a society requires a democratic context (a necessary but not sufficient condition) in order to ensure reciprocal freedom. Some form of 'enlightenment' about the meaning and conditions of freedom may also be necessary as part of a democratic 'praxis'. Further, a stable democracy is ultimately conditional upon a commitment to some kind of individual autonomy, enabling individuals to freely and effectively express their views and mobilise others. Even if Macpherson was not completely successful in resolving these tensions, perhaps any meaningful notion of individual freedom conceived in societal form has to accept the need to work at a number of different interrelated levels.

— FEMINIST CRITICISM —

Macpherson's project was also subject to feminist criticism, especially by Virginia Held. First of all, although he recognised the existence of internal impediments to freedom Macpherson concentrated on external ones. Yet, she argued, internal impediments were often particular to women, and more significant for them rather than men. For example, women suffered more than men from the problem of shame, which led to a sense of inadequacy and therefore inner disempowerment.[84] Secondly, his concept of net transfer of powers was unduly narrow. In relation to human reproduction and sexual satisfaction, women have routinely given more affection than men. Macpherson did not 'contribute to our understanding of how transforming gender relations may be a project as fundamental as ... transforming relations between the owners of capital and those who must sell their labour.'[85] Thirdly, his individualism meant that the concept of self-development was seen in terms of the individual. In other words self-development was not intimately tied to the development of other persons, that is the development of that *relation* with another person. Rather, he conceived of such relations in an instrumental fashion, as beneficial to the individual.[86] He failed to appreciate the value of 'shared, relational activity in itself'.[87] Thus, Macpherson's democratic theory did not include the development of social relations of trust, care and concern, of 'mutually appreciated expression, of shared enjoyment'.[88]

– *Commentary* –

For sure, Macpherson did not devote much time to the feminist agenda and his terminology in referring to 'man' for the whole of the human race was old fashioned. Nevertheless, he was sympathetic to the 'new social movements' of the 1960s of Blacks and students, who were seeking to empower themselves,[89] and to neighbourhood and community movements in the 1970s;[90] later he employed more gender sensitive vocabulary,[91] and in the 1980s he explicitly supported the women's and the ecology movements. He admonished fellow academics who failed to understand these 'post materialist', new phenomena because they still started 'from the maximising atomic individual'.[92] However, the question is whether Macpherson's democratic theory was in principle anti-feminist. This was not so. Against Held's complaint that he ignored the importance of relationships, as already indicated he willingly embraced the communitarians' relational sensibilities and saw people developing through and with others. In other words, there was a concern for sustaining relationships that would promote this process. True, ultimately the test of these relationships was the extent to which people were able to exert, enjoy and develop their powers within them, but there is no reason to suppose that individual/relationship has to be viewed as a dichotomy. And the danger with the way Held poses the argument is the assumption that a relationship might be more important that the 'exertial' and developmental needs of individuals within that relationship. Furthermore, as Lindsay indicates, his list of human powers included the relationship oriented ones of love and friendship.[93] On the question of internal impediments, such as shame, Macpherson did not give them great prominence, but as already indicated, from his viewpoint this could be explained in terms of intellectual strategy. He noted their existence, but gave priority to external impediments partly because he saw internal impediments as externally generated. Thus he could have acknowledged the significance of shame as an impediment, but that it had an external source, for example as part of a system maintaining patriarchal power relations.

This brings us to the question of whether Macpherson's concept of transfer of powers necessarily concealed exploitative relations between the sexes, as Held suggests. His ethic of equal human flourishing would certainly have disposed him towards opposing exploitative relations between the sexes, and as suggested he was sympathetic to feminist concerns. He could also reply that capitalism uses patriarchy in order to maximise the net transfer of powers, either in terms of creating divisions in the workforce, or using women as unpaid domestic labour, or systematically underpaying women. Further, although patriarchy can be seen as separate from capitalism and class relations, the latter can have a major impact on the depth of women's oppression, commodifying women and disempowering men who then proceed to attempt to disempower women. Capitalism thus either serves directly or indirectly to limit women's effective autonomy more than men's. Therefore, the transcending of capitalist, class relations could be seen as one vital element in women's emancipation. Although all this does not to absolve him from the charge that he failed address the feminist agenda seriously, there is nothing to suggest that his theoretical framework is incompatible with a certain kind of socialist feminism.

— CONCLUSION —

Communitarian, Marxist and feminist criticisms in many respects under-estimated the strength of Macpherson's position by attempting to saddle him with a spurious abstract individualism. Like many critics considered in the previous chapter, these critics often did not read him closely. Thus, they ignored his Aristotelian social ontology as well as his Marxist influenced possessive individualist thesis, which criticised liberalism's abstract individu-alism for 'ontologising' market 'man'. Unsurprisingly after these criticisms he emphasised his Marxist and communitarian credentials, and was also poten-tially receptive to feminist criticism because he opposed all social relations that stymied the equal exercise and development of human capacities. Hence his support for struggles against gender, as well as racial, oppression should not be seen as surprising. Nevertheless, because individuality was the name of

Macpherson's game, he would have opposed any idea that individual needs ought to be subordinated to any larger collective or 'relational' whole which did not in some way make for the greater satisfaction of these needs. He made his commitment to the Millian (or Humboldtian) idea of human flourishing loud and clear.[94] Yet this flourishing necessarily had to occur within a social context, hence his acceptance of MacIntyre's description of his project as a 'cooperative and creative individualism'.

Macpherson was engaged in a difficult balancing act in seeking to integrate what he saw as the best in liberalism and Marxism in order to 'retrieve' a humanistic democratic theory. Given the nature of capitalist modernity, in which market imperatives either determine or constrain individual choice and confront the individual with the unrealistic ideal of individual autonomy, such a synthesis can be regarded as essential in answering theoretically and practically the question of what it means to be human in the twenty-first century. And his synthesis did not leave what he took to be the basic liberal and Marxist ontological and ethical postulates untouched, the implication of either his liberal critics on the one hand, or his communitarian and Marxist critics on the other. He teased out the ethical implications of a 'scientific' Marxism, owing to his liberal, Millian (and Aristotelian) sensibilities, and brought to this liberalism a societal and historical awareness (as well as an explicit egalitarianism) found in this Marxism.

– NOTES

1. A. MacIntyre, 'On Democratic Theory: Essays in Retrieval by C. B. Macpherson', *Canadian Journal of Philosophy*, 6/2, 1976, p. 179.
2. S. Lukes, 'The Real and Ideal Worlds of Democracy', in A. Kontos (ed.), *Powers, Possessions and Freedom* (Toronto: University of Toronto Press, 1979), quoted p. 151.
3. Ibid., p. 149.
4. Ibid., p. 147.
5. Ibid., p. 146.
6. Ibid., pp. 145–6, p. 149, reference to *DT*, p. 57.
7. Ibid., p. 150.
8. Ibid., p. 151. See also K. R. Minogue, 'Humanist Democracy': The Political Thought of C. B. Macpherson', *Canadian Journal of Political Science*, 9/3, 1976, p. 380, pp. 386–7.
9. B. Parekh, *Contemporary Political Thinkers* (Oxford: Martin Robertson, 1982), p. 70.
10. Ibid., p. 60.
11. Ibid., pp. 71–2.
12. Ibid., p. 72.

13. Ibid., pp. 72-3.
14. C. B. Macpherson, 'Individualist Socialism? A Reply to Levine and MacIntyre', *Canadian Journal of Philosophy*, 6/2, 1976, p. 198.
15. *DT*, p. 57.
16. Ibid., p. 199.
17. Ibid., p. 199.
18. Macpherson Papers, 8 January 1980, p. 2.
19. *DT*, p. 5, p. 32.
20. This exaggeration could even extend as far as ignoring the significance of his response to MacIntyre, although they had read it, in the case of Lukes and Parekh.
21. *LTLD*, p. 99.
22. For example, *RFEJ*, pp. 50-1.
23. Macpherson, 'Individualist Socialism?', p. 199.
24. Parekh, *Contemporary Thinkers*, p. 72.
25. *DT*, p. 56.
26. Lukes, 'The Real and Ideal Worlds of Democracy', p. 149, reference to *DT*, p. 76.
27. Ibid., p. 150.
28. Parekh, *Contemporary Thinkers*, p. 70.
29. *DT*, p. 4.
30. *DT*, p. 54.
31. *DT*, p. 54. See also C. G. Gould, *Rethinking Democracy: Freedom and Cooperation in Politics, Economy and Society* (Cambridge: Cambridge University Press, 1988), pp. 72-8.
32. This idea is not unproblematic. See F. Cunningham, *Democratic Theory and Socialism* (Cambridge: Cambridge University Press, 1987), pp. 182-3. Perhaps the issue is really about how freedom is maximised in a society, which inevitably involves some kind of interference with individual autonomy.
33. *DT*, p. 54.
34. Macpherson Papers, 8 January 1980, p 1. See also Macpherson, 'Needs and Wants: an Ontological or Historical Problem?' in R. Fitzerald (ed.), *Human Needs and Politics* (Rushcutters Bay, Australia: Pergamon, 1977), p. 34.
35. *RFEJ*, p. 23.
36. F. L. Bender (ed.), K. Marx, *The Communist Manifesto* (New York: Norton, 1988), p. 75. Marx's affinity with Mill can be seen in Marx's claim that the object of political economy ought to be the 'free development of individualities'; *Grundrisse*, tr. M. Nicolaus (Harmondsworth: Penguin, 1973) p. 706. And he saw the 'development of human powers as an end in itself'; *Capital*, tr. D. Fernbach, (Harmondsworth: Penguin, 1981), vol. 3, p. 959.
37. A. Levine, 'The Political Theory of Social Democracy', *Canadian Journal of Philosophy*, 6/2, 1976, p. 191.
38. Ibid., p. 191.
39. Ibid., p. 192.

40. Ibid., pp. 187–8, referring to *DT*, p. 22. In a later piece Levine reasserted these objections, but slightly shifted the emphasis, so that although he acknowledged that Macpherson had effected a radical break with the liberal tradition, he still endorsed its practice, especially because he did not accept the constitutive role of class struggle in transition to socialism, or embrace a class view of the state. A. Levine, *Liberal Democracy* (New York: Columbia University Press, 1981), pp. 197–9.

41. E. Wood, 'C. B. Macpherson: Liberalism, and the Task of Socialist Political Theory', in R. Miliband and J. Saville (eds), *The Socialist Register* (London: Merlin Press, 1978), p. 217.

42. Ibid., p. 222.

43. She did later, however, concede that he did adopt something like a Marxist theory of exploitation in his concept of the transfer of powers, but she insisted that it remained an ethical concept, rather than perceived as the motor of the class struggle. E. Wood, 'Liberal Democracy and Capitalist Hegemony: A Reply to Leo Panitch on the Task of Socialist Political Theory', in Miliband and Saville, *The Socialist Register* (London: Merlin Press, 1981), p. 174.

44. 'C. B. Macpherson ...', p. 226.

45. Ibid., p. 231.

46. Ibid., p. 228.

47. Ibid., p. 231.

48. Wood, 'Liberal Democracy and Capitalist Hegemony', p. 181.

49. Ibid., pp. 173–4.

50. Ibid., p. 173.

51. 'C. B. Macpherson ...', pp. 231–7.

52. L. Panitch, 'Liberal Democracy and Socialist Democracy: The Antinomies of C. B. Macpherson', in Miliband and Saville, *The Socialist Register* (London: Merlin Press, 1981), pp. 145–50.

53. Ibid., p. 164.

54. Ibid., p. 160.

55. Ibid., p. 163.

56. See also M. A. Weinstein, 'C. B. Macpherson', in A. De Crespigny and K. Minogue (eds), *Contemporary Political Philosophers* (New York: Dodd, Mead, 1975), p. 268, and Lukes, 'The Real and Ideal Worlds of Democracy', p. 144, who both noted Macpherson's seemingly inconsistent treatment of these Worlds, especially his support for vanguardism in the Second and Third Worlds and his commitment to democratic change in the First.

57. Ibid., pp. 155–7.

58. Ibid., p. 159.

59. *DT*, p. 151.

60. Ibid., p. 164.

61. V. Svacek, 'The Elusive Marxism of C. B. Macpherson', *Canadian Journal of Political Science*, 9/3, 1976, p. 419.

62. Ibid., p. 421.

63. Ibid., p. 422.
64. Macpherson, 'Individualist Socialism?', p. 196.
65. Ibid., p. 197.
66. Ibid., p. 198.
67. Macpherson, 'Humanist Democracy and Elusive Marxism', *Canadian Journal of Political Science*, 9/3, 1976, p. 425.
68. Ibid.
69. Ibid.
70. *DT*, p. 56.
71. For example, Interview, 'C. B. Macpherson on Marx', in F. Cunningham, *The Real World of Democracy Revisited* (Atlantic Highlands, NJ: Humanities Press, 1994), p. 15.
72. *DT*, p. 8.
73. Ibid., p. 54.
74. There appears to be a slight problem in Panitch's argument in that he notes that intellectuals associated with Marxism have used it in two ways, either as part of a revolutionary socialist movement or as a resource to achieve broadly, but not necessarily Marxist, progressive aims: 'Liberal Democracy and Socialist Democracy', pp. 144-5. Since he locates Macpherson in the second category, he can hardly be regarded as culpable of not taking 'responsibility' for developing Marxism when it was not his intention to do so in the first place.
75. Ibid., p. 159.
76. *DT*, p. 153.
77. Ibid., p. 153.
78. *LTLD*, pp. 112–13.
79. *DT*, p. 22.
80. Ibid., p. 76, p. 140.
81. *LTLD*, p. 103.
82. See also ibid., p. 101.
83. *RFEJ*, p. 53.
84. V. Held, 'Freedom and Feminism', in J. Carens (ed.), *Democracy and Possessive Individualism: The Intellectual Legacy of C. B. Macpherson* (New York: State University of New York Press, 1993), p. 141.
85. Ibid., p. 144.
86. Ibid., pp. 147–9.
87. Ibid., p. 149.
88. Ibid., p. 148.
89. *DT*, p. 50.
90. *LTLD*, p. 103.
91. *RFEJ*, p. 27.
92. Ibid., p. 49.
93. P. Lindsay, *Creative Individualism: The Democratic Vision of C. B. Macpherson* (New York: State University of New York Press, 1998), p. 33. See also, *DT*, pp. 53–4.
94. See, for example, his letter to Lukes, Macpherson Papers, 8 January 80, p. 2.

CHAPTER 6

RETRIEVING MACPHERSON

The previous chapters have evaluated critical commentaries on Macpherson's work showing where they were misguided or posed arguments that could either be plausibly rebutted or led to the need for some kind of reformulation. While this account of intellectual jousting has hopefully been interesting and informative, the question still remains: why bother? This chapter will attempt to show the continuing relevance of his project. Figuratively, this will involve doing a 'Macpherson' on Macpherson. That is to say, his thought will be 'retrieved' in order to focus a critical spotlight on the various current schools of thought which criticised him. Such an act of 'retrieval' is not meant to imply that the world of ideas in many ways has not moved on – and with good reason – since Macpherson's death in 1987: the whole area of so-called 'identity' politics to name but one.[1] Nor does it mean that no contemporary thinkers have, albeit critically, 'retrieved' him in the sense of explicitly acknowledging his influence on their own thought.[2] Nor does it mean that his project can be uncritically be restated, as though to remind us that the wheel had been invented. A 'retrieval' does not simply entail a 'return' to Macpherson. Indeed, there are parts of his project that look dated: his attitude towards 'Second World' and 'Third World' states in the 1960s, and his optimism about the world moving in a socialist direction with an abandonment of possessive individualism deriving from an historical teleology. No: the claim is that his project, if slightly amended, is an important reminder of certain traditions of political thought that have useful things to say about what the world is and where it ought to go. At the very least Macpherson's concerns should not be forgotten, because we still live in a capitalist democracy, even more obviously so than in Macpherson's day, and if political philosophy is to be relevant it should start from that premise. Of equal significance, his project with substantive human flourishing at its centre is a healthy counterpoint to the obsessive proceduralism that implicitly or explicitly underlies much contemporary democratic theory. This chapter is devoted to making good the claim that his thought still has resonance by pointing to some inadequacies of modern approaches to political thought from a Macphersonian standpoint. His relevance for Marxism, feminism and for the study of politics generally will be briefly explored. Then his significance for contemporary political philosophy will be highlighted.

Let us first of all remind ourselves of Macpherson's approach and purpose in order to see clearly how his project provides the ground for a critical analysis of contemporary shortcomings. His project, with the property/democracy relation at its core, was above all a critique of the theory and practice of liberal, capitalist democracy. Methodologically, it embodied positive and normative concerns, combining the 'is' and the 'ought'. Knowledge of the world was vital to the emancipatory ethic, and the pursuit of knowedge had to be in the name of human flourishing. This meant that he was as much concerned to criticise supposedly value-free political scientists who disregarded normative issues as he was to castigate political philosophers for being empirically illiterate. At the same time his project was deeply historical: he urged political scientists and philosophers to have some sense of history; in order to understand the present and future the past had to be understood; not only did past thinkers possess wisdom to be reappropriated, but they also shaped the ruling, liberal ideology of the present. He also wanted contemporary political scientists and philosophers to become sociologically aware, to understand the extent to which their own working assumptions unconsciously involved an 'ontologising' process, thereby unwittingly legitimating production and political relations of exploitation and domination. Substantively, his project involved a critique of liberal democratic political institutions, which were built on social inequality. They fostered political apathy amongst the lower orders and promoted a centrist type of politics, thereby concealing class cleavages. Furthermore, electability was in part determined by the prospect of success in managing economic growth. In essence, liberal democracy was capitalist democracy, and democratic possibility was thus severely restricted. Macpherson, however, devoted most of his time to teasing out the possessive individualist assumptions in liberal democratic theory and recasting it in a way that would make it an instrument of human flourishing rather than of class domination. As we have seen this entailed an immanent critique of liberal democratic theory, as well as offering a tentative, so-called 'perfectionist' account of human well-being. In so far as liberal democratic theory was committed to the capitalist market, it was equally committed to a net transfer of human powers to capital. The liberal developmental vision of Mill (and Marx's socialist version) could only be achieved by the abolition of such a market.

His significance for Marxism has to do with the fact that he was, as he himself declared, only 'five-sixths' a Marxist. He was not a 'Talmudic' Marxist.

Rather, he used Marxism, as Laski and other prewar British progressives had done, as an intellectual resource. His creative engagement with Marxism enabled him to develop his concept of possessive individualism, to look at the type of individual psyche generated and sustained by the capitalist market. Marxism also provided the basis of his sociologically and ethically grounded Millian ontology. The self-exerting and developing individual could only fully develop in a classless society, in which no net transfer of powers occurred. Moreover, while he seemed to rely on Mill for his ethical perspective in many respects he was in reality closer to Marx: he did not prioritise mental 'utilities' over bodily ones, and he stressed the interdependence of human beings, for individual needs could be met only through cooperative activity. In effect, he brought out the ethical dimension in Marxism in a way that did not have to rely on whether Marx was ambiguous on the subject or not, which has recently exercised recent commentators.[3] And given that at the time when he began writing 'scientific' Marxism held sway, his ethical orientation in relation to Marxism proved prophetic. His introduction of Mill enabled his 'Marxism' to have an ethical inflection, as did his net transfer of powers hypothesis, which he contrasted with his 'ethical concept' of power, that is a potential 'for realizing some human end'.[4] Thus Macpherson's approach to Marxism enables us to move 'beyond' Marx and Marxism in a dialectical rather than a mechanical sense of rejection as implicitly advocated by many post-Marxists. Thus, the insights of Marx and Marxism do not have to be abandoned in the construction of an emancipatory ethic, but can be utilised in a creative way. While so-called 'analytical Marxists' have taken this route, many such as John Elster, John Roemer and Adam Przeworski rely on the micro-foundational approach of rational choice theory, rather reminiscent of Hobbes and common to the social sciences, thereby eschewing the holistic and 'ontologis-ing' insights characteristic of Marxism and Macpherson.[5] However, Macpherson would no doubt have applauded the call made by one of analytical Marxism's chief exponents that socialists 'must engage in more moral advocacy than used to be fashionable' in the absence of a proletarian revolution.[6]

As for Macpherson's relevance to feminism, as indicated in the previous chapter, effectively he had a close affinity with socialist feminism. Current feminist concerns are more cultural or more 'post-materialist' in orientation, and have done much to uncover the depth of patriarchy in many cultures. Even here parallels could be made with Macpherson's 'ontologising' method, which in this case privileges men or male values. More significantly, materialist explanations are important for understanding the rise of the feminist movements in terms of changing labour markets, labour-saving technologies in the home and improved contraception. And while capitalism may not always be directly responsible for oppressing women, or only indirectly through colluding with patriarchy, its abolition may be crucial as part of the solution. Without its abolition women have been unable to overcome the oppressive implications of human reproduction under capitalism, which has meant that women have made few inroads into 'public patriarchy', or that a high price has to be paid for the 'double shift'. The implication of this argument is that a majority of women may also have an interest in the eradication of the 'net transfer' of powers along with a majority of men, so that the benefits and burdens in society are not allocated by the morally blind forces of the capitalist market, but open to democratic scrutiny and control.

Macpherson's project also impinges on the study of politics in a general sense. He was a true representative of the Enlightenment, someone strongly committed to the belief that knowledge was vital in facilitating material and moral progress. He saw himself as a scholar, who had an obligation to contribute to this process. Secondly, he viewed the study of politics in a holistic way, disliking its bifurcation into normative and empirical spheres. Although he did not devote much time to the empirical study of politics, he consistently held, following Marx, that ethically principles had to be grounded upon reality. He was concerned with the question of why certain elements of liberal democratic theory could not be put into practice. Indeed, the implication of his project is that liberal democracy has the constant problem of legitimating itself, because it rests on an unstable, class-divided foundation. Normative and empirical questions, as he was never tired of repeating, were for him interlinked. Nevertheless, although a holistic approach to the study of politics was part of his research agenda, his significance lies much more in his treatment of normative issues, and it is his relationship with contemporary political philosophy to which we now turn.

– MACPHERSON AND CONTEMPORARY POLITICAL PHILOSOPHY –

This survey from a 'Macphersonian' perspective of contemporary Western political philosophy seeks to establish his continuing relevance. For obvious reasons, it is suggestive, not exhaustive. The hope is that such a survey will be sufficient to show that at least a case can be made for current political philosophy to acknowledge Macpherson's concerns, especially the problematic relation between human emancipation and capitalism. The areas covered will be liberalism and comunitarianism, and the theories of 'deliberative' and 'radical' democracy.

– Liberalism –

Although contemporary liberal philosophy is much more than Rawls, he is its central figure. And in many respects few liberals have gone beyond the

Rawlsian horizon in stressing the importance of individual autonomy within some sort of capitalist market context, whether of a welfare state or laissez-faire variety, which is proceduralist and 'anti-perfectionist'.[7] Accordingly, this section focuses mainly, but not exclusively on Rawlsian liberalism.

We do not have to speculate about what a Macphersonian critique of Rawls would look like, for Macpherson did in fact assess his work. Unfortunately, Rawls in *Political Liberalism*[8] did not respond to him or his Marxist-inspired critics, only to his so-called communitarian ones. Macpherson first criticised Rawls' account of justice in *DT* before his *A Theory of Justice* had been published (*TJ* hereafter).[9] Macpherson suggested that Rawls had difficulty in applying his two principles of justice in the context of capitalism. The first principle was that all citizens had 'an equal right to the most extensive liberty compatible with a like liberty for all'. The second, which referred to inequalities, was that they were arbitrary 'unless it is reasonable to expect that they will work out to everyone's advantage and provided that the positions and offices to which they attach or from which they may be gained are open to all'.[10] Macpherson, in keeping with his immanent critique of Millian liberalism, granted that his principles made 'very good sense' in a socialist society but were incompatible in a capitalist one.[11] In the former society, inequalities of income and wealth would not be the product of nor the 'means of an inequality of power', which in capitalist societies reaches 'to the liberties, rights, and essential humanity of the individuals in those classes'.[12] Rawls admitted that extreme concentrations of wealth could lead to inequalities of power, and that therefore they had to be limited. Yet he failed to note that even if such limits could be determined, the basic 'extractive' or exploitative power of capital, diminishing the developmental powers of workers, would remain. And in reality his two principles would be 'internally inconsistent'. To promote the first principle of equal liberty either a continuous process of income redistribution from the rich to the poor, or state interference with capital concentration would be required. This could be incongruent with the second principle, which assumes that incentives are needed for economic efficiency. Thus there would be no guarantee that the transfers and interferences entailed by the first principle would be consistent with the efficiency requirements of the second. The penetration of possessive individualism occurred in another way: his second principle assumed that the 'advantage' to be had from inequality referred to individuals as consumers and not as producers. He did not properly consider whether such consumption advantages would compensate for the disadvantages of not developing capacities for employees in a work situation subject to 'capitalist rationality'.[13]

Macpherson's second critique of Rawls, in his review of *A Theory of Justice*, again saw his work vitiated by market assumptions, overlooking the possibility of capitalism as an inherently exploitative system.[14] This meant that he could say that his principles of justice were equally applicable to capitalism and to socialism, without noting the qualitative – exploitation – distinction between them. Thus although he posited a socialist model with publicly owned means of production, workers' control of firms and public control over investment, it was merely a 'modification' of capitalism with firms still regulated by market forces, conducting themselves 'much as before'.[15] They cannot do so if such a system was socialist, because the drive to accumulate capital, that is exploit, would be absent. Perhaps Macpherson's more telling criticism here was his detection of an inconsistent ontology, when discussing his reformed capitalist model. On the one hand the realm of production relied on incentives, that is material maximising behaviour, which produced inequalities. On the other hand, he saw the resultant 'primary goods' as the basis to develop life plans and concepts of the good which were not bourgeois. Thus Rawls 'man' was reminiscent of T. H. Green's valuing individual liberty and yet accepting a class-divided society which created differential life prospects. And like Green, Rawls at the end of *TJ* postulated a harmonious society of non-conflicting ends, while building such a society on an economic model of competitive, market conflict which he saw as unavoidable. Both therefore endorsed the moral values of community and exploitative market relations. Such a critique was reminiscent of the early Marx's dismissal of liberalism on the grounds that it could not overcome the 'bourgeois/citoyen' dichotomy.

More can be said about Rawls' shortcomings in a Macphersonite vein. In terms of his model of 'man' there are problems internal to his theory in attempting to be neutral between different conceptions of the good, because his emphasis on human beings as in effect 'consumerist' choice-makers already privileges one kind of ontology or 'good',[16] for example, in contrast to, say, loyalty to a community.[17] As for his model of society, whether in *TJ* or in the 'late' Rawls of *Political Liberalism* where his self-confessed standpoint in response to communitarian criticism is no longer that of Archimedes but of a Western if not American liberal, there is a lack of understanding of the capitalist system, both its production and consequential political relations. In the economic realm he regarded the question of exploitation as 'out of place here'.[18] Rawls assumes that a democratic society consists of voluntary co-operation among equals in both economic and political realms to secure 'mutual advantage'.[19] While at one level in the political sphere this can conceivably be so, in the economic sphere in a capitalist context, as Macpherson never tired in repeating, the choices made by workers, although formally voluntary, are in reality constrained because there is no equal access to life and labour. As a result the inequalities that his theory of justice would have to deal with are not merely those of wealth and income, but also of authority, power and influence in the workplace.[20] Indeed, Rawls is far more concerned with the question of the distribution of outputs than inputs. Thus the individual behind the 'veil of ignorance' is not asked to consider how 'perhaps the most important' so-called 'primary goods' (which include rights and liberties, powers and opportunities, income and wealth) of self-respect and self-esteem[21] are affected by the authoritarian nature of the capitalist labour process and the alienating effects of the capitalist organised division of labour. Given the demands of energy and time devoted to work, and the constrained choices of occupation, a freely chosen working-life plan would not be available. And the capitalist labour process certainly impacts upon 'life plans' outside the workplace, or as Macpherson would put it, on the exercise of an individual's 'extra-productive powers'. Indeed, why should Rawls' cautious risk-taker behind this veil subscribe to the principle of equality of opportunity, given that the odds are pretty heavily stacked against them assuming a position of power and authority in the productive realm? While the equality of opportunity principle can be justified in material output terms of 'economic efficiency', Rawls' rational and self-interested individual would certainly want to know something about the multitude of opportunity costs involved, and may want to design jobs in a less meritocratic way.

Rawls also does not sufficiently note the impact of the 'economic' on the 'political' within the capitalist system, that is the extent to which the capitalist class and the needs of capital accumulation set the political agenda, especially in terms of economic growth. In reality, a capitalist state cannot be neutral between competing conceptions of the good, not merely because of concerns for economic growth, but also for social and political stability. As the history of liberal democracies has shown in Germany and Spain in the 1930s, and Chile in 1973, the state can become very illiberal when a capitalist order is threatened. And even states that remain formally liberal democracies can behave illiberally, as for example during the Cold War when Communists were persecuted in the West during the McCarthy era in the 1950s, or in periods of intense industrial conflict, as demonstrated for example by the role of the police during the British miners' strike of 1984–5. There is also the question of who has the largest voice in liberal democracies in periods of stability. And it is certainly not the subaltern classes.[22] The argument here is not that Rawls would necessarily collude with the repressive activities of the liberal state in such circumstances. Rather, if his principles are to work, there has to be an acknowledgement that capitalism could be deeply problematic for self-interested choice-makers behind the veil of ignorance.

Further, Rawls did not deal with the problem, raised by Macpherson, of party representation in liberal democracies: the move to the centre-ground to maximise votes blurs class differences and can create political apathy. And as Macpherson, Pateman and others have noted, there exists a significant correlation between 'political efficacy' and class. Although Rawls acknowledges that the wealthy might be able to exercise their political liberties more than the poor, he resorts to the standard liberal defence of distinguishing between liberty and the worth of liberty. Even if this distinction is accepted, the individual in Rawls' 'original position', as Daniels has indicated, would want to choose *both* equal liberty and equal worth, thereby bringing into conflict his two principles of justice.[23] Although DiQuattro has attempted to defend Rawls against his socialist critics by suggesting that Rawls' primary politico-economic model was not welfare capitalism but a 'property-owning democracy' involving a widespread distribution of property 'pooled through insurance firms, investment trusts, and so on', it is not clear whether such a system is really that different from capitalism.[24] Once one admits a system for the competitive allocation of investment, of 'insurance firms and investment trusts', the actual dynamic of capital accumulation is in place with its negative consequences for those participating in the labour process. Thus he does not deal with the question of how primary goods are produced and the expressive disutilities that are often entailed. Nor does he deal with the split, bourgeois/citoyen ontology alluded to by Macpherson that is implicit in Rawls' theory.[25] In sum, while his communitarian critics managed to get him to come clean on the metaphysical nature of the individual in the original position, he was unable to admit to his metaphysical understanding of the capitalist system, which supposedly can be based upon hypothetical, voluntary agreement in the economic and political realms.

Other liberals have attempted to deal with the problem of justice under capitalism. Richard Dworkin in *A Matter of Principle*[26] famously attempted to devise a scheme that was 'ambition sensitive' and that compensated for undeserved differences in natural ability and circumstance. Not only does his complicated scheme of hypothetical auctions and insurance schemes, market mechanisms and taxation policies run up against practical problems of how to initially redistribute resources and rectify natural advantages and disadvantages and differences of circumstance. There is also the problem of how to distinguish between what is achieved as a result of ambition-sensitive choice or natural endowment.[27] In addition, his proposal also runs into the same difficulties as Rawls' two principles: no necessary correlation exists between the incentives assumed to be required for 'economic efficiency' and the resources needed to compensate the less fortunate. These practical problems of welfare liberalism are even more acute than when they were first proposed as a result of globalisation restricting national states' room for economic manoeuvre.

There is also the famous anti-welfare liberalism of Nozick's entitlement thesis. Nozick argued that all holdings are just if they are justly acquired, either in their initial appropriation that left sufficient for others or through exchange and gift. Macpherson may have been referring to Nozick when he talked of the 'gross idealism' of some contemporary liberal political philosophers, although the subriquet as we have seen is equally applicable to Dworkin.[28] Macpherson did not bother to criticise Nozick. If he had he would probably have noted that any attempt to rectify past injustices of acquisition was impossible. He would also have explored in greater detail Nozick's notion of just exchanges under capitalism which has exercised the minds of some Marxists.[29] And he would have characterised him as some kind of hyper Lockean possessive individualist who had made little attempt to justify his ontological assumptions.[30]

– Communitarians –

As already indicated Macpherson was in much agreement with his communitarian critics, not surprisingly since most were leftist in inclination. In response to their criticisms, as already noted, he brought to their attention the communitarian motif in his work, and in his subsequent writings he took pains to declare his communitarian affinity. Thus he would have agreed with much of their subsequent critique of Rawlsian liberalism, that ontologically the 'self' was socially situated, 'thick' and 'encumbered'; further, that the self could not be posited antecedently of its ends, behind a veil of ignorance. He would also have concurred that people become individuated in society, and develop themselves in and through society. In addition, he would have shared the communitarian belief that ethically there was much to be valued, first, in community and individuals identifying with it, and secondly in the republican virtue of democratic participation, as in the works of Walzer and Taylor.[31] Yet potentially there existed differences between him and some communitarians. As already noted in his response to MacIntyre, the fact that humans are communal beings because they have language does not make them any less involved in exploitative relations.

More importantly, he wanted to retain a 'Millian individualist concept of essence'. Thus, he would have been worried by the thought that community would be valued for its own sake, overriding the developmental claims of the individual, even if these individuals had initially agreed to allow the community to do so as a result of 'shared understandings'. Indeed, this worry raises two large issues indicating potentially sharp differences between himself and some communitarians. There is, first, the 'political economy' issue. Even if the shared understandings of a community (if this can be clearly identified) were of a Millian individualist sort, to what extent would communitarians be committed to creating a non-exploitative economy? In other words, to what extent have they adopted an immanent critique of communities that claim to promote such individuation? Kymlicka has complained that communitarians (and liberals) have ignored the 'real issues involved in creating the cultural conditions of self determination'.[32] He could have added the material/political conditions too. William Connelly, in noting Macpherson's importance, suggested that communitarians (and liberals) were unable to 'specify the mode of political economy that best protects and nourishes [their] idealism.'[33]

The unwillingness to explore the relationship between material/political conditions and the culture of 'shared understandings' can be seen in Walzer's *Spheres of Justice*. Walzer recognises that people can disagree over the meaning of social goods, and when such understandings are controversial, then justice requires that 'society be faithful to the disagreements, providing institutional channels for their expression, adjudicative mechanisms, and alternative distributions'.[34] Yet if we look for example at the shared understandings of liberal democracy which attempts to regulate disagreement, such a compromise is the product of a complex balance of class and political forces, and when the masses have attempted to go beyond liberal democracy or significantly interfere with private property rights or capital accumulation, the state and/or the capitalist class has strongly resisted. In other words, there is the question of class power and how it shapes liberal democratic institutions. And in Gramscian parlance, this is not merely a matter of blatant coercion, but of how 'consent' is generated by the mechanisms of 'civil society' − education, mass media, political parties, trade unions, the church and so on. Put slightly differently and perhaps more strongly, as Caney remarks, Walzer, in relying on a 'naive social theory', does not recognise the 'possibility of the coercive generation of values'.[35] Thus individual consent based upon shared understandings can be made in ignorance of values which are the product of unequal and multifaceted power relations.

A further question which might arise related to the promotion of individual flourishing is how to distinguish between authentic and inauthentic communities, between practices and values that genuinely promote it and those grounded in unequal power relations. Here a starting point is Macpherson's use of immanent critique, of seeing whether a community lives up to its professed values, and if not, why not. Walzer quotes Marx to the effect that he did not see the worker/capitalist wage bargain under capitalism as unjust because it was 'internal' to this system, and from this deduced that if injustice occurred it was in the sphere of distribution through the use of the 'surplus' to purchase special privileges, for example in law, education, political office.[36] Yet an important element of Marx's critique of liberalism and capitalism was that equal freedom as buyers and sellers was only formal. The vulnerability of the worker vis-à-vis the capitalist, meant that there was not equal effective freedom for both parties, that the latter exploited the former whose needs were more immediate and ever pressing. This, as we have seen, was the type of critical gambit used by Macpherson and was expressed in his concept of the net transfer of powers, closely modelled on Marx's theory of exploitation.

Thus the question arises as to the grounds for condemning capitalism as unjust, which most of the communitarians assumed. Although Walzer leans heavily towards relativism, his ideal was a 'decentralized democratic socialism' as the answer to the 'tyranny of money'.[37] While he wants people to freely choose such a system, his grounds for why he thinks they ought to do so are because they will find 'plutocracy' objectionable. This arises when they see the power of money undermining a 'complex', pluralist equality in the purchase of privileges outside the economic realm. But this position is not firmly established. What if for a variety of explanations – brainwashing, ignorance, adaptive preferences and so on – people accept plutocracy?

MacIntyre too is concerned to avoid the conservative implications of his (neo)-Aristotelian 'tradition of the virtues' based upon small-scale communities, and wants to resist charges of moral relativism. But equally he seeks to resist embracing a critical standpoint independent of the practices of a given community in order to avoid what he saw as the socially corrosive universalism of Enlightenment rationalism. He refers to the 'distortions and illusions within practices' arising from 'money, power and status' which 'invade the practice' and to the 'deformations and distortions' of existing practices, leading for example to injustices to women.[38] Such a stance is problematic: first it assumes that an existing practice is inherently good. Yet, however defined in the case of women, it is hard to think of many civilisations that have not been deeply implicated in patriarchal practices. In other words, the practice itself may be perfectly coherent, that is, undistorted but oppressive. Furthermore, even if the inherent goodness of a practice is accepted, an external standpoint may be essential in determining *how* it has been distorted or deformed or subject to illusions arising from concepts and insights not available to a given society. Interestingly, MacIntyre invokes an 'external' standpoint when condemning liberal capitalism in asserting that 'the tradition of the virtues is at variance with central features of the modern economic order and more especially of its individualism, its acquisitiveness and its elevation of the values of the market to a central social place', sentiments that Macpherson would have applauded.[39] The Greek tradition of the virtues is used to illustrate the intrinsic moral incoherence of modernity. Yet the justification of this appeal to such a tradition has to be more than its moral coherence, given that the society producing these virtues, to which MacIntyre is referring, was patriarchal, slave-owning and imperialistic. The excellences to be encouraged, judged from another standpoint, could be very oppressive and incoherent indeed. The question then is on what grounds can that standpoint be justified?

The crux of this discussion is that generally the communitarians have a problem with ethical relativism, because their radical dispositions want to avoid its conservative logic. Macpherson's mode of critique implicitly attempts to circumvent this quandary by, in effect, offering a double critique of liberal democratic capitalism, that is both 'local' and 'global'. As indicated many times in this book, what powered his critique of liberal democratic capitalism was its failure to live up to its official, 'Millian' self-description (either actually or potentially), through an understanding of its so-called internal contradictions: the gap between declarations and deeds. This was his 'local' critique. His external, 'global' critique based on his conception of the net transfer of powers was both procedural and substantive. It was procedural in the sense that it was grounded on the Kantian categorical imperative that all individuals had to be treated as ends-in-themselves. And it was substantive in that it was ontologically grounded upon a notion of human essence, of objective human needs. The question is whether both standpoints can be integrated in order to avoid the potential conservatism of the 'local' and the potential authoritarianism of the 'global'. Procedurally, the end-in-themselves doctrine is only authoritarian for those who want to boss, oppress or exploit. So in that sense the local with oppressive and exploitative characteristics could not be combined with the global. Ontologically, as already indicated for Macpherson, the human essence was both invariant and subject to change. The exertion and development of universal human powers occurred in specific contexts. The critical issue was the extent to which the individual – and here we come back to the Millian concept of essence – was in a position to exert and develop these powers. Here the whole question of economic and political relations arises and cuts into the procedural standpoint, because in a class society based upon a net transfer of powers these possibilities are unequally and unfairly distributed. Thus in so far as there were irreconcilable differences between liberals such as Rawls and the communitarians, Macpherson's position is to straddle them by recognising the need for effective individual autonomy championed by liberals, while acknowledging that this cannot occur in a competitive market society that fosters atomistic behaviour.

– Deliberative democracy –

Theorists of so-called 'deliberative democracy' shared a similar concern to resolve the key issue which divided liberals and communitarians, namely how to rescue individual autonomy whilst reconciling it with some conception of a common good.[40] This was to be achieved by establishing a form of democratic legitimacy, where democracy itself was 'a fundamental political ideal and not simply a derivative ideal . . . '[41] And like the communitarians most deliberative democrats were of a radical – if reformist – disposition. These theorists owed much to Rawls and Habermas, in developing ideal models that would promote a consensual, reasoned agreement between individuals through the use of agreed procedures.[42] While different deliberative democratic theorists have defined themselves in slightly ways,[43] their solution to the autonomy/common good problem is a procedural one: collective decisions are legitimate in so far as they are made between free, moral and political equals who deploy reasonable arguments in a process of deliberation. The use of reasonable argument to persuade others constitutes respect for their autonomy, that is their capacity for self-legislation. What is distinct about this model is that it attempts to avoid the aggregating of preferences and bargaining (that is manifestations of 'possessive individualist' behaviour). The hope is that through deliberation, if there are differences, a 'reasonable pluralism' will result, with participants redefining in some way their pre-deliberative preferences because they are committed to the 'values of rationality and impartiality'.[44] The other characteristic of this model is that there is no commitment to direct democracy, merely to 'ongoing accountability'.[45] In other words a political division of labour between professional politicians and citizens is legitimate. Indeed, all explicitly or implicitly endorse liberal democracy, albeit a reformed one, which embodies the 'idealized content of a form of practical reason'.[46] They were merely 'elucidating the already implict principles and logic of existing democratic practices'.[47] A further distinctive feature of deliberative democratic thought is that although it is primarily concerned with democratic procedures and practices, it is to some extent sensitive to the context in which they take place, and that as a result there can be a problematic relation between democracy and capitalism.[48] In an ideal deliberative procedure participants have to be 'substantively equal in that the existing distribution of power and resources does not shape their chances to contribute to deliberation, nor does that distribution play an authoritative role in their deliberation.' And significantly participants can regard the existing system of rights as a 'potential object of their deliberative judgement', provided free deliberation among equals is not undermined.[49]

Again, as in the liberal/communitarian debate, the solution to the autonomy/common good problem runs up against capitalist reality. As already indicated, deliberative democrats are clearly aware of this, but are unable to offer a convincing remedy to this difficulty. One remedy for Cohen initially was by stipulation: the deliberative model allows the problem of social and economic inequality to be on the agenda of the democratic deliberators.[50] But the question is whether *in reality* any agreement is possible – or if so is the product of adaptive preferences where the deliberators initially are not economically and socially equal in a profound sense. In a situation of moderate or individuated scarcity, bargaining and negotiating or not playing by the rules of the game would be the most likely outcome. Nevertheless, Joshua Cohen and Joel Rogers, the two main exponents of deliberative democracy, in their book *Associations and Democracy* [51] attempt to fashion a feasible model of deliberative democracy that seeks to take into account capitalist reality, while promoting greater political participation for the less materially endowed.

However, before discussing this work, their earlier, more full-blooded socialist position in *On Democracy* ought to be noted. Here they unequivocally state that democracy 'requires the abolition of capitalism', because capitalism subverts formal equality.[52] And they observe capitalist democracy's ability to create consent through the satisfaction of short-term material gain, because it encouraged such economic calculation by creating conditions of material uncertainty.[53] Nevertheless, they sought an alternative to 'capitalist democracy', which entailed among other things public control of investment, workplace democracy and equality of educational opportunity, as well as a reduction in working time and public funding of political parties, all to allow for an equal capacity for political action. Material inequalities had to be regulated along the lines of the Rawlsian difference principle. Thus, their deliberative requirements entailed a socialist order.

Nevertheless, in *Associations and Democracy* their ideas took a more concrete, pragmatic turn. No longer is the frame of reference 'capitalist democracy' but 'modern democratic societies'[54] and the 'economically advanced mass democracy' of the United States.[55] Their proposals for 'associative democracy' were, they declared, drawn from the 'social democratic practice in Northern Europe' and from arguments made 'within the 'quintessentially liberal orders as in the United States'.[56] And such a democracy would, they argued, not merely overcome the 'faction' of adversorial politics, but facilitate 'good economic performance and state competence'.[57] Good economic performance meant enhancing the productivity of labour in order to increase, for example, time to deliberate and to generate non-inflationary growth. And state competence would be enhanced by more information and initiatives from those directly affected by state legislation. While state policies to redistribute wealth and income were important background features, along with state aid for political parties, the 'conventional tools of public policy', namely taxes, subsidies and legal sanctions, could be used to promote associative democracy among underrepresented groups, 'other regarding groups', and where associations have greater competence than the state, for example in environmental and occupational safety, vocational training and consumer protection. They acknowledged that there might be strong employers' associations and weak trade unions, consumer groups and women's organisations, but argued that state intervention could rectify this situation through taxes, subsidies and legal regulation. Thus, an effective 'social partnership' between trade unions and employers' associations and representatives from new social movements could be developed to deal also with broad issues such as incomes policies, active labour market policies, and environmental policies at local, regional and national levels. In response to their various critics, what became clear was their aim to establish deliberative arenas 'outside the formal political system . . . not mediated by money and power',[58] especially for the monitoring of and setting standards for occupational health and safety and the local environment.[59] They also suggested deliberative mechanisms for coordinating different private and public agencies in dealing with urban poverty.[60] Their hope was that this associative democratic strategy would eventually yield a 'new form of *political-constitutional order*' with non-governmental organisations helping to define and resolve social problems.[61]

From a Macphersonite standpoint the Cohen–Rogers' thesis encounters an ends/means problem and is an eminently suitable candidate for immanent critique. The ends, which ultimately seek to unite individual autonomy with the common good, are perfectly laudable. The question is whether they can be delivered by democratising capitalism. In other words, can the ideals of democracy and liberty be detached from socialism?[62] Or from the question of propety rights? [63] Put in a Macphersonian way, do Cohen and Rogers posit a consistent ontology? From this perspective they run into the same difficulty as Rawls and his developmental liberal forebears of being committed to the capitalist market, competition and individuated scarcity and therefore to possessive individualism, yet wanting to transcend this through the creation of deliberative arenas. Why should atomistic, factional behaviour become transformed into genuinely solidaristic behaviour? Moreover, they appeal in this work as in their socialist *On Democracy* to the Rawlsian difference principle designed to legitimate 'fair' inequalities, but this raises the question of whether it can be realised in such a way as to secure genuine acceptance by the least fortunate under capitalism, especially a strongly globalised one. Nor do they deal with the argument that capitalism is inherently exploitative and therefore is bound to create conflict, which again makes the applicability of the difference principle under capitalism difficult.

In other words, if they accept 'economic competence' as one of the overriding considerations, they also accept that in any dialogue between deliberators profits are ultimately trumps. For instance, in the realm of work relations in certain situations the imperative of profitability might favour – to use old-fashioned Maxist parlance – 'class collaboration', and at other times not. Therefore, the context in which deliberation takes place is a crucial consideration. In many respects the Cohen–Rogers proposals, whatever their disclaimers, have something of the *déjà vu* about them of a pre-globalised capitalism and of the postwar Keynesian welfare state settlement against a Cold War background. There is much evidence to show that the type of collaborationist politics they prefer comes in historic cycles, often when managerial authority is effectively challenged from below.[64] And joint management–worker bodies end up either deliberating about trivial concerns or becoming an instrument of management, especially as a channel for communication, or transformed into bargaining arenas. Further, the incomes policies in Britain in the postwar period, in response to a strong labour movement, full employment and an overall decline in international competitiveness of industry, set the scene for participation in the 1960s and 1970s. Hence, the kind of corporatist recommendations that they make appear to be at the wrong historic juncture of enfeebled labour movements and relatively high unemployment, and global markets limiting the kind of reformist economic policies that can be pursued. A question mark must hang over the long-term stability of such schemes, given the fundamental differences of interest between workers and capital and contextual variation.

Another Macphersonite consideration relates to the nature of liberal democratic politics. Ultimately majority parties tend to win or lose elections or rewrite their agendas in order to demonstrate 'economic competence'. Capitalist markets quickly judge the degree of business confidence in a government, and by and large electors dependent on such confidence would not be happy with any deliberative proposals that appeared to cause economic instability.[65] Whether 'capitalist democracy', to use their earlier term, could get into a position of sustaining a deliberative democracy that significantly contributed to a 'new political-constitutional order' over the longer period is questionable.

In sum capitalism, or a 'possessive market society', owing to its owns needs of accumulation, presents a huge obstacle to the creation of a context in which all citizens can deliberate freely and equally and extend the horizon of deliberative possibility.

– Radical democracy –

Laclau and Mouffe, post-Marxist theorists of 'radical democracy', in common with deliberative democrats take liberal democracy as the starting point of their analysis, and like Cohen and Rogers they came to see socialism as no longer integral to the expansion of democracy. Socialism was merely a 'moment internal to the democratic revolution', which began with the French Revolution of 1789.[66] However, unlike deliberative democrats they held that any aspiration towards consensus needed severe qualification, because antagonism was an invariant feature of the human condition. The reason for this was that human identities were inherently unstable or 'precarious'. For the self there existed an 'irresoluble interiority/exteriority tension'.[67] The perceptions of self and the world, subjective desires and dispositions could never be taken as constant. Identities were subject to the 'continuous movement of differ-ences'.[68] Antagonism arises because within this context of the 'contingent' world of unstable identities, the existing discursive and social '"Other" prevents me from being totally myself'.[69] The a priori 'essentialism' of Marxist discourse, which 'fixed' identities on the basis of class, had to be abandoned. So too had the presumption of a necessary relationship between the working class and socialism. Rather it was merely 'contingent'. Indeed, the 'essentialist' discourse of Marxism contained an authoritarian logic of 'privileging', of privileging the working class and ultimately privileging the 'Party' over and above other emancipatory non-proletarian movements as well as the working class itself, as evidenced in the Soviet Union. This could be said to be the 'bad' couplet of essentialism/totalitarianism, and it had to be replaced by the 'good' couplet of contingency/democracy. The virtue of liberal democracy for Laclau and Mouffe is that it takes antagonism, the product of contingency, for granted and has the flexibility to incorporate and recognise new forms of identity, as for example manifested in the rise of the new social movements. Accordingly they did not 'renounce liberal-democratic ideology'. Rather they wanted to 'deepen and expand it in the direction of a radical and plural democracy'.[70] This required therefore a 'multiplication of spaces' within and the 'institutional diversification' of liberal democracy, allowing for new forms of representation on the understanding that the democratic project would always be incomplete owing to the 'unfixity' of human identity.[71]

Laclau and Mouffe's approach contained explicit and implicit parallels with Macpherson's project. Not only was there a positive reference to 'possessive individualist' nature of earlier liberal discourse in *Hegemony and Socialist Strategy*,[72] more interestingly they too adopted the strategy of immanent critique in relation to liberal democracy. The 'symbolic resources', the ideals of freedom and equality, of the liberal democratic tradition could be utilised by radicals, because they were 'a long way from being implemented'.[73] They also shared Macpherson's lack of faith in the idea of the working class becom-ing a hegemonic subject. Finally, they acknowledged Macpherson's import-ance in opening a way to the 'radical historicization of the categories of political theory', especially through his demonstration of the contingent relation between democracy and liberalism.[74]

However, their similarities with Macpherson were superficial, and their differences, apart from those noted in the previous chapter, can be expressed through contrasting their immanent critiques of liberal democracy which led to different political trajectories. Invoking the 'the tragic experience' of Soviet socialism, their immanent critique did not require the 'construction of a completely different society'.[75] Significantly, this invocation performs the act of closure in considering how socialism might be integral to key elements of new social movement agendas. By contrast, as we have seen Macpherson's immanent critique had revolutionary socialist implications because his egalitarian developmental ontology entailed the abolition of the capitalist 'net transfer of powers'. In other words, socialism was the completion of the liberal project, at least of a Millian kind. Laclau and Mouffe's immanent critique did not imply drastic institutional revision, wheras Macpherson's did. He wanted to subvert the language of liberal democracy to inspire fundamental social transformation. In contrast, Laclau and Mouffe used its vocabularly to reform its institutions in the light of social changes demanded by the developing new social movements. This difference in part stemmed from their different ontological and methodological approaches. Macpherson's employment of the language of 'essentialism', of 'human essence'and of 'essential human powers' was one of his trade marks. Further, an essentialist 'identity' can be attributed to the working class because, although not a revolutionary subject, it had a essential interest in translating its formal political equality into social equality. For Laclau and Mouffe, however, such language contained totalitarian danger. It could only serve to privilege interests of the working class above other emancipatory movements, potentially legitimating the totalitarian power of political parties claiming to represent its interests. Moreover the language of human essence did not allow for the flux of human identity, limiting the democratic 'imaginary'. Differences over the question of class and essence also informed their different attitudes to liberal democracy in the institutional sense. For Macpherson liberal democracy played an important role in containing class conflict and ensuring that politics worked to a capitalist agenda, and he understandably wanted new economic and political institutions that would genuinely empower people. Laclau and Mouffe on the other hand see in liberal democratic institutions a positive virtue, because they take antagonism for granted: 'We must accept the permanence of conflicts and antagonisms.'[76] Accordingly they rejected the 'idea of a perfect consensus, of a harmonious collective will', which they implied Macpherson thought possible, thereby rendering liberal democratic institutions unnecessary in a classless society.[77]

We can now show that Macpherson's project had a far richer emancipatory import. That Macpherson rejected the idea of a society based upon a 'single harmonious pattern' has already been discussed in Chapter 4,[78] and requires no further comment. Rather, we can start by subjecting Laclau and Mouffe's principles and prescriptions to an immanent, Macphersonian critique, by asking whether a genuine diversity of identities can be promoted within a liberal democratic framework and within their theoretical, anti-essentialist schema. If the promotion of diversity is to go beyond the traditional liberal principle of toleration, then the question of the production and distribution of material resources has to be addressed. Laclau and Mouffe, following traditional liberal thought on this matter, tend to assume that freedom and equality stand in opposition to each other, with liberty, as negatively defined, encouraging diversity and equality meaning sameness.[79] They seem to assume that increases in social equality, which may merely involve more free time (required one would have thought for the promotion of their ideal of 'active citizenship'), will encroach upon individual freedom. Yet in aggregative terms, and accepting that positive liberty does not have to be totalitarian, such equality may be basic to enhancing the ability of people to make effective choices. And we only have to think, in the absence of social equality, of how oppression impacts differently upon upper and middle class gays, blacks and women in comparison with those from the working class. Therefore the property/class question is of profound importance. And if we accept Macpherson's argument that liberal democracy functions to uphold capitalist property relations, then there may be severe limitations as to the extent to which it can be widened and deepened in a meaningful way to allow for meaningful representation and individual autonomy. In not arguing for the necessity of socialism, Laclau and Mouffe have committed themselves to working within the liberal democratic institutional framework. In other words, the relation between capitalism and democracy central to any emancipatory project worthy of the name becomes obscure.

Their anti-essentialism also performs an act of emancipatory closure for a number of reasons. First, their worry is that the very *language* of essentialism, especially in its Marxist form, contains a totalitarian logic. They argue that essentialism lies at the root of other related 'isms' in Marxist discourse – 'reductionism', 'monism', 'classism', 'a priorism' and 'economism' – which legitimated Soviet rule. What they do not sufficiently distinguish between is Marxism as an ideology of domination and as a conceptual vocabulary. Hence, they do not give due weight to the fact of the Soviet appropriation of Marxist discourse for its own purposes. While there was a connection between Marxist ideology and concepts, especially surrounding the teological conception of history, Laclau and Mouffe in championing 'contingency' junk all significant Marxist concepts apart from 'hegemony'. Thus, class gets written off as 'classism', economic analysis is reduced to 'economism', historical directionality becomes 'monism', and scientific method is reduced to 'reductionism'. In other words, by becoming tainted with the status of an 'ism' these concepts can no longer be used to analyse and understand the world for emancipatory purposes.[80] Rather than asking whether these concepts are well or badly used, they suggest their abandonment. From Macpherson's viewpoint an essentialist methodology was crucial because of the need to analyse 'real underlying relations between people, or between things or between people and things.'[81] Otherwise one would be trapped in the realm of appearances.[82] The use of such concepts to explain the 'extra-discursive' world may help generate agreement between people as to what the world is, thereby overcoming various kinds of antagonism which they regard as endemic to the human condition.

This brings us to a second objection to their anti-essentialism. All essentialism is written off in favour of contingency. Yet there is no reason why there cannot be different kinds of essentialism and necessity which are not innately oppressive. Obviously, an 'a priori' essentialism that fixes human identity as seen in Aristotle in relation to women and slavery, for example, does have oppressive implications. But Macpherson's notion of 'human essence' or 'essential powers' with individual, developmental and 'exertial' autonomy factored in does not. Macpherson's only 'oppressive' requirement is that this autonomy should not reduce the autonomy of others. Within a broader Macphersonian picture *both* necessity and contingency are at work. He recognised the existence of objective, universal human needs, yet how they are met is a matter of choice and contingency. As Terry Eagleton puts it:

> It is no disproval of ... human universals to point out that all ... features are differently constructed in different cultures. One has only to ask oneself *which* activities are differently constructed to find the universal question stubbornly reposing itself.[83]

And

> we cannot jettison essentialism because we need to know among other things which needs are essential to our humanity and which are not. Needs which are essential to our survival and well-being, such as being fed, keeping warm, enjoying the company of others and a degree of physical integrity, can then become politically criterial: any social order which denies such needs can be challenged on the grounds that it is denying our humanity, which is usually a stronger argument against it than the case that it is flouting our contingent cultural conventions.[84]

And the way needs are met can be judged as good or bad, depending upon whether individuals, to put the matter at its simplest, 'harm' themselves and/ or others. Thus 'contingent' capitalist relations of production exploited the 'necessity' of workers for life and labour in a way that diminished their human 'essence'.

Moreover, such relations encouraged a self-owning 'possessive individualism' which diminished the recognition of the needs of others. In a sense contingency becomes a problem for Laclau and Mouffe precisely because they reject essentialist categories. With identities precarious and the never ending play of difference, antagonism and its containment through 'protective' liberal democracy becomes an overriding consideration. A common recognition of a common humanity, of a common human 'essence' which acknowledged *similar* needs being met in *particular* ways might make human individuation less threatening.[85] Indeed, their 'non' ontological anti-essentialism raises the question whether democracy itself would be sustainable, because there seems to be no obvious basis for lasting agreement grounded in shared understandings at the procedural level. Why should particular groups either seeking to defend or promote their 'identities', especially if the political goods are indivisible, be committed to liberal democratic procedures? This of course is a problem for democratic theory in general, but having eschewed the possibility of appealing to a 'thick' ontology of a common humanity and the use of rational-scientific discourse(s) to understand the extra-discursive world means that such commitment becomes contingent and unstable. (Even 'radical' democratic theorising in its attempt to persuade others of its arguments cannot but help appeal to shared understandings implicit in the use of language.)

Thus Laclau and Mouffe, owing to their profound distrust of the socialist commitment to human diversity arising from a deep suspicion of the power-laden nature of Marxist discourse, put their faith in the capacity of liberal democratic regimes, not merely to tolerate difference, but to deliver it. Macpherson, however, was far more sceptical about such regimes' ability to promote individual flourishing because they were grounded upon capitalist property relations. His argument in effect is that actually existing liberal democracy is capitalist democracy and as such requires supplanting with a politico-economic system that is genuinely democratic, both in a procedural and substantive and 'radical' sense, and provides the basis for effective individual autonomy. And his argument was based upon what we might call a 'reasonable' essentialism, expressing a radicalism that means to get to the root of things, especially the relationship between property and democracy.[86]

In sum, what virtually all contemporary political philosophers examined above seem to do is to ignore the real world of capitalism. They seem more concerned ultimately with a proceduralism deriving from questions of toleration, whether of individuals or communities, or of justice within a capitalist market, at a time when global capitalism has been politically and ideologically on the ascendant. Liberal democracies are increasingly powerless in pushing forward political agendas at variance with such a capitalism. Implicitly or explicitly contemporary political philosophers seem to have narrowed their critical horizons and lost the willingness to subject the prevailing liberal democratic ideology to a meaningful immanent critique. On the whole from the point of view of political economy these philosophers are conservative, leaving capitalism broadly as it is, and therefore the existence of exploitation.[87] Liberty they take to be negative, implying forbearance on the part of the state or other individuals; positive liberty, which has clear resource implications, they reject. They assume the free floating 'possessive individual' whose freedom merely depends on the non-interference of others. As for a positive view of freedom, which acknowledges human interdependence, the question of the terms of productive cooperation become paramount. And justice they take to be broadly consistent with a capitalist market economy, thereby ignoring the fact that justice cannot be enacted because the market is not in business to distribute benefits and burdens on the basis of visible ethical criteria. This of course has not prevented pro-market economists from attempting to develop some kind of ethical criteria based upon marginal utility. However, even if this could be justified in theory, they have an even greater problem in jusifying it in practice, in a world of oligopolistic competition. Macpherson's critique of liberal democratic theory and practice points to the need for alternative production relations.[88]

— MACPHERSON FOR TODAY —

While a case can be made therefore for Macpherson's relevance for modern political philosophy, this does not mean that his views can be uncritically defended. As we have seen although he saw the need for empirical analysis, he provided little to show how his post-capitalist democracy would operate except in the one, lonely chapter in *LTLD*. His importance lies as a critic of liberal democracy rather than as an institutional designer. We can also note that as far as an emancipatory ethic is concerned he shared some of the weaknesses of classical Marxism. This was not in the sense of focusing exclusively on the proletarian redemption of humanity, but in the optimism of a historical teleology where the 'real' and the 'good' coincide, especially in the form of a technological 'fix' to produce the abundance needed to transcend the possessive individualist mentality, and in his faith in the Second World's ability to create societies based upon humane principles. And allied to this is an assumption that the root of most human antagonism is material in origin. Similarly, although he embraced an ontology, he had little to say about the psychological aspects of the self and about the myriad of sites of asymmetrical power relations between people, and of the 'internal impediments' to freedom beyond those of class. In other words, he did not fully embrace the analysis and concerns of different types of new social movement theorists and those influenced by postmodernism.

Yet perhaps the least satisfying element in his theoretical edifice, as already suggested, is *the way* in which he extended the definition of democracy beyond a 'proceduralist' system of government to include society: not in the sense that one cannot speak of a democratic society, but in defining it as an end, as a society of flourishing individuals. This move, which stemmed from his strategy of immanent critique, as we have seen, led him at one time to be accommodating towards blatantly totalitarian regimes described as 'democratic' in their ends. His position would have been strengthened if he had kept to a procedural definition of political equality, and expanded the notion of the 'political' to wherever unequal power relations occurred in a collective sense. Normatively, the end of human flourishing could have been maintained in order to justify the widening of democracy into the private realm, but also to sustain such a widening. Thus a democratic society would be much more visibly one in which individuals would be able to participate in decisions affecting their day-to-day lives. Although this was Macpherson's clear intention and although his motives for reducing tensions in the Cold War were laudible through his substantive definition, a procedural definition linked to substantive ends would have made his argument less vulnerable to the accusation of a 'left' totalitarianism.

This discussion raises the question of the relationship between foundationalism and democracy.[89] While many democratic theorists are wary of anything that smacks of 'pre-political' foundationalism because it would appear to restrict the scope of democratic decision, Macpherson could be seen as suggesting why it is essential to democratic theory. This could be so in at least two senses. First, foundationalism suggests that democracy has to be justified on grounds more worthwhile than merely the reconcilation of human antagonism, and linked to this it provides an argument for democracy's extension into an exploitative, capitalist 'civil society' as well as into 'cosmopolitan society'. Secondly, foundationalism can be connected to democracy, because the latter could be seen as having a vital mediating role in reconciling the 'universal' with the 'particular', of giving particular expression to universal human needs. Putting to one side the whole issue of deciding between needs and wants and whether this would be necessarily significant in a democratic forum, there can be some agreement as to what constitutes universal human needs.[90] Yet differences can obviously arise as to how they are to be prioritised and how they are to be met in particular circumstances. Thus, far from a 'needs' discourse foreclosing democratic debate, such debate is essential if substantive egalitarian goals are to be achieved. This becomes even more pressing where production relations are not driven by the needs of capital accumulation, where the benefits and burdens of productive activity are not arbitrarily distributed but regulated according to some transparent, if complex, combination of principles of justice and human needs, the outcome of practical reasoning.

The importance of the relation between democracy and foundationalism or essentialism can be put another way if the environmental agenda is addressed. Macpherson was sensitive to environmentalist concerns, yet *seemed* to imply that the planet had infinite resources because he argued that technologically created abundance was the answer to the infinite desire of the possessive individualist. His point, though, was made at the 'justificatory' level, because for him the problem of scarcity was not so much material as psychological/ socio-economic in origin, deriving from the capitalist market itself. Capitalist society consists of competitive individuals, in which labour and its products are no longer authoritatively allocated, and the 'carrot' of incentives is required to get people to work.[91] In such a society 'the chief purpose of man is an endless battle against scarcity in relation to infinite desire.'[92] Technological advance meant that the scarcity argument required as an incentive, the product of the ontology of infinite desire, became less tenable. Even if Macpherson's argument has not been widely endorsed, within the context of declining natural resources and environmental degradation some kind of needs discourse becomes important as an alternative to a wants (infinite desire)/profits regulated market. Thinking more clearly about the purposes of consumption and about qualitative issues generally could mean that the question of time utilisation for individuals and communities could become more important than material consumption. Cooperation and agreement about resource production and distribution for these purposes would be more easily facilitated and legitimated through democratic decision-making. All this of course has implications for the ownership and control of the planet's natural resources and productive assets.

Macpherson also represented a number of traditions in political thought which are relevant. He was prepared to ask the big questions that Plato and Aristotle addressed, even if he did not adequately answer them: what kind of principles should inform political and economic institutions which are most favourable to our human essence? Macpherson was also representative of a rich liberal-socialist tradition, which saw socialism as the completion of a certain kind of non-possessive liberalism, not as its antithesis, as partisans on both sides of the Cold War would have it. Finally, he shared with the Marxist tradition an unwillingness to separate the political and philosophical from the economic. Perhaps what 'retrieving' Macpherson really means is to be part of an ongoing dialectical process in contemporary Anglophone political philosophy: Kant inspired Rawlsian liberalism, and Hegel certain kinds of communitarianism. Maybe Macpherson is telling us to stand critically on the shoulders – if with a little help from Mill – of the last in that trinity of intellectual giants: Marx.[93]

Above all, what Macpherson's project provides us with is a moral benchmark. This his critics were unable to destroy, and needs 'retrieval' in the face of a liberal and 'radical' ethos that has abandoned the universalistic claims of a common humanity which a globalised world has made so self-evidently concrete.

– NOTES –

1. See also A. Wright, 'C. B. Macpherson, Democracy and Possessive Individualism', in L. Tivey and Wright (eds) *Political Thought Since 1945: Philosophy, Science and Ideology* (Aldershot: Elgar, 1992), pp. 167–8.
2. For example D. Held *Models of Democracy*, 2nd edn (Cambridge: Polity Press, 1996), C. Gould, *Rethinking Democracy: Freedom, and Cooperation in Politics, Economy and Society* (Cambridge: Cambridge University Press, 1988); F. Cunningham, *Socialism and Democracy*, and *The Real World of Democracy Revisited* (Atlantic Highlands, NJ: Humanities Press, 1994); P. Lindsay, *Creative Individualism, The Democratic Vision of C. B. Macpherson* (New York: State University of New York Press, 1998).
3. For example, N. Geras, 'The Controversy about Marx and Justice', *New Left Review*, 150, 1985, pp. 47–85.
4. *DT*, p. 9.
5. See T. Carver and P. Thomas (eds), *Rational Choice Marxism* (London: Macmillan, 1995).
6. G. A. Cohen, *History, Labour and Freedom* (Oxford: Clarendon Press, 1988), p. 9.
7. The notable exception is of course J. Raz, *The Morality of Freedom* (Oxford: Oxford University Press, 1986).
8. New York: Columbia University Press, 1993.
9. Cambridge, MA: Harvard University Press, 1971.
10. Quoted *DT*, p. 88, in *TJ* of course this became more specific: 'to the greatest benefit of the least advantaged' (p. 83).
11. See also D. F. B. Tucker, *Marxism and Individualism* (Oxford: Blackwell, 1980), p. 124. For comments on, and developments of, Macpherson's criticisms see K. Nielson, 'On the Very Possibility of a Classless Society, Rawls, Macpherson, and Revisionist Liberalism', *Political Theory*, 6/2, May, 1978, pp. 191–208, and Macpherson's reply, 'Class, Classlessness and the Critique of Rawls: A Reply to Neilson', in the same issue, pp. 209–11.
12. *DT*, p. 90.
13. Ibid., p. 94.
14. 'Rawls' Model of Man and Society', *Philosophy of Social Science*, 3, 1973, pp. 341–347.
15. *TJ*, p. 280.
16. R. Beiner, *What's the Matter with Liberalism?* (Berkeley: University of California Press, 1992), p. 8.
17. M. Luntley, *Reason Truth and Self* (London: Routledge, 1995), ch. 9 *passim*.
18. *TJ*, p. 310, noted by D. Schweickart, 'A Democratic Theory of Economic Exploitation Dialectically Developed', in R. Gottleib (ed.), *Radical Philosophy, Tradition, Counter-Tradition, Politics* (Philadelphia: Temple University Press, 1993), p. 101.
19. *TJ*, p. 383.
20. See C. Pateman, *The Problem of Political Obligation: A Critique of Liberal Theory* (Cambridge: Polity Press, 1985), p. 131.

21. *TJ*, p. 440.
22. See N. Daniels,'Equal Liberty and Unequal Worth of Liberty', in N. Daniels (ed.) *Reading Rawls* (Oxford: Blackwell, 1975), p. 258.
23. Ibid., p. 263.
24. A. DiQuattro, 'Rawls and Left Criticism', *Political Theory*, 11/1, 1983, p. 56.
25. See I. Shapiro, *The Evolution of Rights in Liberal Theory* (Cambridge: Cambridge University Press, 1986), pp. 266-300 for an extended critique of DiQuattro.
26. Cambridge, MA: Harvard University Press, 1985.
27. M. Ramsay, *What's Wrong with Liberalism? A Radical Critique of Liberal Political Philosophy* (London: Leicester University Press, 1997), pp. 90-1.
28. 'Rawls' Model of Man and Society', p. 347.
29. See G. A. Cohen, *Self-Ownership, Freedom and Equality* (Cambridge: Cambridge University Press, 1995), chs 1 and 2.
30. See Tucker, *Marxism and Individualism*, p. 129.
31. M. Walzer, *Spheres of Justice* (New York: Basic Books, 1983), p. 318. C. Taylor, *Philosophical Arguments* (Cambridge, MA: Harvard University Press, 1995), p. 200.
32. *Contemporary Political Philosophy* (Oxford, Clarendon, 1991), p. 231.
33. Quoted Lindsay, *Creative Individualism*, p. 159.
34. *Spheres of Justice*, p. 313.
35. S. Caney, 'Liberalism and Communitarianism: A Misconceived Debate', *Political Studies*, 40/2, 1992, pp. 287-8.
36. *Spheres of Justice*, p. 315.
37. Ibid., pp. 317B18.
38. J. Horton and S. Mendus (eds), *After MacIntyre* (Cambridge: Polity, 1996), p. 289.
39. A. MacIntyre, *After Virtue* (London: Duckworth, 1981, p. 237.
40. A. Gutmann, 'Democracy' in R. E. Goodin and P. Petit (eds), *A Companion to Contemporary Political Philosophy* (Oxford: Blackwell, 1995), p. 417; S. Benhabib, 'Toward a Deliberative Model of Democratic Legitimacy', in S. Benhabib (ed.), *Democracy and Difference: Contesting the Boundaries of the Political* (Princeton, NJ: Princeton University Press, 1996), pp. 77-80; J. Cohen, 'Deliberation and Democratic Legitimacy', in A. Hamlin and P. Petit (eds), *The Good Polity: Normative Analysis of the State* (Oxford: Blackwell, 1991), pp. 23-6.
41. Cohen, 'Deliberation and Democratic Legitimacy', p. 17.
42. For example, Cohen, Deliberation and Democratic Legitimacy, p. 33, S. Benhabib, 'Towards a Deliberative Model of Democratic Legitimacy', p. 68.
43. J. Elster (ed.), *Deliberative Democracy* (Cambridge: Cambridge University Press, 1998), p. 8.
44. Ibid., p. 8.
45. Gutmann, 'Democracy', p. 418, and Cohen and Benhabib in effect accept this too, although they clearly want to strengthen the deliberative state through extending deliberative democracy to the secondary associations of civil society.
46. Benhabib, 'Towards a Deliberative Model of Democratic Legitimacy', pp. 68, 72.
47. Ibid., p. 84.
48. Ibid., p. 85.

49. Cohen, 'Deliberation and Democratic Legitimacy', p. 23.
50. Ibid., p. 23; also S. Chambers, *Reasonable Democracy, Jürgen Habermas and the Politics of Discourse* (Ithaca, NY: Cornell University Press, 1996), pp. 206-7.
51. London: Verso, 1995.
52. Harmondsworth: Penguin, 1983, pp. 148, 193.
53. Ibid., pp. 51-2.
54. Ibid., p. 7.
55. Ibid., p. 77.
56. Ibid., 34.
57. Ibid., pp. 35, 50.
58. Ibid., p. 256.
59. Ibid., p. 257.
60. Ibid., p. 250.
61. Ibid., p. 240, emphasis in the original.
62. A. Levine, 'Democratic Corporatism and/Versus Socialism', in Cohen and Rogers, *Associations and Democracy*, p. 166.
63. I. Katznelson, 'On Architectural Syncretism', in Cohen and Rogers, pp. 196-7.
64. For example, H. Ramsay, 'Participation: The Pattern and Its Significance', in T. Nichols (ed.), *Capital and Labour: Studies in the Capitalist Labour Process* (Glasgow: Fontana, 1980), pp. 381-94; T. Nichols and H. Beynon, *Living with Capitalism: Class Relations and the Modern Factory* (London: Routledge & Kegan Paul, 1977); P. Brannen, *Authority and Participation in Industry* (London: Batsford, 1983).
65. As I write (March 1999) the fall of the leftish Oskar Lafontaine, the German Finance Minister, has been met with much relief in the financial markets and in the media.
66. *Hegemony and Socialist Strategy: Towards a Radical Democratic Politics* (London: Verso, 1985), p. 156, hereafter *HSS*. Although some quotations below are taken from works which they separately authored, the assumption here is that they have a joint perspective.
67. *HSS*, p. 111. See also C. Mouffe, in C. Mouffe (ed.), *Dimensions of Radical Democracy* (London: Verso, 1992), p. 13.
68. *HSS*, p. 122.
69. Ibid., p. 125.
70. Ibid., p. 176.
71. Ibid., p. 191.
72. Ibid., p. 175.
73. *Dimensions*, p. 1; see also C. Mouffe, 'Liberalism and Modern Democracy', in J. Carens (ed.), *Democracy and Possessive Individualism: The Intellectual Legacy of C. B. Macpherson* (New York: State University of New York Press, 1993), p. 176.
74. E. Laclau, 'The Signifiers of Democracy', in ibid., p. 221.
75. Mouffe, *Dimensions of Radical Democracy*, pp. 1-2.
76. Mouffe, 'Liberalism and Modern Democracy', p. 178.
77. Ibid.
78. See *DT*, p. 111.

79. *Dimensions of Radical Democracy*, pp. 7, 14.
80. See also G. McLellan, 'Post-Marxism and the "Four Sins" of Modernist Theorizing', *New Left Review*, 218, 1996, pp. 53-74.
81. Macpherson, 'Humanist Democracy and Elusive Marxism: A Response to Minogue and Svacek', *Canadian Journal of Political Science*, 9/3, 1976, p. 430.
82. See also M. Fisk, 'Post-Marxism : Laclau and Mouffe on Essentialism', in R. S. Gottlieb (ed.), *Radical Philosophy: Tradition, Counter Tradition, Politics*, pp. 144-65, for an argument in favour of methodological holism required to explain the 'backgound totality' in which different struggles occur in order to foster unity between them.
83. *The Illusions of Postmodernism* (Oxford: Blackwell, 1996), pp. 48-9, emphasis in the original.
84. Ibid., p. 104; see also M. C. Nussbaum, 'Human Functioning and Social Justice: In Defense of Aristotelian Essentialism', *Political Theory*, 20/2, 1992, pp. 202-46 for an essentialist defence of needs theory.
85. This brings to mind Marx's statement that 'Hunger is hunger, but the hunger gratified by cooked meats eaten with a knife and fork is different from that which bolts down raw meat with the aid of hand, nail and tooth': Marx, *Grundrisse* (Harmondsworth: Penguin, 1973), p. 92. Although this of course applies here to biological needs, the argument is that it also applies to mental needs. M. Saward appeals to the notion of a 'common humanity' in justifying democracy. For him this consists of the 'autonomous capacity for the exercise of reason': *The Terms of Democracy* (Cambridge: Polity, 1998) p. 45. The discussion here appeals to a somewhat 'thicker' concept.
86. In *DT*, written in 1973, Macpherson presciently discusses 'post-Marxism', and like the term 'post-capitalism' it suggested that the 'thing now hyphenated has in fact disappeared and has been replaced by something really quite different. If one cannot deny, in either case, that something superficially similar to the old thing is still around, one can perhaps exorcise its spirit by calling it "post"'. (*DT*, p. 171).
87. Of course many liberals can deny that capitalism is inherently exploitative, but as we have seen few when criticising Macpherson bothered to refute his net transfer of powers theory. See G. A. Cohen, *History, Labour and Freedom* (Oxford: Clarendon, 1988), ch. 11 *passim*, and T. Carver, 'Marx's Political Theory of Exploitation', in A. Reeve (ed.), *Theories of Exploitation* (London: Sage, 1987), p. 76 for interpretations of capitalism as exploitative, independent of Marx's theory of surplus value. Macpherson's concept of the net transfer of powers is also independent of such a theory, arising from the monopolising of the means of production by a minority of society.
88. See Lindsay, *Creative Individualism*, ch. 5 for a speculative attempt to theorise what these might be.
89. See Lindsay's intelligent discussion of this, which attempts to justify foundationalism in terms of democracy rather than the converse, in *Creative Individualism*, pp. 106-8.

90. See M. Ramsay, *Human Needs and the Market*, pp. 170–8, demonstrating how much empirical agreement there is among needs theorists on the question of universal human needs.
91. *DT*, p. 18.
92. Ibid.
93. Raymond Plant nearly completes the circle with a call for a 'left Hegelianism': *Modern Political Thought* (Oxford: Blackwell, 1991), p. 375.

INDEX

Abstract individualism, 137–8, 141
Abstraction, 101, 107–8, 110–11, 122–3, 137, 141–2, 145
Abundance, 21, 89
   see also scarcity
'Agrarian capitalism', 90
'Analytical Marxism', 162
Aristotle, 1, 10, 11, 19, 20, 23, 51, 118, 148, 183
Ashcraft, Richard, 67, 72, 77

Barker, Ernest, 10
Bentham, Jeremy, 34, 57, 144
Berlin, Isaiah, 3, 5, 51, 53
Bernstein, Eduard, 119

'Cambridge School', 8, 86
Caney, S., 169
Carmichael, D. J. C., 46–7, 48–9, 52
Categorical imperative, 171
Chapman, J. W., 103–4, 106, 109–10, 116–19, 120, 129
'Class collaboration', 174–5
Cohen, Joshua, 172–5
   Associations and Democracy, 173–4
   On Democracy, 173
Cold War, 2, 4, 12, 99, 183
Commodity fetishism, 19, 33, 113
Common humanity, 127, 180
Communitarians, 168–71
   see also Macpherson
Connelly, William, 124–5, 126, 169
Cuban missile crisis, 20

Damico, A., 107, 120–1
Daniels, N., 167

Democracy, 8–9, 12, 101, 106, 111–12, 121, 126, 153, 181–3
   Definition, 13, 21
   'Deliberative', 171–5; *see also* Macpherson
   'Developmental', 21
   'Equilibrium', 22, 144–5, 146
   Liberal, 163, 172, 176, 180, 201; *see also* political parties
   Participatory, 23, 119, 140
   Procedural, 21, 125–6
   'Protective', 21
   Substantive, 21, 126
DiQuattro, I., 167
Dunn, John, 67, 69, 70, 71, 76, 102, 105, 114, 115, 119, 120
Dworkin, Ronald, 167, 168

Eagleton, Terry, 179
Ecology, 128–9, 183
   see also Macpherson; scarcity
Enlightenment, 1, 113, 163
Essentialism, 112, 176, 178, 179, 180
Ethical pluralism, 127
'Extractive powers' *see* net transfer of powers

Fact/value problem *see* 'is/ought'
Feminism, 162–3
   see also Macpherson
Filmer, Robert, 81
Foundationalism, 182–3
Freedom, 113, 119, 141–2, 154, 169–70
   Impediments, 137, 140, 141
   see also Macpherson, human nature; net transfer of powers; power
Friedman, Milton, 3